HANDBOOK OF
LEISURE AND TOURISM

HANDBOOK OF
LEISURE AND TOURISM

Edited By

Praveen Sethi

ANMOL PUBLICATIONS PVT. LTD.

NEW DELHI - 110 002 (INDIA)

ANMOL PUBLICATIONS PVT. LTD.
4374/4B, Ansari Road, Daryaganj
New Delhi - 110 002
Ph.: 23261597, 23278000
Visit us at: www.anmolpublications.com

Handbook of Leisure and Tourism

First Published, 1999

Reprint, 2006

ISBN 81-261-0440-6

PRINTED IN INDIA

Published by J.L. Kumar for Anmol Publications Pvt. Ltd., New Delhi - 110 002 and Printed at Mehra Offset Press, Delhi.

Contents

Preface

Handbook of Leisure and Tourism is a new area of tourism which tackles issues that will affect the sector into the next century including globalisation, virtual leisure, and the grey and green revolution.

Deciding on a comprehensive definition of the terms 'leisure' and 'tourism' is no easy matter. Most people associate leisure with either leisure time or leisure activities; they choose to use their spare time in ways which give them the most satisfaction. To many people, tourism is their annual holiday.

To the leisure tourism professional, the simple ideas mask a highly complex industry, arguably the fastest-growing in the world, which spans many activities, such as, sport and physical recreation; international tourism; Arts and entertainment; Heritage and other attractions; community leisure provision; Hotels and the accommodation sector; Hospitality; Transport; Travel agents and tour operators; Home based leisure; countryside recreation, etc.

As an industry, leisure and tourism is developing rapidly at local level, with new facilities being opened to meet the needs of the local community.

Above all it is hoped that this text will create a lasting

interest in the leisure tourism and generate a spirit of critical enquiry into leisure tourism issues affecting consumers, producers and hosts.

This book is an essential guide for those who are involved in the tourism, leisure and hospitality industry.

Editor

1

Leisure Tourism

Introduction

Information is the key to effective management. Without reliable data, on profitability and facility usage for example, managers in leisure and tourism are not able to carry out their many functions with any degree of certainty and are liable to make incorrect assumptions and poor decisions. The provision and use of management information systems in many leisure and tourism organisations is not given a high priority, due in part to insufficient resources and partly because of a lack of awareness of the capabilities of the resources that do exist. The fact that the industry is still in its early stages of evolution is another reason why systems are still under development.

Systems for gathering information in one form or another have existed since the beginning of human enterprise. A glance at any history textbook will produce countless examples of military campaigns and power struggles that relied heavily on the establishment of systems to ensure a flow of information to the decision makers. The same principles still apply today, the only difference being the rapid rise in technology and communications that have expanded both the amount and variety of available information, and the speed with which it can be accessed, processed and communicated.

Since the introduction of the computer, information systems have been revolutionised, with many mundane tasks previously carried out manually being transferred to automated systems. Sophisticated computer systems can now give managers a whole host of information, from occupancy rates in hotels to break-even points for new leisure and tourism projects.

What is a management information system?

It is difficult to find a universally-accepted definition of a management information system applicable to the leisure and tourism industry, because of the vast range of activities that go to make up the industry and the very different information needs that the management in each sector has. The owner of a small seaside hotel, for example, has quite different information needs to, say, the manager of a local authority leisure centre; the information needed by the administrator of an art gallery will not be the same as that required by the manager of a high street travel agency, and so on.

There are, however, areas of common need and similarity of approaches that could be applied to all of the above examples, and a definition of a MIS that could encompass the whole of the leisure and tourism industry is as follows:

> A management information system is a mixture of manual and automated resources which is concerned with the collection, collation, storage, retrieval, communication and use of data for the purposes of an organisation's sound management and forward planning.

Not all management information systems are computer based. Smaller organisations may prefer to continue with a manual information system that has served them well for many years. A small hotel, museum, cafe, restaurant or tourist information centre can function quite well with a system based on card indexes, charts or files. The type of system, whether manual or automated, should not be a prime concern when setting up a MIS; far more important is deciding exactly what information is required, in what form and at what speed. If the answers to these questions point to a manual system, then a manual system should be used. Too many organisations make the decision to computerise their information system for the wrong reasons, quite often persuaded by sales staff with an eye on their commission rather than the needs of the client. Many organisations find that, rather than cutting down on paperwork, computers actually create more paper, and sometimes fail to provide the information needed for effective decision making.

Information needs

Deciding what information is required from a MIS is crucial to its success; get it wrong at this stage, and all that follows will be rendered useless. Some managers overestimate the quantity of data they think they will need and are often confronted with reams of computer printout, which they have no time to read, let alone use for management purposes! Decisions as to what is needed should start with basic data and finish with more elaborate statistics. The fundamental question to ask at all stages is, 'will this data really help in decision making?'.

Information needs should be primarily determined by the decisions that need to be made, which in turn are determined by the objectives of the organisation.

Let us look at the case of British Airways as a simple way of explaining the relationship. BA's goal is 'to be the best and most successful company in the airline industry' . In order to reach this goal, BA has a series of objectives ranging from being a safe and secure airline to being a global leader. To be successful in achieving its objectives, the airline employs managers to make decisions that will effect change and thus secure its aims. To be sure that its decisions are sound, BA will need the sort of information on finance, operations and the 'market', which we discuss below.

Every leisure and tourism organisation has different information needs, meaning that every MIS will have different characteristics. There are, however, common features that should apply to the information produced by all management information systems. The information should be:

— Reliable,
— Consistent.
— Appropriate.
— Accurate.
— Timely.
— Precise.
— Clearly understood.
— Regular.

The information needed by managers in leisure and tourism organisations is likely to fall into one of three broad categories:

1. Financial data.
2. Operational information.
3. Market information.

Financial data

Many management information systems are introduced in the first instance to provide accurate financial data so that managers can monitor performance and plan for the future. Income figures can be produced in a number of different ways, and in the case of a leisure centre could include:

— Income related to type of customer, e.g. adult, child, senior citizen, groups, off-peak, concessions, etc.

— Income related to type of activity, e.g. squash, badminton, basketball, indoor football, aerobics, etc.
— Income related to facility used, e.g. swimming pool, sports hall, bar, catering, sports shop, all-weather pitch, fitness suite, equipment hire, etc.
— Income related to time of use, e.g. weekdays, weekends, different times of day, different months of the year, etc.

Income and expenditure information can be organised into revenue centres and cost centres. In a typical hotel, for example, revenue centres, i.e. activities that generate income, are likely to be:

— Rooms.
— Conference and banqueting facilities.
— Food and beverage.
— Telephone and business services.
— Valet services.
— Retail operations and vending.
— Special events.

Cost centres, which make it easier to analyse performance, are likely to include:

— Staffing.
— Food and beverage purchase.
— Marketing and publicity.
— Laundry.
— Maintenance and equipment purchase.
— Telephone and postal costs.
— Energy costs.
— Administration costs.

The arrival of CCT in local authority leisure services has introduced more managers in the public sector to the notion of financial ratios and performance indicators, which have been widespread in private sector leisure and tourism for some time. The range of financial ratios that can be calculated by a MIS is very broad, and could include:

— Total income: staff costs.
— Total income: number of admissions /visitors.
— Total income: operating expenditure.
— Income per facility: staff costs per facility.
— Income per facility: costs per facility.

As well as these ratios which are of use to those managers involved in day-to-day management of facilities, other financial ratios for senior management can be produced by the MIS, including:

— Net profit: sales.
— Overheads: sales.
— Gross profit: sales.
— Fixed assets: sales.

These ratios will give the policy makers the necessary information to be able to plan effectively for the future, as well as making any modifications that the figures suggest.

Operational information

As well as information relating to financial performance, leisure and tourism organisations need data concerned with the use and operation of their facilities, for example:

— *Occupancy and usage rates a* hotel will want to know what percentage of its available bedspaces are occupied, a holiday centre will need to know how many of its self-catering units are let and a leisure centre will need information on the use of the facility as a whole and the take-up on individual activities. Tourist attractions, tour operators, airlines and travel agencies will also need basic data on the use of their facilities and services.

— *Stock control leisure* and tourism organisations that operate retail outlets will use their MIS to check availability of stock, for example equipment in a sports centre shop, food in a cafeteria and drink in a bar. Many computer-based POS systems will automatically update stock availability figures as goods are sold or used.

— *Personnel records any* organisation will need to keep information on its staff, their conditions of employment and record of performance. Subject to confidentiality this information can be held on a MIS, which can also handle the payroll function, providing an automated system for the calculation and payment of wages and salaries. The MIS can also give information on staff turnover and the uptake of staff training.

Market information

An effective leisure and tourism organisation must have detailed information about its customers in order to be able to provide them with the facilities and services they want, and to do so with attention to their desire for a good standard of customer service. A management information system is invaluable for providing such information on the 'market' and can help highlight under-exploited opportunities or areas of.an organisation which need more promotion. A theatre's database, for example, may indicate that residents of a particular area of a city do not visit the theatre in anything like the same proportions as those who live in other areas. The management may investigate why this is so, and may feel it worthwhile to mount a publicity campaign in the under-represented area in order to increase attendance.

As well as these types of information on its 'internal' market, an organisation may use its MIS to store data on the market outside its own organisation; the 'external' business environment. For example, details of competitors and their performance, government statistics and specialist reports may be part of the MIS. Such data will give the management an idea of its position in the marketplace relative to other organisations; and will be an invaluable aid in planning and decision making.

Components of a MIS

In the early days of computer-based management information systems, organisations followed a task-by-task approach to solving their information needs, often starting with specific financial data concerning income and expenditure analysis. Having satisfied one particular need for information, the organisation would move on to another data problem to solve. It is only in the last 15 years or so that UK leisure and tourism organisations have begun to commission integrated management information systems that can perform many tasks and provide a multitude of management information from a single source.

In his book on information systems in management, KJ Radford identifies five separate subsystems, which together form the MIS. These are:

— *Administrative and operational* systems these are the components created to support the routine functions within the organisation which revolve around the processing of data. Typical functions served by these systems are:

- Personnel records.
- Pensions details.
- Payroll.
- Accounting ledgers.

- Internal audit.
- Maintenance of inventories of equipment.
- Purchasing.
- Maintenance schedules.
- Market research databases.
- Sales planning and promotion.
- Production of documents.

— *Management reporting system the* function of this system is to provide managers at all levels of an organisation with the necessary information on which to base their decisions. These 'reports' will be concerned with either the control of the use of resources, the efficiency of operations or the effectiveness in achieving goals and objectives; depending on which level of management has requested the reports, it may be a mixture of all three.

— *Common database this* is the 'hub' of the MIS to which all the other subsystems are connected. It acts as a storage compartment for information accessed by more than one department or individual in the organisation. The accessible nature of the information in the common database means that security of data is an important concern for management. The database is continually updated and altered, as the organisation goes about its normal operations. Choice of hardware for the MIS will play an important role in the operation of the common database, since, with inappropriate equipment, the expansion of the database will result in a slowing down of the speed of response of the MIS. This can be to some extent overcome by the establishment of an 'archive', a separate system into which is transferred data that is not current but may be required at some time in the future.

— *Information retrieval system this* has a similar function to that of the management reporting system (MRS) described above, the main difference being that while the MRS provides structured reports for use by managers in their day-to-day tasks, the information retrieval system gives them the opportunity to receive information from the system on demand, and in a form that is not structured in advance. The manager of a leisure complex, for example, may be asked by a senior executive to give her up-to-date figures on the usage of one of the facilities immediately; an effective information retrievals stem should be able to handle such information requests speedily.

— *Data management system this* is the part of the MIS which arranges and controls the flow of information between the other components of the system. Its major functions are supervising the capture and updating of data on the common database, the accessing of the common database by the other subsystems, generating reports in the formats required by management and providing security for the data in the database against accidental damage, intentional malice or inquisitiveness.

The concept of 'front office' and 'back office'

The design of any MIS for a leisure and tourism organisation will need to take into account the growing trend for organisations to divide their functions into 'front office' and 'back office'; in simple terms, the 'front office' (sometimes referred to as 'front of house') refers to the reception area of any leisure and tourism facility, the point at which the customer first makes contact with the organisation. The 'back office' (also known as 'back of house') refers to the organisation's functions that take place behind the scenes, e.g. accounting, which the customer is unlikely to be aware of. There must always be a strong link between front and back offices for a management information system to be truly effective; for example, when a guest books into a hotel at reception, information must be conveyed, possibly manually but more likely via a computer system, to the other departments that need to know, such as housekeeping, accounts, food and beverage, laundry, marketing, etc.

The concept of front and back office is widespread in the leisure and tourism industry. As we have seen, hotels operate on this basis, as do leisure/sports centres, travel agencies, visitor attractions, educational establishments, transport providers, catering outlets, entertainment venues and tourist information centres. The division into front and back office allows management to focus resources on particular functions and train staff in these areas. The selection and training of staff to work in the 'front office' is particularly important since it provides the visitor with his or her first impressions of the organisation. Staff with an understanding of customer needs and expectations and who are committed to providing excellence in customer service should be chosen to work in this high-profile area. The environment in which the 'front office' is positioned also needs to be carefully planned, and should provide a clean, warm, efficient, welcoming and friendly atmosphere.

The use of computers in leisure and tourism

The dynamic and responsive nature of the leisure and tourism industry has meant that it has always been at the forefront of developments in new technology. The travel industry, including retail travel agencies, tour operators, airlines and other transport providers, has been particularly noteworthy in its willingness to take on-board new developments in computers and telecommunications equipment. The leisure sector has also adapted quickly to the rapid growth in the demand for leisure, sport and recreation services by installing computer systems to handle many financial and operational aspects of the business.

Why have a computer system?

The principal reason for installing a computerised MIS will be that it will increase the efficiency and improve the effectiveness of the organisation in which it operates. More specific reasons for choosing a computer system will vary enormously between the different sectors of the leisure and tourism industry but could include:

— As a means of expanding the organisation a small company may wish to expand its number of customers but realises that its manual system will not be able to cope with the extra information.

— To make better use of staff resources it is unlikely that a computer system will actually reduce the number of employees once it is introduced, but it will enable the same number of people to do much more, thus improving staff efficiency.

— As a way of accessing a remote database a leisure and tourism organisation may introduce a computer system so that it can gain access to data from other organisations. A travel agent, for example, will be able to access information and make bookings with tour operators and airlines directly via a computer link. In the same way, a public sector leisure centre may set up a direct link with its local authority mainframe computer in order to transfer and process data.

— In order to provide a better standard of service to its customers a computer system is likely to speed up the processing of such items as bookings, membership details, cash handling, credit transfers, invoicing, letters and mailing of, publicity materials.

— To provide information for management purposes, which is regular, accurate and in a form that is easily understood.

Microcomputers in leisure and tourism

In addition to large-scale, integrated computer management information systems, which can handle complex data management functions, microcomputers have grown rapidly in popularity in the leisure and tourism industry over the last ten years or so. It is becoming increasingly common to find these personal computers (PCs) not only on the desks of administrative staff but also on the desks of the managers themselves. Modem business computers, most of which conform to the standards established by the IBM personal computer, will run word processing, spreadsheets, database and DTP programs, depending on the type of software used. Smaller leisure and tourism organisations are able to provide acceptable levels of management information with a MIS based solely on the use of microcomputers.

Security of the MIS

With so much confidential, personal and commercially sensitive information being held by leisure and tourism organisations, the question of security of the MIS must be taken very seriously by management. Loss of any part of the system may affect the viability of the whole MIS. The system must be secured against:

— Accidental interference.

— Inquisitiveness.

— Theft.

— Fraud.

Loss of part of the information contained in the MIS will be particularly acute if its loss results in an advantage to a competitor organisation; industrial espionage, involving the deliberate and unlawful entry into a system by unauthorised personnel, is not unheard of in the highly competitive leisure and tourism industry.

Simple security measures can give good protection against theft and wilful damage to components of the MIS. In the case of computer-based systems, these include strict control of access to processing facilities and data storage, and careful screening of the staff who are given access to these facilities. Steps can be taken to prevent or at least minimise damage resulting from fire, flood, power failure and civil disorder, including the provision of secure premises and storage facilities designed to combat these threats. Special measures are necessary to protect data in the MIS and to enable the management to reconstruct files from archive material stored in a different location, should the need arise. Issues concerning security of data are particularly important when employing consultants and staff from computer bureaux; rigorous screening of such companies and their personnel is vital.

The data protection act 1984

Since 10 May 1986, all organisations that hold personal data about individuals on automated systems have been required to register with the Data Protection Registrar and to comply with the Data Protection Act (DPA). The exact definition of an 'automated system' is open to debate, but in general terms information held on computer falls within the scope of the Act and that which is processed manually does not. Indeed, some organisations choose to store certain data on manual systems in order that it is not covered by the DPA. The Act seeks to regulate the way in which data is gathered, stored and disclosed to third parties. The extent to which computers are used throughout leisure and tourism means that the Act has important implications for the industry.

The Act establishes eight Data Protection Principles with which data users must comply (data users are defined as individuals, corporations or other agencies that control the automatic processing of data). The eight principles, which in reality are a set of points of good practice to which data users should aspire, are as follows:

1. That the information held on computer shall be obtained and processed fairly and lawfully. Data would be said to have been obtained unfairly if the provider was deceived or misled about the purpose for which the information was being obtained.
2. That personal data shall be held only for one or more specified and lawful purposes. A contravention of this particular principle would, for 'example, be when an organisation holds personal information for staff training purposes but chooses to use it for the selection of staff for redundancy.
3. That data shall not be disclosed to persons other than those named in the registration document, nor for any other purpose than that registered under the Act. A tour operator, for example, which collects information on its customers to offer them discounted holidays, cannot then sell the data to another company without contravening this principle.
4. That personal data held for any purpose or purposes shall be adequate, relevant and not excessive in relation to the registered purpose. An organisation that holds data unrelated to the purpose for which it is registered or is clearly holding far more than is needed to satisfy the purpose will be in breach of this principle.
5. That personal data shall be accurate and updated as and when necessary. If an organisation, for example, holds a list of customers who have exceeded their annual credit limit, but the organisation makes no

attempt to update the list when further payments are made, it is likely to be considered as having contravened this principle.

6. That personal information held for any purpose or purposes shall not be kept for longer than is necessary. A leisure centre that holds a prize draw and uses a computer to store the names and addresses of those entering, should destroy this data at the end of the promotion.
7. That an individual shall be entitled, at reasonable intervals and without undue delay or expense, to know whether information is held on him or her and to have access to any data that does exist; also to have any data corrected or erased as appropriate.
8. That the data user shall take reasonable security measures to guard against unauthorised access to, alteration, disclosure, accidental loss or destruction of the personal data.

Under the Act, individuals who have data held on them have a range of rights in civil law, including:

— Rights of access to the data.
— Rights to compensation for inaccuracy of data.
— Rights to compensation for loss, destruction or unauthorised disclosure of data.
— Rights to apply to have any inaccuracies in the data rectified and, in certain circumstances, rights to have the information erased.

We have seen earlier that leisure and tourism organisations are avid users of computers and other automated information systems. Membership lists, databases for marketing and promotional work, guests' accounts in hotels, travel agencies and tour operators, to name but a few, all involve the collection and storage of personal data on individuals. As such, managers need to be aware of the principles of the Data Protection Act and the extent to which it affects their own particular organisation.

MIS evaluation

Much of the early development work with computerised management information systems in leisure and tourism proved disappointing when it came to examining their cost-effectiveness. This was a result of a lack of clarity in terms of defining management information needs coupled with inadequate and inefficient hardware and software. The last ten years has seen great strides in the reliability and capabilities of the technology and an almost universal acceptance of the computer as a useful management tool. This has led to improvements in price/performance ratios of the various systems in use in leisure and tourism organisations; in other words, an evaluation of the benefits of the MIS when compared with its costs has given favourable results. While it is sometimes difficult to fully evaluate all the benefits of a system, since some may be intangible and therefore hard to quantify, it is important that evaluation of the system once it is operational is seen as an important element of the introduction of the MIS. Formal and informal feedback from staff, customers and managers themselves will prove invaluable in making the system as effective as possible.

On the negative side, an evaluation of the MIS may highlight actual or potential problem areas, which could include:

— Lack of adequate terminals or work stations.
— Insufficient storage capability of the system.
— Lack of operational support, including training and maintenance

— Bottlenecks in interfacing.
— Lack of awareness of capabilities of the system.
— Inadequate security of the system.
— Inadequate expansion capability.

If the process of choosing the MIS has been objective, planned and thorough, it is to be hoped that many of these problems will have been anticipated and that the system will function according to the specification drawn up by the purchasing organisation.

Leisure centres

Irrespective of whether a leisure centre is in private or public sector control, it will need to be effectively managed, with the assistance of an efficient management information system. In the UK today, this will invariably mean the use of a computer-based MIS. Leisure centres need reliable information to be able to control costs and provide value-for-money services and facilities for their current and future customers. A good computer system can handle a great deal of tedious administrative work, can provide a database of users, membership lists for promotional work and will enable the centre to handle its finances far more effectively. The management of the centre will be able to track its performance over time, identify trends and compare performance against targets.

The introduction of CCT in local authority leisure services has hastened the need for very detailed information on income, expenditure and usage, both for the operators (known as the 'contractors') of the centres and the 'clients', the local councils themselves. Figure 6.3 shows the type of detailed information that the contractor of a hypothetical local authority leisure centre would be required to provide under the terms of the CCT contract.

Just one small element of what will be needed to satisfy the demands of most CCT contracts concerning the management of leisure centres. As well as detailed data on income, the contractor will have to provide information on a regular basis, covering:

— Levels of usage of the facility as a whole and by categories of users.

— Total attendance and demand for individual facilities.

— Expenditure levels.

In addition, the management of the leisure centre will be required to furnish information concerning:

— Staffing.

— Cleaning.

— Maintenance.

— Publicity.

— Health and safety.

— Plant and equipment.

— Operational issues.

The collection of this information, and its subsequent checking by the 'client', is all part of the process of monitoring the CCT contract to see if the operator of the leisure centre is meeting the performance standards set out in the specification and is providing the level and quality of service demanded. The need to collect this detailed management information, which has been common practice in private sector providers for many years, has resulted in an increased demand from leisure centre managers for computer systems that can provide the information both in the detail and format required by the local authority and at the intervals laid down in the CCT contract. The difficulty that has faced many such managers is how to go about choosing the 'right' MIS for the job.

Choosing a computerised MIS

There are countless numbers of stories heard about

computer systems costing many thousands of pounds which have failed to live up to the claims of those who provided them in the first place; systems that can provide complex management information but can't handle the basics, systems that are too slow in many of the routine operations they are asked to perform and systems that 'crash' with alarming regularity. If you add to these tales of woe, the fact that many good systems can be out of date by the time they are 'on-line', then it is no wonder that leisure centre managers exercise a great deal of care and attention when it comes to installing or updating a computerised MIS.

There are four basic steps in deciding on a system and its supplier:

1. Decide exactly what information is required.
2. Write a specification based on the stated information needs.
3. Invite tenders from prospective MIS providers.
4. Choose the company that best meets your needs.

Decide exactly what information is required

This is no easy task, since it involves a methodical appraisal of everything that happens in the centre at the moment, as well as an attempt to predict what additional information may be needed in the future. All the centre's facilities and services will need to be itemised, and all procedures, both formal and informal, will need to be documented. If the system is being introduced as a result of winning a CCJ' contract for the management of the centre, the process may be somewhat easier, since the operator will have a specification contained in the contract to which he or she will be expected to work. This will list the information that the client will expect to see and will form the basis of the MIS under consideration.

Write a specification based on the stated information needs

The written specification will be used by the companies that submit tenders, and will give them a detailed picture of the centre's needs and requirements. The secret in writing the specification is to clearly express what the management of the centre expects from the MIS, while at the same time not making it so specific that any of the tendering companies would have to devise a completely new system in order to comply with it, with all the added expense this would involve. The specification is likely to include detailed information on the following items:

— The objectives of the system the general principles on which the system must be based.

— Details of the facilities, activities and services which the system will have t cope with.

— Front office operations. goes on in the reception area.

— Back office functions for example programming cash control etc.

— Membership systems.

— Point of sale (POS) systems, including stock control.

— Format of the management information required.

— Security of the system.

— Support and training needs.

— Hardware requirements capability of expansion, portability, flexibility, etc.

Invite tenders from prospective MIS providers

Once the specification for the system has been agreed, the process of inviting tenders can begin. Advertisements can be placed in relevant leisure magazines such as *Leisure Week, Leisure Manager* and *Leisure Management* asking interested parties to request a specification and tender application form. Details may also be distributed direct to other organisations that may have worked for the organisation before or are known to have carried out similar work at other centres. The need for impartiality, however, must be paramount, particularly in the case of local authority centres where public money is involved. The information sent out must indicate the latest date by which the completed forms should be returned.

Choose the company that best meets your needs

The evaluation of the tenders that come in needs to be a very thorough and methodical process carried out in an objective a manner as possible. A company's 'track record' will be an important consideration; it will be necessary to establish whether any companies new to leisure centre systems, although they may have worked in another business sector for some time, are looking for a 'guinea pig' on which to try out their ideas. On the positive side, however, such a company may be willing to offer a very good deal if it is new to leisure, and, if it is open in its negotiations, it may secure the contract on a lower tender price than a more established company.

It will be necessary to establish what proportion of the specification each company can meet without having to make major changes to its 'base' system. It is unlikely that any company will be able to meet all the details on the specification without some adjustments, but it is important to find out how long each modification will take and if it will incur extra costs.

Cost is likely to be a significant factor in the selection process, although it should not be assumed that the company that submits the lowest tender will get the contract. Cost must be considered along with all the other variables such as experience and expertise. The companies should be asked to itemise the various costs involved in supplying the total system and providing an ongoing support and maintenance service.

Another important consideration when comparing tenders is the support that the company can give, both before installation and once it is on-line. Training for staff will be a vital part of this support, as will updating to software and hardware, and on-site maintenance and repair.

Having evaluated the tenders, a short list of possible suppliers should be drawn up and the companies invited to make presentations to managers and staff, and council representatives in the case of a local authority centre. The companies should formally present their systems and state how they will meet the requirements listed on the specification. Site visits to look at systems in action may also be part of the 'sifting' process.

Although the process of choosing a supplier for the MIS is planned to be as objective as possible, it is sometimes the case that there are two or three companies that could equally well carry out the job. In these circumstances, the company that eventually is successful in winning the contract may be the one that the management and staff of the leisure centre felt most comfortable with or the one that came across as having the most confidence in being able to get the job done to the necessary specification and in the agreed time-scale.

Pubs, bars and catering outlets

When it comes to management information systems, there is something of a mini-revolution going on in pubs, bars, restaurants, fast-food outlets and cafes all over the UK. Driven by the constant need to reduce costs, increase revenue and provide the high level of customer service that today's consumers are increasingly demanding, these leisure outlets are introducing new technology systems at a frantic rate in what has always been a highly competitive sector of the leisure market. Many operators have replaced their old-fashioned tills with sophisticated electronic cash registers, preprogrammed with prices for food and drinks. Most large organisations are now giving serious consideration to full-scale EPOS (electronic point-of-sale) systems, the sort that have long been used in retail outlets to help control stock and cash.

EPOS

Electronic point-of-sale (EPOS) systems are being introduced in ever increasing numbers to many leisure sector premises, especially pubs, clubs, bars and fast-food outlets. The only way the customer is likely to know that a facility has an EPOS system is when the staff use their 'touchpads' or 'scatterpads', the small touch-sensitive panels located behind the bar or counter, sometimes on the cash register itself. The benefits of EPOS are:

1. It gives the management control over cash transactions.
2. It improves stock control.
3. It frees staff to concentrate on improving customer care rather than having to calculate prices and issue bills.

As well as performing all the normal functions of an electronic cash register, an EPCS system will log all transactions with time, date, items served, cost, method of payment and the member of staff who dealt with the customer. This not only reduces the possibility of fraud by staff but also allows management to introduce incentives for staff who are meeting and exceeding their sales targets. The system will also mean that the busiest times can be better anticipated and allow better management of staff generally. The detailed management information given by EPOS will mean that stock levels can be monitored more closely enabling the outlet to hold much smaller levels than would otherwise be the case.

The public house MIS network

A very good example of state-of-the-art management information systems in the leisure industry is the introduction of a fully integrated system by Bass Taverns into its public houses throughout Britain; Bass is the UK's largest brewer and the fourth largest in the world. By using a front office system combining 'scatterpads' and touch-screen tills, flowmeters that automatically monitor how much beer is drawn from the kegs and a back office system that can review stocks and cash-flow, Bass can monitor the operation of all pubs on the system from a central control.

The system begins with staff entering transactions using a scatterpad and touch-screen tills. As a security measure, each till only operates with the electronic identity card of a member of the bar staff. Flowmeters located on the kegs measure the amount of beer used and input data into the network. Each pint pulled is recorded by the flowmeters, which measure to the nearest quarter pint how much beer has been dispensed, while the till is automatically alerted by the flowmeter to expect a payment. If no payment is received, the system sends a warning to the pub manager who operates the back office system. Here, he or she monitors transactions and prepares data for the network. The data is downloaded to the network control in Birmingham which supervises the operation of more than 2,000 pubs.

All 3,000 of Bass's pubs were scheduled to be on this integrated MIS network by the end of 1993, less than two years since the start of the project in January 1992. Every pub manager will have a networked PC in his or her office, linked to the network control so that stock details, work rates and cash takings can be downloaded during the night. Using this sophisticated technology, managers at network control have an exact upto-the-minute picture of what business it is doing in which areas. Regional managers are able to supervise more than 100 pubs in an area by simply connecting a PC or notebook computer to the central network and calling up the data. The system has enabled Bass to manage its public house operation more effectively and has given individual pub managers the chance to use their resources, particularly staff, more efficiently.

Bass plans to integrate an automatic delivery system in to the network to further refine the operation. By analysing the stock control data downloaded every night, the system will automatically activate deliveries of beer to the individual pubs. The system will be linked to the brewing arm of Bass in order that demand for beer can be estimated more effectively and wastage can be kept to a minimum.

Looking to the future, Bass sees this as only the start of a revolution in pubs and the way they are managed. There is likely to be even greater use of new technology equipment to monitor, for example, energy use and to offer other services such as cash machines and ordering of theatre tickets.

Theatres and other entertainment venues

There have been great strides in the development of management information systems for theatres, large and small, and the indoor and outdoor entertainment venues that exist throughout the UK, e.g. Wembley Stadium and Wembley Arena, GMEX in Manchester, Sheffield Arena and the Royal Albert Hall, to name but a few. Most venues serving a regional catchment, and quite often many catering only for their local population, will have a computerised MIS controlling front and back office functions. The national venues employ sophisticated systems that can handle the large volume of enquiries and sales they attract.

The functions carried out by staff in the front office of such venues are in many respects similar to the work carried out by reception staff in leisure centres. The one big difference, however, is that theatres and other entertainment venues sell most of their tickets in advance, rather than taking casual bookings on the day. The main functions are:

— Selling tickets either in person, by telephone, by post or by fax.
— Providing information.
— Cash and cards handling.
— Controlling entry and exit.

The front office or reception of an entertainment venue will almost certainly have a VIDU (visual display unit) showing a seating plan, seat availability and the prices in the various parts of the venue. This system will include a ticket printer to issue tickets automatically and speedily. The front office system will be connected to a back office computer, responsible for:

— Accounting.
— Sales analysis.
— Promotion and marketing.
— Personnel.

Many venues make extensive use of their database of customer details to market their services. Customers can be targeted according to their tastes and preferences; for example, a person who books a seat at the snooker championships in the Wembley Arena will automatically be sent details of the same event the following year via the database. Separate files can be created according to different types of performances, e.g. opera, comedy, music, drama, light entertainment, sport, etc., enabling customers to be sent promotional material suited to their interests.

Leisure complexes

Leisure complexes, including country clubs, health resorts and golf courses, are a growing part of the leisure industry in the UK today. Offering facilities for individual and business (corporate) clients, they need fully integrated management information systems that link all the elements of their operation. Effective systems must provide a fast and efficient service for customers and allow staff to concentrate on developing the highest levels of customer service.

Like many systems available for leisure complexes, the Baron MIS offers three integrated 'modules', covering membership, bookings and point-of-sale systems (see Figure 6.4), all of which can be tailored to the requirements of an individual resort. This modular approach offers the management, staff and customers a system through which all operations can be channelled for enhanced administrative and financial control.

The membership system is often at the heart of any leisure complex and needs flexibility, speed and accuracy of operation. The Baron MIS can record subscription information to speed up renewals and members' account spends can be controlled by levies or credit controls. The ledger module ensures an efficient storage of transactions and allows the collection of finance at regular intervals.

The membership system can be used for marketing purposes with the capability of producing personalised letters for mailing direct to clients.

The bookings system can control all the bookable functions at the complex, including tennis, squash, sauna, spa treatments, golf courses, etc. Figure 6.6 shows part of the Baron MIS, which lists details of golf course bookings for a particular day. Good booking systems should offer the facility for bookings to be taken at more than one point in the complex and enquiries for bookings to be made at multiple locations. Various options within the bookings module of the Baron MIS allow the recording of information on hired equipment and the control of members' use of facilities, via magnetic strip cards. The point-of-sale system is specifically designed for shops within complexes and clubs. It ensures control of all aspects of the shop's operation, including stock movements, stock taking and stock control.

The POS system gives the option to barcode all items giving a faster method of recording sales and stock control information. Analysis of sales can be made under a number of categories, including by supplier, by location, by category of goods, by colour, by size, etc. One of the most important points about each of the three elements of this MIS, bookings, membership and POS, is that reports can be generated from all three modules for use by management. Information on usage and financial performance can be generated by the system.

Fully integrated management information systems offer the leisure complex with many facilities and a mix of clientele, the opportunity to make maximum use of its resources to provide a professional service backed up with sound management practices.

2

Impacts of Leisure Tourism

There are three main types of impacts that leisure tourism can have at national, regional or local level:

1. Economic impacts.
2. Environmental impacts.
3. Social/cultural impacts.

It is important to remember that within each of these categories, the impact that leisure and tourism can have may be either positive or negative or, as is often the case, a mixture of the two.

Economic impacts

Income generation

'The leisure and tourism industry generates income and wealth for private individuals, local authorities, companies, voluntary bodies and national governments. At the international level, tourism can make a considerable contribution to a country's balance of payments, which is a statement of the inflows and outflows of currency to and from a particular country. Tourism and leisure are services and are known as invisible items on the balance of payments, while visibles include goods such as food and manufactured items. As you can see, the balance has gone into a negative situation in recent years reflecting the growth in overseas holidays taken by British people and a slowdown in the growth of overseas visitors to Britain. At a local level, revenue generated by leisure and tourism facilities is often vital to the economic wellbeing of an area and is boosted by an important concept known as the multiplier effect. Research has shown that the amount spent by visitors to an area is recirculated in the local economy and is actually worth more to the area than its face value.

The actual value of the multiplier varies between regions and different sectors of the leisure and tourism industry. The multiplier for, say, a farm guesthouse is likely to be greater than for a city centre hotel which is part of a large multinational chain. This is because the farm guesthouse is likely to buy its food and other services locally, while the goods and services for the large hotel may well be brought in from outside the area as part of a national distribution contract; i.e. income is lost to the area.

Job creation

We have seen already that leisure and tourism is a significant employer in the private, public and voluntary sectors, providing around 1.5 million jobs nationally. The creation of new jobs is one of leisure and tourism's major benefits.

Investment

Investment in large and small leisure and tourism projects not only provides short-term benefits for an area in terms of jobs in construction, for example, but also offers a base for the longer economic regeneration of regions by providing employment and revenue for many sectors not directly related to the industry, e.g. more business for petrol stations, printers, accountants, etc. Leisure and tourism is increasingly used as a 'springboard' for the regeneration of rundown areas of towns and cities; the Albert Dock in Liverpool and the

Castlefields development in Manchester are excellent examples of this.

Environmental impacts

Although leisure and tourism can have positive environmental benefits to a local area, for example the Britain in Bloom scheme, restoration of redundant buildings and improvements to derelict areas, there is much evidence to suggest that the industry could do a lot to improve its negative environmental impacts. In Britain, the coast, countryside, towns and cities all suffer from the pressures of increasing numbers of visitors and their transportation. Some of the worst problems include:

- *Physical erosion the* wearing away of soil and vegetation by walkers, horseriders, cyclists, cars and motorcycles.
- *Litter* both an eyesore and a threat to safety
- *Congestion and overcrowding in* popular holiday areas we all see the effects of too many people and too many cars.
- *Pollution of* water and air, not forgetting noise pollution.
- *Loss of habitats* for flora and fauna.
- *Spoiling of the landscape* that people have come to see and enjoy.

Better education, improved visitor and traffic management techniques, use of the price mechanism and better signposting, are some of the possible solutions which are being tried in our towns and countryside to reduce the harmful envirornmental effects of leisure and tourism.

Social/cultural impacts

Some people believe that the negative social and cultural

impacts of leisure, and particularly, tourism are far more harmful in the long run than the environmental problems we have just seen. This is based on the belief that many of the negative environmental impacts can be easily corrected with the right management and funding. The social and cultural problems, however, can be far more deep-rooted and may take generations to improve. Some of these problems are:

- Overcrowding, which may cause a reduction in the quality of life for the 'host community'.
- Traditional activities may lose labour to the seemingly more attractive jobs in leisure and tourism.
- Tourists' behaviour can distort local customs.
- Religious codes may be altered to adapt to the needs of visitors, e.g. Sunday opening of facilities.
- Local languages may be lost through under-use.
- Traditional crafts may be lost in favour of mass-produced souvenirs.

Leisure and tourism can, however, have positive impacts, such as the revitalisation for visitors of neglected regions, the rebirth of local arts and crafts, refurbishment of local architecture and greater understanding of cultures.

The growth of sustainable tourism

Concern about the harmful environmental and social/cultural impacts of tourism has led to a lively debate about 'green' or sustainable issues in relation to the industry. The Tourist Boards and private sector companies are developing principles and practices which all sectors of the leisure and tourism industry will need to consider in order to ensure a healthy industry for the future.

The underlying *leitmotif* is that tourism is concerned with the quality of the holidaymaker's experience of travel and place. This experience includes travel to the place, the nature of the holiday destination, the return journey, and the interactions between tourist, host, fellow tourists and representatives of the tourist industry that occur in this process. This perception of tourism is not the only perspective. Tourism can be construed as an economic activity, and might be defined as a study of the demand for and supply of accommodation and supportive service for those staying away from home, and the resultant patterns of expenditure, income creation and employ-ment'. But, from the experiential view it can be argued that the attitudes, expectations and perceptions of the holidaymaker are significant variables in setting goals, influencing behaviour and determining final satisfaction. It is also noted that tourists retain, while on holiday, the social skills used to establish acceptable parameters of action.

Accordingly, this chapter reviews literature relating to motivation for recreational activities, and levels of derived from such activities. Ryan notes that the relationship between motivation, performance and resultant satisfaction invites consideration of number of variables, including:

(a) the expectation and perception of the place and its attributes;

(b) the importance of the activity to the individual in meeting personal needs;

(c) the expected outcomes of the activity;

(d) the role of intervening variables which are twofold in nature:

 (i) internal, personal factors such as perceived ability to bring about a desired outcome; and

(ii) external factors which affect the probability of a desired outcome such as the availability of human and other resources;

(e) the presence of significant others, and the importance attached to them; and

(f) the degree to which an individual is able to adopt adaptive behaviour, such as goal adjustment and search behaviour, given the frustration of initial objectives.

The chapter is also based on the assumption that variables thought to be appropriate to recreational activities by researchers in leisure studies can be of use in understanding the nature of holidaytaking and the satisfaction derived from it. Holidays include a series of behaviours in which needs for relaxation, skill acquisition, self-development etc. form a complex set of relationships, and it is argued that parallels with other leisure activities can be drawn.

Equally, any brief consideration of this area should take into account some theories of consumer behaviour. If satisfaction is seen as the congruence of need and performance, then dissatisfaction can be perceived as a negative gap between expectation and experience. Therefore, some form of gap analysis might be helpful in analysing tourist satisfaction. Equally, if cognitive dissonance is thought to play a role, then it is arguably 'triggered' by some event, some 'critical incident' in the holidaytaker's experience of place or activity. Research would apparently indicate that such events can serve as powerful 'confirmers' of positive experience.

The concepts of fun and leisure

The question as to what are the roles and functions of leisure; its contents, the distinctions between leisure and fun, the motivations for, and determinants of, satisfactory leisure experiences are well recorded in the literature relating to leisure studies. For example, Podilchak examines the meaning of leisure and fun, and argues that there is indeed a distinction. Fun is perceived as being:

(a) doing things on the surface, being silly, laughing;

(b) as growing out of an activity, being purposeless; and

(c) exciting, exhilarating—unique, not everyday.

Fun is qualitative. Leisure, on the other hand, is seen as being more serious and more institutionalised and, since it involves choice, by implication is more premeditated. Podilchak argues that in the definitions of leisure as a means of 'recreation', the fun and instantaneous enjoyment associated with it has been deleted from the analysis of leisure and its role in contemporary society. Gunn makes a similar point when he writes:

> As it was formalized and institutionalized, recreation became whatever the proponents and agencies created as policy. Some recreational professionals draw a strong distinction between that which is an end in itself and that which is purposeful, claiming that the former is negative whereas the latter is positive. Leisure, engaged in for its own sake, provides no focus; those recreational activities accepted by society as wholesome, creative and uplifting are worthy of public support.

Yet, in the case of tourism, reference is made to tourism as a 'sanctioned escape route', a 'regression into childhood', and in that sense the role of fun within the tourist experience has been recognised, albeit not always analysed in terms of its relationship with other components of the tourist experience.

Leisure and tourism—conceptual overlaps

As evidenced by a perceived need to devote a special

issue of the Annals of Tourism Research to the relationship between leisure and tourism studies, there have been few structured attempts to apply variables thought to contribute towards a satisfactory leisure experience to the phenomenon of holidaytaking. Tourism literature has tended to concentrate more on the determinants of tourism choice and holiday behaviour. One reason may lie in the definitions of tourism used in both commercial and academic research. Tourism activity has been defined in terms of travel away from home requiring overnight accommodation. Such a definition attracts attention to questions of where people go, and seeks to explain travel in the language of economic variables and social processes as well as of motivational drives.

Equally, the objective or perceived attractiveness of destinations is viewed as being important, particularly from the geographical viewpoint of finding measures of attractiveness for spatial modelling. Arguably, the psychological perspective of tourism as an experience of place, and events at that place, has tended not to feature as strongly in the literature. A review of standard texts, such as those of Mathieson and Wall, Murphy, and Burkart and Medlik, would seem to support this contention. This is not to say that psychological modelling is absent from the literature. Far from it, and the work of Pearce is a notable contribution here; but it might in part explain why the gap between recreational and tourism literature has occurred at a conceptual level. (In saying this, it is recognised that structural components of academic departmental organisation might well, in the final analysis, be at least as important a contributing factor.)

Also it can be argued that there is a distinct difference between leisure activities undertaken as part of one's daily life, and those undertaken whilst on holiday. Put simply, by definition, the holiday trip requires a stay away from home, and thus holiday activities occur within a geographical space with which the tourist may not be familiar. Thus, holiday experiences involve degrees of exploration which might not be present in the normal pattern of leisure activity. Yet even this argument must be modified. For example, Lyon, in analysing the attraction of timeshare, argues that geographical familiarity and destination loyalty might be motivators for the use of such types of holiday accommodation. Gunn, in common with many other authors, points out that the tourism experience has a time dimension. He argues that there are three stages: the creation of pre-image, participation and evaluation. Ryan refers to the fact that the holiday experience commences with the collecting of information about destinations prior to actual booking, and that the brochure is used as a source of reference and confirmation of the travel decision prior to departure. Pre-departure behaviour is characterised by special purchases, and post-participation is experienced through souvenirs, the development of photographs and other forms of behaviour designed to recall the holiday. Hence, holiday experiences have both spatial and time dimensions.

The overlap between leisure and tourism is, on the other hand, more apparent when the phenomenon of VFR (visiting friends and relatives) tourism is considered. It can be hypothesised that the trip activities so undertaken are akin to family daytrips; there are high degrees of familiarity with the holiday destination, and the nature of the activities may be more home-based than would otherwise be the case. Certainly in MacCannell's term the 'backroom' is certainly more open. Yet, from the viewpoint of an attraction operator counting visitor numbers, there may be little distinction between those on daytrips or those who come further afield, or in the nature of their activities once they arrive.

Yet even where familiarity with a destination is present, the experience of the visit is never the same. Interactions with different people can make it seem a different place, while the nature of the search for information about a place may be conducted less strenuously.

Having indicated some differences between tourism and recreation, Smith and Godbey emphasise their commonality. They write:

- Many authors link both recreation and leisure, as well as tourism to a spiritual search. The desire for authenticity as a driving force in tourism is a familiar hypothesis to tourism scholars, but the same theme exists in leisure studies. The two fields of study share the same dialectic between a theoretical, descriptive, cross-sectional and applied research to a new form of scholarship that emphasises theory, conceptual development, analytical rigour and eschews the concept of immediate application. It thus is attacked by academics as not having legitimacy, and from industry as not being practical.

Concepts drawn from leisure studies

There are many concepts drawn from leisure studies that can be of use to the tourism researcher seeking to understand the nature of the tourist experience, and some reviews of these can be found in the literature. From the perspective of tourist activity classification, the concept of the Recreational Opportunities was expanded by Butler and Waldbrook into a Tourism Opportunity Spectrum. These authors and others have identified a number of principles that might help to understand tourist behaviour and satisfaction. Dimanche et al. have noted the importance of involvement in the recreational activity, and this might be thought to be important in holidaytaking, given the levels of planning that might precede it and the anticipation which accompanies the period prior to departure. Laing found when analysing reasons given for independent holidaymaking, 'freedom' and 'independence' were the most quoted reasons (by 50% of the sample), while the primary reason for selecting a package holiday was that little planning was needed, and, in 16% of cases the primary reason was that 'no risk was involved'. Laing also found that for package holidaytakers, the lack of risk was the most frequently quoted secondary reason for taking package holidays, and concludes 'perceived risk... seems to play an unique role as an enforcer rather than a prime motivator to stay at home'.

However, close analysis of Laing's data shows that while risk aversion is a factor, other factors may be more important—notably the force of habit. He notes:

> for many people package holiday taking is an habitual action—they rarely consider the reasons behind the preference... (the) preference for packaged travel may be more an outcome of personal and highly individual factors which demand particular detailed analysis.

Specific risk-aversion strategies and indeed the reliance upon habit are means of avoiding the stress associated with the unfamiliar. Yiannakis and Gibson identify as two of three dimensions in their model the strange—familiar axis and the high structure-low structure dimension. Their results show that organised mass tourists score high in their needs for familiar, highly organised structures—findings which support the work of Laing. The inexperienced tourist might also show similar preferences, and from this perspective the comment by Norton that the decline of transatlantic traffic in 1985 and 1986 in the face of aircraft hijackings and other terrorist action was in part due to the inexperience of American tourists is consistent with this contention.

Gray proposes a categorisation of four components of stress that is applicable to recreation and tourism. The 'stressors' are:

(a) *intensity*—the demands of the task and self-assessment of ability to cope with those demands;

(b) *social interaction*—the relationships incurred in being part of a group;

(c) *novelty*—the creation of concern by being in a new and unfamiliar environment; and

(d) *specific situations*—the development of perceived threat within a specific set of circumstances.

Each of these factors may be viewed as possessing the characteristics of a continuum ranging from high to low intensity, high or low social interaction etc. It may therefore be possible to plot the nature of the tourist experience upon each of the dimensions Gray identifies.

The overlapping nature of the debate relating to leisure motivation is further evidenced by the concepts of boredom and frustration which are reported in the leisure literature. Patrick, Hill and Perkins, IsoAhola and Weissenger and Voelkle and Ellis, are amongst those who describe boredom as being a sense of dissatisfaction, disinclination to action, longing with an inability to designate what is longed for, a passive expectant attitude, a sense that time hangs heavy or stands still, and a sense of emotional bankruptcy and being found in situations characterised by high degrees of familiarity, lacking novelty, and having too much time for a task posing little challenge. Given such conditions it can be hypothesised that within a holiday experience low levels of satisfaction may be recorded. However, perversely, holidaymakers may also respond with low levels of dissatisfaction. Pearce, builds upon the work of Larger and Piper in suggesting that large parts of a holiday may be accompanied by a degree of mindlessness'. This might be described as being akin to the state sometimes experienced by drivers when they arrive at their destination with little ability to recall the events of the journey. A process of automatic reaction has taken place.

Within the holiday, Pearce suggests, there are a large number of potential occasions for such mindless behaviour which induces little recall. Many are highly scripted occasions where a series of familiar steps are followed in a programmed sequence. The checking in of the baggage, the ordering of a hamburger at a fast food outlet, the driving of long distances through uniform scenery would be examples of little challenge, little novelty, and hence little cause for either high or low levels of satisfaction. Would it he true to argue that the experienced holidaymaker is likely to descend into such a state of mindlessness where diminishing returns to scale have been experienced? The first Gothic cathedral visited may be fresh in the mind, but what of the fifth, sixth or twenty-sixth?

In 1988 Pearce proposed the concept of the tourist career as a progression along Maslow's hierarchy of motivation, and from this perspective the 'self-actualised' tourist would indeed find something fresh and new in the fifth, sixth or indeed the twenty-sixth Gothic cathedral that is visited. However, the tension between familiarity on the one hand, and the degree of involvement on the other is more likely to be a predictor of the degree of satisfaction to be derived from such a visit. Hence, familiarity would induce boredom, unless there is a very strong interest in Gothic architecture. However, the evidence for Pearce's concept is weak—indeed the evidence from Pearce's study of visitors to Timbertown in Australia and the study he quotes by Mills are not conclusive. Mills in his study of skiers notes, 'The context validity in terms of numbers of items and diversity within some of the operational measures in this study is admittedly weak'.

A significant concept that might incorporate the concepts of boredom, excitement, familiarity and involvement that is widely reported and used in the leisure studies literature and which can be of help in understanding tourist behaviour is the concept of flow. The concept has, for example, been used by Mannell et al. in a study of retirees undertaking exercises in Ontario, while Chick and Roberts used the dimensions of challenge and skill and resultant 'flow' in a study of Americans playing in pool leagues in bars on a Monday night. Csikszentimihalyi defines the 'flow' experience as 'one of complete involvement of the actor with his activity' and identifies seven indicators of its frequency and occurrence:

(a) the perception that personal skills and challenges posed by an activity are in balance;

(b) the centring of attention;

(c) the loss of self-consciousness;

(d) an unambiguous feedback to a person's actions;

(e) feelings of control over actions and environment;

(f) a momentary loss of anxiety and constraint; and

(g) feelings of enjoyment or pleasure.

Additionally, for the flow experience to be felt there are four prerequisites:

(a) participation is voluntary;

(b) the benefits of participation in an activity are perceived to derive from factors intrinsic to participation in the activity;

(c) a facilitative level of arousal is experienced during participation in the activity, and

(d) there is a psychological commitment to the activity in which they are participating.

It is not difficult to assume that these prerequisites are present in many holiday environments. The perception of flow thus occurs where there is a balance between the skills of the participant and the challenge inherent in the situation. If the skills possessed are inadequate for the task, frustration results. Such frustration can be evidenced by a process of annoyance, anger and possibly a collapse into sullen lethargy. Does this describe the attitude of the package holidaymaker at a foreign airport faced with a delay of an unknown number of hours of his or her charter flight with no couriers or other representatives of the company at hand? On the other hand, a situation of insufficient challenge, or lacking in an ability to involve the tourist, results in boredom. The concept has its antecedents in the Yerkes-Dodson 'Law' of arousal, and so has a long pedigree of psychological support.

It is obvious that the concept of 'flow' is applicable to work settings, but Baldwin and Tinsley conclude it is 'more readily perceived in leisure than in work'.

If, however, it is to be argued that the concept of 'flow' is applicable to holidaymaking situations and not simply to sports-orientated leisure, and if the concept of involvement is thought to be important, a necessary addition to any model of tourist behaviour and resultant satisfaction is a recognition of the role of motivation. Csikszentimihalyi notes that a prerequisite is that the activity is voluntary, thereby implying that a decision to participate has been made. Mannell et al. also argue that the concept has to incorporate a role for expectation and purpose (motivation). Arguably, within a context of holidaying activities, it is a balance between challenge, skill, motivation, and expectation that determines the experience of flow. Mannell et al. found that 'there was strong evidence for the prediction that higher levels of flow accompany freely chosen activities... freely chosen activities are not only more likely to be labelled leisure, but to be accompanied by higher levels of flow'.

The motivation for holidaytaking and holidaymaking

There are many studies of tourist behaviour that identify potential sources of holidaytaking and holidaymaking motivation. Incidentally, although the terms holidaymaker and holidaytaker are often used as interchangeable descriptions of the same thing, the distinction between the two could well be important—the 'holidaymaker' being proactive, the 'holidaytaker' more passive. Thus the abovementioned works of Yiannakis and Gibson and those of Pearce are amongst those who have proposed tourist typologies based on responses to motivational questionnaires subjected to cluster analysis or similar responses. As with all such questionnaires, the validity of the results depends not simply upon correlations of items, but upon the validity of underlying theory. The problem of reporting results simply based on the emergence of factors that are strongly correlated has been described by Bagozzi thus:

> One drawback with this procedure is its atheoretical character. Rather than proposing a structure of perceptions based on conceptual arguments and prior research, the researcher relies on the pattern of responses found in the particular data under scrutiny

> to arrive at perceptual dimensions. This can lead to fortuitous, but erroneous, solutions and tends to promote a multitude of variables and interpretations, since little consistency results across studies. A second drawback is that principal components and common factor analysis can sometimes generate many dimensions within any particular study and thus yield cumbersome models.

Again, there are motivational studies within leisure theory that may be applicable to tourism. One such concept that has been tested by other than the original authors is the Leisure Motivation Scale of Ragheb and Beard. This scale possesses four dimensions and is derived from Maslow's theories of motivation. The dimensions are:

(a) The *intellectual* component, which 'assesses the extent to which individuals are motivated to engage in leisure activities which involve... mental activities such as learning, exploring, discovering, thought or imagining';

(b) the *social* component 'assesses the extent to which individuals engage in leisure activities for social reasons. This component includes two basic needs... the need for friendship and interpersonal relationships, while the second is the need for the esteem of others';

(c) the *competence-mastery* component assesses the extent to which 'individuals engage in leisure activities in order to achieve, master, challenge, and compete. The activities are usually physical in nature'; and

(d) the *stimulus-avoidance* component of leisure motivation 'assesses the drive to escape and get away from overstimulating life situations. It is the need for some individuals to avoid social contacts, to seek solitude and calm conditions; and for others it is to seek to rest and to unwind themselves'.

The content of these dimensions are similar to those identified by commentators on tourism motivation, but the Leisure Motivation Scale has been replicated in other studies, and found to possess significant degrees of stability. Ragheb and Beard also devised two other scales of Leisure Satisfaction and Leisure Attitudes, but these have not proved so consistent. Within a UK context, Ryan reported being able to replicate the factors of the Leisure Motivation Scale.

Given the dimensions identified by Ragheb and Beard, it becomes possible to incorporate them into a more conventional attitudinal model as identified by a series of writers including Vroom, Fishbein, Bagozzi and Warshaw, and as have been developed within the tourism literature by various authors including Moutinho and Witt and Wright, amongst others. These models seek to measure the strength of the attitude held by assessing the importance of product attributes to the respondent, and the respondents' perception of the degree to which a product actually possesses the attributes. Thus, for example, a holidaymaker's attitude towards say, Benidorm, may be gauged if they value peace and quiet highly, and perceive Benidorm as lacking these attributes. Given the attitude held, then the attitude may be a precursor to action in this case to avoid having a holiday in Benidorm! The same distinction can also be held to be the basis of a gap analysis similar to that incorporated in part by the SERVQUAL model of Parasuraman, Berry and Zeaithaml. Here satisfaction is measured as a gap between client expectation and client perception of a service—a congruence between the two being a measure of satisfaction. Given that the dimensions of the SERVQUAL model incorporate tangibles, reliability, responsiveness, assurance and empathy, the application of a gap approach using the two-dimensional modelling technique inherent in both the SERVQUAL and multi-attribute models begins to provide a methodology to implement a questionnaire that utilises the attitudinal concepts of these models with a content derived from flow theories, the Ragheb and Beard Leisure Motivation Scale with additional questions designed to measure familiarity and involvement.

In short, a number of potential approaches exist in the explanation of holidaymaker behaviour, but such paradigms must recognise the:

(a) constructs of risk aversion and risk taking inherent in travel;

(b) relationship between holidaymaker and significant others—e.g. family, other tourists;

(c) relationship between tourist and tourist;

(d) use of the tourist destination zone by the holidaymaker;

(c) relationships between tourist and agencies of the tourist industry;

(f) relationships between tourist and members of the host community not employed in the tourist industry;

(g) constructs of familiarity, mindlessness and novelty;

(h) constructs of involvement and flow;

(i) constructs of motivation;

even while adhering to an accepted mode of attitude measurement.

To attempt a general model of such a nature is perhaps inconsistent with today's thinking, especially if one takes into account concepts of tourism as a postmodern activity devoid of consistency on the part of its participants as they indulge in role play. Indeed Foxall refers to the erosion of paradigms as psychologists have sought to refute, incorporate or improve understanding of human behaviour. He also comments that:

> A comprehensive plurality of paradigms is inescapable if authentic understanding of consumer behaviour is preferable to the doctrinaire parochialism that would follow the domination of consumer research by one ontology and associated methodology.

Hence a general model can only serve a limited function in the sense of providing a context of behaviour and choice. Additionally, it must not only take into account the personal factors of individual choice as listed above, but also:

(a) marketing variables—product design, pricing, advertising/promotion channels;

(b) tourist variables—previous destination experience: fife cycle, income, age, lifestyle, value system;

(c) destination awareness—unavailable or considered sets (inert, inept, evoked);

(d) affective associations of destinations—positive, negative;

(e) tourist destination preferences;

(f) formation of intention to visit;

(g) specific situational variables.

As initially noted, the holiday consists of further components, namely:

(a) travel to the destination; (b) the nature of the destination;

(c) the nature of the interaction with significant others; and

(d) activities undertaken.

Implications of the model

Once the outward journey begins, so too does a process of evaluation. The nature of the trip, its comfort, ease of journey, delays, and the ease of accessibility to the destination become part of the total experience. It is tempting to describe these experiences, in Herzberg's terms, as hygiene factors. That is, the availability of ease and comfort etc. are not in themselves predictors of high degrees of satisfaction, but their absence can generate dissatisfaction. They create dissatisfaction in two senses. Initially expectations are high, and an early disappointing experience might cause initial dissatisfaction. Second, on completion of the holiday, tourists become concerned about the need to return home in time for work, the need to make connections, or for the need to be picked up at airports by friends and relatives. Delays etc. at this stage of the holiday can cause a revaluation of the past, otherwise satisfactory, experience. If, however, the journey goes according to plan, then an expected service is delivered, but no addition to total satisfaction may occur.

This scenario may be true of mass package holidays, but not necessarily true of all types of holidays. For the explorer type of tourist, the actual journey may be the purpose and rationale of the holiday. Indeed, acceptable levels of discomfort might actually enhance satisfaction with the holiday, Furthermore, the journey, like the rest of the holiday, consists of a series of events, and to refer to satisfaction with the trip as a whole implies a process of compensating between 'highs' and 'lows'. In short, inherent characteristics of the journey do not retain constant values, but can only be evaluated by reference to the tourists' needs and expectations.

The same is true of the destination tourist zone. Conventionally the tourist literature refers to destination attributes as having different appeals to different types of tourists. Although a number of writers have sought to modify this by reference to changing tourist behaviour within a tourist zone, or from evidence of search behaviour by tourists in terms of physical exploration of sites, it is none the less recognised that the nature of the tourist destination is an important variable in determining satisfaction. It is the milieu of the goal-seeking behaviour, and must permit the sought goals to be achieved. If it does not possess this potential, the tourist will be dissatisfied. Thus, the inherent characteristics of the destination are evaluated against this matrix of needs, and expectations.

A destination may possess the right type of attributes, but still not generate a satisfactory holiday experience. This can arise for at least two reasons. The first is that the holidaymaker perceives the destination as lacking in quality. A mass tourist might view a zone as possessing hotels, bars, clubs, beaches etc., but also perceives them as being 'tacky', or overpriced, or otherwise not delivering 'value for money'.

A second reason for dissatisfaction might lie in the nature of the interactions between tourist and significant others. For example, the 'explorer' might find a destination to be 'authentically ethnic', but is unable, in McCannell's terms, to penetrate the 'back room'. The failure to establish contact with local people at what is thought to be a 'meaningful' level will leave the tourist frustrated, and hence dissatisfied. Equally, the mass-organised tourist returning to a destination which is known to meet the terms of both product mix and quality of provision, might have a less than satisfactory experience because of a failure to get on well with fellow tourists. Also, although both staff and destination characteristics remain the same, the staff cannot sustain the same quality of service as fatigue occurs on the part of service providers. Thus, the quality of the product towards the end of the high season might not be as high as at the beginning of the season (or at the end of season when pressures abate). (It is for this reason that some tour operators switch personnel at mid-season in an attempt to retain 'fresh staff' on site.)

However, the model does not predict that satisfaction will be generated by a congruence of expectation and perceived reality at the time of the initial meeting of tourist and destination. It argues that there will be a process of information acquisition, evaluation of that information, and a process of either changing evaluations of place and/or behaviour. For example, if the 'explorer' finds that the destination is more builtup than expected, a choice of reaction exists—first, accept the destination on its own terms, and so have a 'relaxing' holiday by the swimming pool, and hence return both physically relaxed and satisfied; second, decide to use the destination as a base from which to explore surrounding areas; or third, leave the area altogether. Alternatively, they may complain bitterly to the tour operator. The model postulates a process of site evaluation, and a process incorporating an ability to suspend disbelief and a search for alternative and more satisfactory sources of potential goal solution. It does postulate a model of the tourist as a goal-seeking, active participant making either internal motivational or external behaviour changes where initial expectations are not met.

What is being discussed is some form of operant performance within complex and open social settings. In short a process of contingency management is involved. Contingency management may be defined as programmes of behaviour modification based on the negotiation and implementation of a contract that specifies rewards and punishments contingent upon the performance of particular behaviours. The situation of the holiday is one where there is high motivation to achieve goals, within an at least moderately high informational context. Foxall proposes a behavioural perspective model which 'stresses the situational factors that are systematically related to such behaviours'. It is interesting to note that Foxall includes within the reinforcement component the level of informational content. It can be noted that almost by definition the holiday experience would form a 'pleasurable' context requiring hedonic responses. From the viewpoint of the above model the informational context provided by the tourist destination is important. Wearden, reviews some of the literature relating to experimental reinforcement schedules with human respondents, and concludes that 'reinforcers' are informational rather than hedonic or response-strengthening; they inform subjects of the accuracy of their performance or that it has been otherwise satisfactory. Whether adopting Foxall's or Wearden's perspective, the conditions of the destination zone and consumer experience are such that they lead to extended problem solving (EPS).

Two apparent caveats to this approach might be mentioned. The first queries the degree to which the holiday experience is entirely one where EPS occurs, and the second is whether behavioural approaches are entirely valid bearing in mind Pearce's concept of the travel career based in Maslow's work. It was previously argued that at least parts of the holiday are characterised by 'mindlessness' and by scripted occasions. For example, it can be contended that frequently repeated actions become routinised, and hence are characterised by a lack of distinguishing features. It becomes difficult for respondents to differentiate between the same action carried out on different occasions. Here the concept of the 'critical incident' as developed by Bitner et al. may be significant. It can be contended that the scripted occasion is one which meets a set of not particularly high expectations—arousal levels are low, and the tourist goes with the 'flow' involved in a low arousal-low challenge-low skill situation. On the other hand, if the occasion becomes marked by a critical incident where performance either exceeds or is significantly below expectation, the situation ceases to be a scripted occasion.

If the characteristic of the scripted occasion is one of repeated action, then by definition it is unlikely to occur in the early stages of a holiday when a tourist is learning about the destination zone. Again, caveats need to be mentioned. The scripted occasion may occur early in a holiday if it is a situation where the tourist has repeatedly returned to the destination (e.g. a 'holiday home'). Assuming that in most cases tourists are exploring new situations, it can be hypothesised that scripted occasions tend to occur only in the latter part of the holiday period, or where the tourist has significant levels of past experience of that type of situation. In short, the scripted occasion occurs through familiarity, and, from the context of information theory, not at points of discontinuity. Such an analysis is from the perspective of the tourist. From the viewpoint of the provider of the service, what is to the tourist a new situation, may in fact be a very familiar one, and the skill of the service provider is shown by their ability to 'persuade' the customer of the 'novelty' of the tourist experience. Essentially a situation perceived by the tourist as a 'scripted, mindless' experience is one that is not generating high levels either of satisfaction, or of dissatisfaction. It might be said to be satisfaction-neutral. On the other hand, a series of scripted encounters might generate satisfaction if the motivation for the holiday is primarily one of relaxation and escape from daily pressures of family and work life. The 'mindless' occasion requires little decision taking or mental exertion and poses little challenge and thus might be entirely appropriate as a holiday experience.

However, the question also remains as to the degree to which the above model can fully explain holiday satisfaction. It is a deductive model based on observation, and like many behaviourist models it can only make inferences about cognitive mediation. The question is important because the motivational models which are reviewed above, and which give rise to the items used in the Ragheb and Beard questionnaire, were based on concepts of autonomy and cognition associated with authors such as Maslow. But can such incidents be incorporated into the model of determinants of tourist satisfaction, and is it legitimate to incorporate concepts derived from humanistic psychology into a seemingly deterministic model? Skinnerian thought can be described as the proposition that observable behaviour can be explained in terms of contingent environmental stimuli; and the process whereby the rate of response is brought under the control of consequent stimuli (reinforcers and punishments). The model has not indicated the nature of reinforcement schedules, and is relativistic in its approach. It incorporates a plurality of paradigms. For example, while primarily arguing that the holiday experience by its nature uniquely meets a series of needs (for example, escape and fulfilment needs) and primarily consists of extended learning behaviours, as discussed above, it recognises routinised procedures where, arguably, Skinnerian approaches are apt descriptors. The model accords to cognitive, internalised processes important functions as motivators for holidays. The cognitive processes are also called into play as means of adjustment to initially less than satisfactory scenarios where the holidaymaker can subsequently derive satisfaction from the holiday. These internalised processes are important, because a basic premise in the argument is that similar motivations and similar holiday settings are not sufficient to predict either behaviour or the final level of satisfaction experienced.

Finally, it must be noted that the model is, at best, only a partial model. The outcome with which it is concerned is a measure of satisfaction, not behaviour. The link between satisfaction and behaviour is viewed as a reiterative process. That is, where performance meets or exceeds expectation, satisfaction is deemed to be an outcome. Where performance is inferior to expectation, then it is expected that adaptive behaviour results in achieving satisfaction because the motivation for satisfaction of wants is high within the holiday context. Where it is not possible to achieve those initial wants, alternative wants are substituted, behaviour changes, and again the goal is the satisfaction of those alternative wants. The consequence of achieving satisfaction from the holiday as to future holiday behaviour is not explored. Rather there is an implicit assumption that the link between satisfaction with a given type of holiday and repeat purchase of that holiday is, in fact, weak. The assumption is that holidaymakers use different types of holidays to meet different types of needs. The realisation of a satisfactory holiday is no guarantee of a repeat purchase. Repeat purchases may be a function of a changing prioritisation of the needs that motivate holidays, or the ability of a holiday type to meet different needs. Those needs are primarily determined not by the nature of past holiday experiences, but by other socioeconomic factors such as lifestyle, life-stage and the interpretation of the resultant experiences through the psychological network formulated by personality and learning abilities. The model also tends credence to the theories of Plog in that specific destinations will be selected by tourists because those destinations possess the attributes that permit the fulfilment of primary leisure motivations.

The formulation of propositions

Having generally discussed some of the implications of the model, the question arises, does it help to formulate specific hypotheses that can be tested? Briefly the model utilises a gap analysis approach drawn from the SERVQUAL model that satisfaction is a consequence of expectation being met. The components of expectation, and the criteria against which performance will be judged is composed of two types of attributes. Extrinsic attributes refer to specific tangibles of the holiday destination—namely accommodation, scenic and other valued physical and cultural components of the destination, the types of people that reside in the resort (both indigenous people and other visitors). Intrinsic attributes refer to the motivations, which can be categorised on the basis of the four clusters described by Ragheb and Beard.

It is now possible to formulate a series of specific search behaviour; propositions. These are:

(a) satisfaction arises from the perceived attributes of the destination matching expectation;

(b) expectation is formulated by reference to four primary leisure motivations, as described by the Ragheb and Beard Leisure Motivation Scale, namely:

the intellectual component;

the social component;

the competence-mastery component; and

the stimulus avoidance;

(c) the destination selected by a holidaymaker will possess attributes that match the primary source of motivation for that holidaymaker;

(d) the more experienced the holidaymaker, the better is the match between primary motivation source and destination attributes;

(e) the more experienced the holidaymaker, the better the match between perception and expectation, and the higher the level of satisfaction;

(f) less experienced holidaymakers will tend to have lower satisfaction scores, but a higher standard deviation of scores. Their inability to more correctly match destination with motivation will lead to a greater chance of disappointment or expectation being surpassed, hence the greater variation in the distribution of satisfaction scores;

(g) from the concept of the 'travel career' it is expected that more experienced holidaymakers will score more highly on intellectual motivations;

(h) more experienced holidaymakers will tend to show less evidence of adjustment behaviours at the holiday destination. Their ability to better select destinations that match needs requires less exploration as a sign of search behaviour designed to overcome initial disappointment;

(i) a congruence between expectation and perception of a place may not in itself lead to high levels of satisfaction being recorded. Intervening variables such as the need to select a holiday destination that meets the needs of significant others, or constraints imposed by availability of time or income, may mean the selection of a destination that does not meet the primary motivation of the holidaytaker. Therefore, where dissatisfaction occurs in spite of the congruence between expectation and perceived attributes of location, intervening variables can be identified as being important in the choice of location;

(k) the more experienced the traveller, the smaller is the number of holiday destinations considered prior to choice; and

(l) the more experienced the tourist, the more homogeneous is the selection of holiday destinations considered before a choice is made.

In a study of 1127 holidaymakers derived from the MOSAIC geo-demographic database in order to be representative of British holidaymakers, it was found that the concepts of the Ragheb and Beard Leisure Motivation Scale were applicable. Using a shortened version of the scale after a pilot study, the four dimensions of the scale could be replicated. The factors did not correlate with each other. Additionally the scale also possessed reliability as measured by Cronbach alpha coefficients, in that using a stepwise procedure which measured the total scale, and the contribution of each item to the scale, the score was consistently above 0.75. Ryan also reports that it was possible to derive clusters of holidaymakers and that significant differences existed between them both in terms of their scores on the scale, and in their requirements of holiday destinations.

The gap concept as a measure of satisfaction was also used, as indicated in Table 30.4, when seeking to correlate the gap with other measures of satisfaction derived from the conventional measures used on tour operator monitoring forms such as 'how strongly would you recommend this holiday to a friend?' and 'To what extent would you say you were satisfied with the holiday?', strong correlations emerge. In Table 30.5 the score of total satisfaction is the sum of responses to questions about:

(a) the extent to which they enjoyed the holiday

(b) the recommendation of the holiday to a friend (c) satisfaction with accommodation

(d) satisfaction with the holiday area

(e) assessment of value for money

(f) perception of enjoyment of travelling companions

What is not supported by the results is the thesis that, given initial disappointment with the holiday destination, higher search activity occurs. There was no evidence that the less satisfied conducted higher levels of exploration activity, indeed the reverse was true—namely those who explored more had higher scores of satisfaction.

It has also been shown that the situational framework of the holiday is important. For example, using the same sample Ryan reported that life-stage was an important consideration in holidaytaking decisions, and this confirmed the recent work of Lawson and Bojanic. The research is continuing and currently the relationship between familiarity and tourist satisfaction and behaviour is being examined. Early results would seem to indicate that familiarity with the type of holiday being undertaken is not significant, but familiarity with the destination, as measured by the number of previous visits to the same destination, is important.

3

Products in Leisure Tourism

The marketing mix in leisure and tourism

The marketing mix is one of the most important concepts in marketing today. It is commonly referred to as the 'four Ps':

— Product.

— Price.

— Place.

— Promotion.

Just as the ingredients must be in the correct quantities to make a successful cake, so the four ingredients of the marketing mix must be in the right proportions to make an organisation's marketing activity successful. Different leisure and tourism providers will vary the emphasis between the four Ps to meet their particular objectives. For example:

— A newly-opened hotel will spend a lot on promotion to attract customers.

— A tour operator who has just discovered that a major competitor has undercut its prices by 5 per cent may restructure its prices in order to remain competitive.

— A visitor attraction which notices that it is receiving 50 per cent more school parties than it had anticipated may need to look again at its product to see if the needs of this important sector are being met.

— Market research for a major leisure company shows

that there is an upsurge in electronic games played at home. It decides to shift resources from its chain of fast-food outlets into home-based leisure to exploit this demand.

The above examples show that emphasis on the elements of the marketing mix will vary over time, as well as between the various sectors of the industry.

Product

The leisure and tourism 'product' is very different from many other products that we buy and use. The term 'product' is something of a misnomer since leisure and tourism is a service industry; it is true that a set of golf clubs, a garden spade or football shirt are all products in the strict sense of the word, but the bulk of the leisure and tourism sector is concerned with the customer's experience and how the many elements of the sector are delivered to the customer. Below are a few examples of leisure and tourism products:

— Short breaks.
— Leisure centres.
— Nature reserves.
— Sports facilities.
— Museums.
— Holidays.
— Art galleries.
— Sports equipment.
— Events.
— A 30-minute session on the squash court.

As you can see, some products are tangible, i.e. you can touch sports equipment and see a leisure centre and its facilities. However, many leisure and tourism products cannot be seen and are, therefore, intangible. You can't, for example, see or touch a session on the squash court or a short break holiday, but you can experience it. It is this aspect of intangibility which makes leisure and tourism products so different.

It could be argued that the tangible products, such as hotels, leisure centres, tourist attractions, etc., are simply the facilities in which the intangible products are experienced; for example, the session on the squash court may well take place in a leisure centre, and the short break may well involve staying at a hotel. As well as being intangible, leisure and tourism products are also perishable; an airline seat or ticket to an event not sold today cannot be resold tomorrow.

Leisure and tourism products are also non-standardised. In other words, it is difficult to guarantee the same experience every time. A tour operator, for example, does not have control over all the elements of a package holiday. This highlights the importance of quality control in leisure and tourism. Products in leisure and tourism also tend to be unpredictable and fragile. A customer treated badly in a leisure centre, for example, may 'vote with his feet' and go elsewhere. Training in customer care is, therefore, essential for a successful organisation.

Branding

Many leisure and tourism products are given brand names, e.g. Reebok, Slazenger, Thomson, Happy Eater and Harvester, to name but a few. A brand name gives a product a certain identity, which, when coupled with promotional activities such as advertising and direct mail, helps persuade the customer to buy that particular product. Many customers show brand loyalty, meaning that they will only buy a particular brand above all others. Branding is often linked to the concept of segmentation, with brands being developed to meet the needs of a particular segment of the market. One of the best examples of this is the wide range of products on offer from Thomson Holidays. Their brands range from 'Small and Friendly', through 'Thomson Cities' to 'A la Carte'.

The product fife cycle

All products, whether they are in the leisure and tourism sector or the consumer goods market, have a life-span. There will come a time when the product is no longer in demand at all, or needs remodelling in some way to keep its customers. We are all familiar with the rise and fall of products such as the 'chopper' bike and tenpin bowling. The product life cycle concept argues that all products go through similar stages during their useful life.

1. *Launch the* product is launched with heavy promotional effort, which hope fully results in encouraging sales.
2. *Growth sales* grow steadily with increasing profits for the commercial organisation.
3. *Maturity sales* begin to decline. Perhaps competitors are offering a product with greater benefits. It is often at this point that the organisation will need to decide to either let the product die, remodel it or increase marketing support to generate more sales.
4. *Saturation sales* have reached a plateau.
5. *Decline sales* are dropping off quickly.

Programming

Programming is an often overlooked element of marketing within the leisure and tourism sector. It is most commonly associated with leisure and sports centres, but is equally applicable to theatres, local community centres or a concert hall. In tourism, tour programmes are devised to meet particular customer needs. Programming is all about making sure that a facility is used to its full capacity at all times and, certainly in the public and voluntary sectors, is used by as wide a cross-section of the local community as possible. It involves planning, scheduling, time-tabling and implementing action and should take into account not only the needs of customers but also the availability and expertise of staff and the physical resources at the organisation's disposal. Programming will help to eliminate any problems concerning the competition for use of facilities by clubs or societies and use by individuals. It will also allow better off-peak use of facilities by those customers with flexibility in their leisure time.

Price

The pricing of products and services is a crucial aspect of the marketing mix. Price is just as important as place, product or promotion; if the price is wrong, no amount of advertising or other promotional work will make the customer buy the product. Getting the price right in leisure and tourism is no easy task. The fact that it is a service industry and that most of its products are intangible makes pricing difficult. It is an industry where it is customary to charge different amounts for the same product at different times of the year and even different times of the day. An all-inclusive family French camping holiday with Eurosites, for example, will cost nearly £500 more in August than the same package in late September. Similarly, a round of golf at the local municipal course may well cost more on a Sunday morning when compared to a Tuesday afternoon. Pricing in leisure and tourism, therefore, is often related to demand.

Price is also closely allied to value, a concept that is notoriously difficult to define since it varies so much between individuals. Some people put a very high value on a particular leisure pursuit, while others will not be interested at all and it is clearly of little value to them.

Value will also fluctuate according to particular circumstances; windsurfing on a local lake in high summer will have a greater value than the same activity taking place in the freezing temperatures of February. Pricing is clearly a far more complex subject than simply adding up all the costs associated with providing a product or service, then adding a small margin of profit. The idea of what something is worth to the individual comes into play, a feature that will influence the amount he or she is willing to pay.

Before we look at some of the methods used to price leisure and tourism products, it is important to understand some of the factors that influence pricing.

— *Costs* it is important for the organisation to be aware of the costs of providing a particular product or service when deciding on its price. This may, however, only be the starting point of a much more complex pricing policy revolving around many of the concepts discussed above.

— *Demand* we have shown that the same product can command a higher price at different times according to customer demand. People will often pay high prices for exclusivity, e.g. a trip on the Orient Express or a flight on Concorde. *Competition in* the highly competitive leisure and tourism industry, an organisation will need to be aware of what competitors are charging and adjust its own prices accordingly.

— *State of the economy in* times of recession, products may be reduced in price in order to gain revenue, e.g. hotel rooms are heavily discounted, particularly at weekends when the use by business clients is low, on the assumption that it is better to get a little income for the rooms rather than nothing at all if they are left empty.

— *Objectives of the organisation clearly* a private sector company will need to maximise revenue and will try to set prices which help achieve this objective. Public sector and voluntary bodies may be able to offer more concessionary prices to achieve their social aims.

Pricing policies in leisure and tourism

From the many different pricing policies in use in leisure and tourism, the following are some of the most common:

1. *Skimming* when a high price is charged initially for a new product that is unique and that attracts people who are willing to pay the high price for status reasons. The pricing of virtual reality facilities is an example of market skimming.
2. *Cost-plus pricing sometimes* known as 'accountant's pricing', this is the rather simplistic approach that totals all fixed and variable costs and adds a small profit margin to come up with the price to charge. It assumes that an organisation can calculate its costs accurately, something that a large leisure complex,, for example, may find it difficult to do.
3. *Penetration pricing this* is used by organisations wanting to get into a new market where there are existing suppliers of the same product or service. The price will be set sufficiently low to persuade customers to switch their allegiance. It is important that this pricing method is seen as a long-term strategy since customers will resent an early rise in price.
4. *Competitive pricing sometimes* referred to as 'the going rate', competitive pricing assumes that where products or services are similar, the organisation *win* charge the going rate, i.e. will match the price of competitors. This method often leads to very low

margins and, in the long run, the collapse of some organisations, e.g. tour operators, who find their profitability is too low.

Place

Place in the context of the marketing mix, is concerned not only with the location of where leisure and tourism activities are undertaken, but also with how they are made available to the customer, sometimes referred to as the chain of distribution. We shall look at each of these in turn.

Location

The right location can often mean the difference between success and failure for a leisure and tourism facility. A farm guesthouse, for example, which is deep in the countryside and well off the beaten track, will not benefit from 'passing trade' and, unless the proprietor is skilled in marketing, will struggle to attract guests. A travel agency, on the other hand, in a busy high street location should attract a constant stream of clients. For a leisure development company looking for a suitable site for a new theme park, the prime location is likely to be close to a major centre of population. Location, therefore, is closely linked to accessibility, at the local, regional and national level. In the public and voluntary sectors of leisure and tourism, accessibility is not just about physical access to buildings, although this is important when it comes to catering for those with special needs. In these sectors, accessibility is also about providing facilities for the whole community and giving everybody equal access.

Chain of distribution

When we think of the distribution of products, images of huge container lorries full of chilled food or fashion garments driving up and down the motorway come to mind. This has little to do with how leisure and tourism products are bought or used. It is true that some tangible leisure products, such as sports goods, CDs and computer games, will pass through standard channels of distribution. The difference with many leisure and tourism products, however, is that they are consumed at the point of production so there is no need for distribution channels of any sort. For example, a round of golf takes place on the golf course, just as a game of tennis is played on a tennis court. In cases such as these, the important point is to make sure that the facilities are made accessible to the customers and that they are promoted effectively to the intended audience.

The way that holidays are sold in Britain is a good example of distribution channels in the service sector.

The tour operator assembles the 'raw materials' of a typical package holiday by buying in bulk such items as hotel rooms and airline seats. Taking on the role of the wholesaler, these are then divided into smaller proportions, the package holidays themselves, and are offered for sale through travel agents to the customers. While this is the usual method of selling holidays, there are certain companies that specialise in selling direct to the customer without using the services of travel agents. Some of the best-known of these 'direct sell' operators are Tjaereborg and Portland Holidays, which profess to being able to offer the public cheaper holidays because they don't have to pay commission to travel agents.

4

Tourism's Impact on Host Lifesyle

The past decade has witnessed the appearance of alternative tourism designs that both recognize tourism's negative impacts and portray a more positive role for tourism linked to sustainable development. Often grouped tinder the title of alternative or appropriate tourism, these forms of tourism include ecotourism, nature trave, ethnic tourism, and adventure travel. Common to all of these is the tourist's desire for a participatory experience in a distinctive and often remote natural and/or cultural environment.

With a combined annual growth rate estimated at 20% to 27%, these alternative models of tourism are the fastest-growing segment of the world travel market. Much of this growth has been associated with third world destinations, such as the Himalaya regions of Tibet, Nepal and Bhutan, the coastal and rain-forest regions of Central and South America, and the savannah regions of Africa. Currently, however, conflicting opinions abound on the role of alternative tourism in third world development. Those who champion its core principle of sustainability argue that alternative tourism can be of assistance in solving difficult third world dilemmas about conservation and economic development, as well as promoting a more equitable distribution of tourism earnings. Others suggest that the discussion on alternative tourism may be distorted, and argue that it may merely be an initial phase in an evolving system of conventional tourism which is more likely to be the ruin of ecologically and culturally sensitive areas of the third world.

A destination which has come to typify the intense debate over the role of tourism in conservation and economic development is that of Sagarmatha (Everest) National Park in Nepal. While adventure travellers continue to be graciously welcomed to this area, and massive increases in visitors have generated a variety of economic and social benefits at both the local and national levels, there has also been increasing international concern expressed about tourism's negative impacts on this fragile mountain environment and its indigenous Sherpa population. Although a large body of literature exists that has portrayed Sagarmatha National Park as both a cultural and ecological catastrophe in the making, more recent reports suggest that these criticisms are premature and have ignored the adaptive strategies which have been developed to reconcile the stresses of tourism with local capabilities and needs.

The purpose of this chapter is to describe and reappraise the economic, sociocultural, and environmental changes that have been associated with the rapid growth of adventure travel in Sagarmatha National Park. In this context, the paper examines both tile benefits and contradictions that tourism poses for sustainable development in Sagarmatha National Park, and outlines adaptive strategies that have been formulated to limit negative impacts on the local culture and environment. In seeking to further the discussion on the role of tourism in third world development, the case study of Sagarmatha National Park serves to illuminate the processes that underlie the expansion of tourism into frontier regions of the world that would not otherwise be expected to develop mass tourism, and offers lessons to guide the development of policies to promote locally directed rural development and natural resource protection in other remote and sensitive tourism destinations.

The information presented in this paper draws on the author's research experiences during two periods (five months in total) of fieldwork in Sagarmatha National Park and Kathmandu, Nepal, in the fall of 1990 and the spring of 1992. This fieldwork involved meetings with Ministry of Tourism officials in Kathmandu, general field observations in both the popular and less frequented trekking districts of the national park, discussions with the national park wardens, and interviews with Sherpas residing in the national park. This information is set against recent reports of change in the region from the tourism research literature.

In a manner similar to many other third world countries that have large external debts, poverty, and scarce natural resources, Nepal has increasingly embraced tourism as a source of easily generated revenue. Having experienced unprecedented tourism growth in the past 25 years, Nepal is now among the more popular of the international tourism destinations. Today, tourism is Nepal's foremost source of foreign income and its major industry. Nepal's fame lies primarily in trekking and mountaineering, and it was here in the 1960s, that the world's first commercial treks took place. Trekking and mountaineering visits to the Himalaya region of Nepal (which includes the protected national parks of Sagarmatha, Langtang, Shey Phksumdo and Rara, and the Annapurna Conservation Area) currently account for approximately 25% of all tourist visits to this country. This represents an increase from a mere 650 trekkers and mountaineers in 1966 to over 46 000 in 1989 (although this number fell to 35 750 in 1990 owing to major political uprisings in Nepal during 1990 and the impact of the Gulf War on international travel) Hoping to maintain the growth of high mountain visitation, the Nepal Ministry of Tourism is planning infrastructure development in existing mountain parks, and plans to open up new trekking areas where they hope to divert some of the growing number of adventure travellers.

The most renowned tourist destination in Nepal is Sagarmatha National Park, Established in 1976 and declared a World Heritage Site in 1980, the park is famous for both its towering mountains, including Mount Everest, and the culture of its Sherpa people. The park is home to approximately 3000 Sherpas who live within its 1243 km^2 borders and is associated with the Sherpa culture more than any other Nepalese park. Migrating from Tibet in the early 16th century, the lives of the Sherpa are interwoven with teachings of Buddhism, and their communities have traditionally been based on agropastoralism and trade with Tibet. The main trekking area in the park consists of four valleys near Mount Everest which are known as Khumbu region. Within Khumbu are eight Sherpa villages and over 100 seasonal herding and secondary crop sites. These villages and secondary settlements are not part of the park proper, although all Sherpa grazing and forest lands are administered by the national park

Since Nepal opened its borders to foreigners in 1951, Sagarmatha National Park has experienced a rapid increase in visitor numbers. The opening of the region's only commercial airstrip at Lukla (9000 feet) in 1964 reduced the travel time from Kathmandu to 40 minutes (as opposed to a walk in of one week from Jiri or two weeks from Kathmandu) and significantly boosted visitor numbers to the park. This region annually hosts mountaineering and trekking tourists numbering approximately twice the local population: in 1988 11366 individual trekking permits were issued for the park, although the Ministry of Tourism's most recently available statistics indicate a decline to 5144 in 1990 (which was associated with domestic political problems and the impact of the Gulf War on international travel).

With tourism as the driving force during the past 20 years, the Khumbu has undergone a rapid transition from a subsistence to a cash economy and has experienced a rapid expansion of its local economy. An increasing dependency on tourism-generated income has brought considerable local economic benefits, and the Sherpas now enjoy a standard of living which is as high as any of the country's ethnic minorities.

Although Sherpas have a reputation for mountaineering skill, mountain-climbing was not a traditional Sherpa occupation. Sherpa involvement with mountaineering began inauspiciously in the 1920s when the British hired Sherpas for the servile work of portering (load-carrying) and guiding in the pioneering explorations to Everest as well as Himalayan expeditions in North India. When trade between Khumbu and Tibet was severely impacted by the Chinese annexation of Tibet in 1959, trekking and mountaineering emerged as a new and lucrative financial opportunity. When commercial trekking began in Khumbu in the 1960s, entire Sherpa households were able to get involved in the industry. Sherpas were hired as high status guides and later as office personnel in charge of hiring in foreign-owned trekking agencies in Kathmandu. These Sherpas, in turn, ensured high employment rates for their family and friends in Khumbu villages as porters, cook staff, and camping staff.

In the 1970s, many young Sherpa men and families began to move to Kathmandu where greater employment opportunities existed in the trekking and mountaineering industry. Those with enough capital opened their own trekking agencies and hired villagers to work for them.

Sherpa entrepreneurship has continued, and of the 100 trekking and travel agencies in Kathmandu in 1989, 26 of the 56 larger agencies registered with the Nepal Trekking Agent Association were controlled by Sherpas. Five of these larger agencies employed a total of 94 permanent salaried staff, 70 employees during part of the year and 670 at peak season.

Employment in the mountaineering and trekking industry in Khumbu itself has flourished at a wide range of levels. In the villages, many Sherpas have converted their homes into teashops and lodges to accommodate the growing number of foreign visitors, and today most households earn income from providing food, lodging, clothing, equipment or handicrafts. Khumbu Sherpas control most of the region's highly profitable tourist lodges, inns and teahouses and have virtually monopolized tourism employment in the region. Young men and boys often gain low-paying jobs as porters, kitchen assistants or mail-runners on treks or expeditions. Those with more experience tend to gain salaried positions with an established trekking agency as cook or *sherpa* (a kind of general assistant to a trekking party). The most experienced Sherpas who possess leadership abilities may secure positions as trek or expedition leader (*sirdar*), which enables them to hire other villagers for daily wage work on a trek or expedition. Overall, the economic benefits appear to have been spread quite extensively throughout Khumbu; Adams reports that 80076 of the 141 village households and 92% of the urban Sherpa households from Khumbu currently earn income from tourism.

It is typical for Sherpas to earn cash wages only during the high tourism seasons of autumn and spring, and although this is only four or five months per year, their incomes are nevertheless high by Nepalese standards. The owner of a popular lodge may gross over

US$10 000 a year, and many are now among the wealthiest families in the region. In 1992, even a kitchen boy could earn more than 1500 rupees (US$50) per month, which is the equivalent to the salary of many office workers in Kathmandu. *Sirdars* may earn more than five times as much, for besides then base-salary they often make considerable extra money by making use of their own family members, servants, and packstock on treks and by over-reporting porter costs and other trail charges to their companies. Since young Sherpas contribute to their parents' household until they marry in their mid- to late-twenties and establish their own households, several members of a Sherpa household will often earn income from trekking. While women from poor households have often earned some income from portering, trekking employment to date has been male dominated, and it is only recently that women have begun to work as members of kitchen and camp crews. There are today only one or two examples of women *sirdars* in the Khumbu.

A frequent criticism of tourism in third world areas, and one that has been applied to this region, is the often exploitative nature of the tourist-host financial labour relationship. Although Sherpas have been involved in tourism through traditional wage relationships, Adams's examination of the Sherpa economy indicates that the Sherpas have become neither 'commoditized' nor 'domesticated' as part of a subordinate local economy serving a Western dominated tourism industry. Rather, increasing Sherpa ownership of trekking companies and unique tourist-Sherpa relationships have provided the Sherpas with opportunities to reconstitute their traditional social relationships, which were mixtures of both reciprocity and wage labour based upon the Sherpa ideals of individualism and independence.

Today, tourism is extremely popular with the Khumbu Sherpas. Although some disaffection with tourism does exist, the Sherpas know that most of the region's inhabitants have gamed substantially in financial terms, in standard of living and through improved medical and educational facilities, Sherpa ownership of a substantial proportion of tourism businesses means that 'financial leakage' has undoubtedly been less than in many other third world tourism areas. Primarily through tourism, this somewhat remote and poor rural society has rapidly become comparatively affluent—a situation which Stevens and Sherpa and Adams have characterized as representing one of the world's foremost examples of successful local economic development through tourism.

However, notwithstanding the Khumbu's current positive economic situation, the course of subsequent events will require careful attention. Not all Sherpa families have benefited equally from tourism, and neither have all Khumbu villages benefited from tourism. Related to the increasing demands from trekking and mountaineering groups, the inflation of the price of food and supplies in Khumbu has financially burdened those poorer families not involved in tourism. Also, while the region's tourism centre of Namche (11000 feet) has experienced massive economic benefits, those villages remote from the main trekking routes, such as Thame, have changed very little.

Despite the aims of the Nepal government, there would appear to be little scope for further growth of tourism in Khumbu. This is primarily because the two airlines that fly into Lukla are severely limited in the number of tourists they can transport. Lukla's rudimentary landing strip, as well as the frequently turbulent flying conditions between Kathmandu and Lukla, have generated for better or worse—a significant transportation bottleneck. Trekkers, however, will always have the option of a one to two-week walk in, and helicopter charters from Kathmandu are becoming popular. Yet, even though the number of tourists is likely to remain fairly constant, new lodges continue to be built in Namche and along the lower Khumbu trekking route leading to Namche. As Fisher has noted, should the number of lodges proliferate too rapidly in this region, then earnings will be divided into an increasing number of shares, with average incomes diminishing or some businesses prospering at the expense of others. Khumbu Sherpas are also facing increased competition for trekking and mountaineering employment from neighbouring Solu Sherpas and other ethnic groups, such as Rais, Gurungs and Tamangs, who migrate seasonally into Khumbu in increasing numbers to seek primarily portering employment. A new trend of foreign ownership of accommodation facilities, such as the newly reopened Japanese-owned luxury Everest View Hotel near Namche, also threatens Sherpa domination of the lodge industry.

The greatest apparent risk for large-scale tourism employment in the region is that tourism itself is susceptible to many events that can cause a major decline in the industry. The ramifications of such events as domestic political problems, a change in the government's tourism policy (Nepal establishes new tourism goals and policies every five years), economic recession, or another international oil crisis could be financially catastrophic to the region's newly monetarized economy. However, given that many 'tourist Sherpa' still return to their traditional lifestyles in the summer monsoon and winter seasons, most Sherpas do not as yet appear to have severed either their traditional economic or psychological ties to customary village life. As both Adams and Fisher have suggested, unlike inhabitants of other parts of the world who are heavily involved in tourism, most Sherpas would still be capable of returning to their customary ecological niche, and those who have been sufficiently educated would have the option of obtaining office jobs in Kathmandu and elsewhere.

Acculturation of indigenous peoples, where entrepreneurs transform remote destinations into tourist places, has become an important issue for a growing number of scholars. While acculturation is difficult to determine or measure because it hinges on the resiliency of the culture, a number of anthropological, geographical and general impact studies indicate that the region's economic transformation has not been achieved without some social and cultural cost to the Sherpas.

Since the advent of tourism in this region in 1950, a profound change in patterns of livelihood has occurred, with many local occupations having declined in importance. For many young people, particularly men, trekking employment is more attractive and certainly more lucrative than both traditional village-based agricultural work or work in the more skilled professions such as local schoolteacher or carpenter. Moreover, although there are exceptions, even young Sherpas from wealthier families tend to prefer the short-term financial rewards of trekking employment to the delayed benefits of higher education. Although these changes could eventually rob 'he region of an important facet of its traditional culture, his seems unlikely to occur given that the Sherpas still value (and indeed are required to retain) the traditional village-based skills essential to their 'off-season' agropastoral subsistence lifestyle. However, these changes livelihood patterns have contributed to a variety of changes in both the social structure and cultural fabric of the Khumbu.

For example, while land and animal ownership was

the traditional source of local social status, nascent class differences have now developed based on cash income from tourism and the overtly different lifestyle associated with it. Those families with high earnings from tourism businesses, large numbers of pack animals, and sirdar positions have become both increasingly more affluent than neighbouring villagers and increasingly more influential than local religious leaders and regional elders. Owing to their involvement in the tourism industry, many of the new Sherpa elite also spend more time out of Khumbu than at home, with many spending 10 months a year away from their villages. This social restructuring has in some instances adversely affected Khumbu political institutions. To serve effectively in a *panchayat* (village government) it is necessary to live in the area, but given the large seasonal outflow of the region's most capable young men, *panchayat* members are often either capable but absentee leaders or are villagers with minimal interest in local affairs. According to Fisher, this has fragmented village interests, with different individuals or groups promoting often disparate goals, and a lack of consensus occurring on important issues, such as management of common pasture lands or the development of new hotel facilities.

Social restructuring associated with tourism has also impacted the region's demographic makeup. For example, seasonal migration among the Sherpas has contributed to a decrease in the birth rate and a concentration of births nine months after the summer monsoon. While the family-planning service now available through the Khunde Hospital has contributed to the lower birth rate, this decline has been generated in part by the lesser economic importance of children in a tourism dominated economy than in the formerly agropastoralism dominated economy. A further demographic change wrought by Sherpa involvement in the high-altitude mountaineering industry is the region's notably high mortality rate among its young male population: Fisher indicates that from 1950 through to the middle of 1989, 84 Sherpas died on mountaineering expeditions in Nepal, the majority of whom were Khumbu Sherpa.

While the impact of tourism on social structure has often been quite explicit, the Westernization of the Sherpa culture is a much more difficult and value-laden issue to address, with much depending on how one perceives the dynamics of culture. Sherpas certainly admire the West because their association with it to date has been financially very lucrative and has opened up new avenues of social mobility and wealth. Because of this, the Sherpas have inevitably adopted some facets of Western culture, lifestyle, and values. Thus, other than for ceremonial occasions, traditional robes (chubas) are rarely worn by many Sherpas; rather, both young and old Sherpas now prefer Westernstyle dress (often garments given to them by foreign visitors) and some flaunt Western accoutrements such as a Walkman and headphones. In the new cash economy, many Sherpas also purchase more readily available manufactured items, such as cooking utensils or cloth, from Asia.

Foreign sponsorship (in the form of monetary or material gifts, business partnerships, and trips to a sponsor's home) is also currently provided to over one-third of Khumbu families, and has contributed to many Sherpas having travelled extensively in foreign lands and to an increasing number having gained university training abroad. Through contact with tourists, as well as their own international travel, Sherpas have certainly gained a broader understanding of modern hygiene, Western languages, and material culture generally.

As the foregoing passage indicates, certain facets of

cultural change related to tourism are now quite apparent in Khumbu; yet if the essence of culture, as Greenwood has defined it, is something that people believe in implicitly and something that gives them the very meanings by which they organize their lives, then the Sherpa culture is both intact and strong. Buddhism has always been the centralizing agent of Sherpa culture, and recent studies by both Fisher and Stevens and Sherpa concur that there seems to have been no lessening of the Buddhist faith or weakening of its core values among the Sherpas. Indeed, local interest and involvement in many Buddhist rituals, such as the annual Mani Rimdu festival at Thyangboche Monastery, appear to be as strong, as ever, Moreover, unlike in some third world tourism places, tourism has not fostered any sense of cultural inferiority among the Sherpa people. Indeed, rather than becoming overly Westernized, Sherpas tend to think of themselves primarily and uncompromisingly as Sherpa and have come to value some of their traditions even more strongly than they did prior to the advent of tourism.

The resiliency of the Sherpa identity has been supported by Western respect and admiration for Sherpa culture and by the unique nature of the social relationships which often develop between Sherpas and Western visitors during a mountain adventure. The image that Westerners have developed of the Sherpa—that of an egalitarian, peaceful, industrious, independent, and compassionate people—in many ways represents a dramatic realization of what Westerners would like to be themselves. Mountaineering and trekking also afford a great deal of personal interaction between tourists and hosts, with the foreign visitor often feeling what Adams has termed an 'unfulfilled gratitude' toward their Sherpa companions at the close of an arduous trip. Fisher contends that, because of a very positive Western perception of the Sherpa culture, coupled with distinctive host-client interactions, the Sherpa have been massively reinforced by Westerners for being Sherpa and have every reason to value and maintain their Sherpahood.

Tourism, however, is still recent to this region; it is only since the late-1970s that visitors have begun to outnumber the local Sherpa population and Sherpa involvement in tourism has become widespread. While the Sherpa have to date effectively embraced tourism within the confines of their own culture, one is drawn to ponder the nature and extent of change that further development will inevitably bring. Given the 'independent explorer' type of tourist who is most commonly attracted to destinations such as Sagarmatha, further sociocultural change may prove to be minimal: independent explorers tend to be culturally sympathetic toward host communities and to travel in small numbers, and therefore tend to have less impact on a host culture than does mass tourism. Such optimism, however, may prove to be unfounded for a number of reasons.

For example, in a given trekking group the average Sherpa-to-tourist ratio is two-to-one and often greater, the trek usually extends from two to four weeks, and most tourists trek toward Mount Everest through a narrow corridor that is inhabited by fewer than 1000 Sherpas. Consequently, contact with local Sherpas is extensive and penetrates deeply into the personal lives of the Sherpas, and the potential for change is therefore greater than in mass tourism. Moreover, research suggests that Khumbu tourists are typically more concerned with environmental rather than cultural degradation and many arrive in Khumbu quite naive of local customs and manners and often display inappropriate tourist behaviour. (In an effort to educate tourists about Sherpa customs Stevens and Sherpa have recently posted guidelines for

'Responsible Tourism in Sagarmatha National Park' in all Khumbu lodges.)

While tourism has helped to finance the rebuilding of the Thyangboche Monastery and other religious places in the region, the fear exists amongst some Sherpas and scholars that while preserving the artefacts of Buddhism, tourism may eventually destroy the spirit needed to maintain it. To thrive, the Buddhism religion requires knowledgeable specialists and the commitment of local people, but the prolonged absence of Sherpas from the villages may result in many Sherpas having little experience of Buddhist rituals.

Despite the efforts of both regeneration projects and local initiatives, the region still faces the possibility of a major fuel crisis at some point in the future. Given the fuel demands of the massive seasonal influx of tourists, as well as the demands of both local Sherpas and seasonal migrants seeking employment, the region's greatest long term need is for a readily available alternative source of fuel to that of wood, The national park and Nepal government are urgently required to take more initiative in introducing alternative energy resources, such as mini hydro projects (as currently exist in Namche and Thame) or the use of kerosene stoves for high-altitude lodges. These energy sources are, however, very expensive for local people, and would require subsidizing if they were to be widely adopted in the region. Given that Nepal's major parks currently generate in excess of US$800000 in entry fees, US$230000 for trekking permits, and US$300 000 for mountaineering fees, the government would be wise to substantially increase its expenditures on maintaining the parks. A fuel subsidy would have ample economic justification given that severe impacts related to deforestation could lead to an economically disastrous decline in visitor numbers.

Forest degradation and loss of ground-cover have been aggravated by pastoral land-use changes associated with tourism. Recent reports suggest that the increasing importance of packstock (yak or yak crossbreeds), rather than porters to transport trekking and mountaineering goods, has contributed to the collapse of some communal pastures and has substantially increased grazing pressure in some neighbouring woodlands and grasslands. The loss of herbaceous ground-cover in the higher alpine elevations has also exacerbated the problem of soil loss associated with increased harvesting of juniper shrub. These changes may have long-term Impacts on forest regeneration, as well as on grassland productivity and soil erosion.

While tourism has also increased regional demands for food, most of this demand has been satisfied by increased imports of food generated by agricultural restructuring in the area to the south of the park. The state of agricultural production in Khumbu itself is subject to conflicting reports. Fisher reports that in 1974 Khumbu Sherpas began hiring Solu Sherpas in large numbers to work their fields while they pursued more lucrative trekking jobs. However, as the Solu Sherpas increased their involvement as load carriers in the tourism industry, the marginal fields were increasingly abandoned for lack of workers to cultivate them. Stevens and Sherpa dispute this, and report that long-abandoned marginal land has often been mistaken for recently abandoned land, and that during recent years the area of crop production has actually expanded such that regional production is now at an all-time high.

An increasing problem in this area, and one that has been extensively documented, is that of waste-disposal. The indiscriminate disposal of human waste, and the dangerous threat to health associated with it, remain serious problems in the more popular trekking areas.

Reckless surface disposal and watercourse disposal have led to widespread water contamination in the region, and increased construction of sanitation facilities by the national park is urgently required. The more popular trekking routes and mountain base camps are also infamous for the quantities of refuse left by an increasing number of travellers. In recent years, the importation of plastic and glass bottles, and other non-biodegradable products such as alkaline batteries and tin cans, have conspicuously heightened the problem. The situation has also been exacerbated by the Sherpa concept of pollution, which concerns only the self, or human creations and artefacts, and is unrelated to Westernstyle perceptions of litter. Ironically, Sherpas themselves are responsible for the bulk of litter along the trekking routes.

In recent years, the refuse problem has been compounded by the Ministry of Tourism removing the traditional limit to the number of mountaineering expeditions which are allowed on major peaks in any given climbing season. This ruling, as well as a recent massive increase in the growth of commercial (client funded) mountaineering expeditions to the region, resulted, for example, in over 350 climbers residing at the Everest base camp during the spring of 1992. Everest base camp sites are littered with the detritus of scores of expeditions, and Byers et al. estimate that since 1963 over 500 empty oxygen bottles have been dumped above base camp at the South Col. Unfortunately, the Nepal government ignored recent remonstrations in 1992 from the international climbing community to restore the mountain's sanctity by imposing drastic limits on the number and size of future expeditions. Instead, the Ministry of Tourism chose to increase the fee per climber from US$1100 to US$10000 and to reintroduce laws and a deposit system requiring all expeditions to pack out their litter and discarded mountaineering equipment. How strictly this system will be enforced remains to be seen. Hampered by a lack of funding and shortage of staff, the national park has been unable to implement clean up projects of trekking routes and mountaineering base camps. Rather, cleanup expeditions continue to be conducted by concerned environmental groups from abroad, as well as by trekking agencies who frequent the region. More recently, Sherpa concern has led them to initiate their own cleanup campaigns, such as the Sagarmatha Club of Namche project, and Stevens and Sherpa report that the newly formed Sherpa Pollution Control Committee, supported by an endowment from the World Wildlife Fund, will work with the national park to coordinate future cleanup projects in the region.

The foregoing reappraisal of the nature and extent of tourism-related change in Sagarmatha National Park suggests that while the region is not without notable detrimental impacts, its characterization as an ecological and cultural catastrophe in the making has been premature. Some reports of adverse environmental impacts appear to have been overstated, and many of the worst impacts are being alleviated through both local and international efforts, Sherpas have also become highly affluent by Nepalese standards and, despite a changing economy and some social restructuring, their culture is strong and in many ways appears to have been intensified rather than adulterated by the presence of tourism. Other impacts, however, especially those of forest degradation and loss of ground-cover, remain serious problems, despite efforts to address them.

Many remote alternative tourism destinations in the third world operate in tourism development contexts that are not dissimilar to that of Sagarmatha National Park: most have a sizeable indigenous population that possesses strong cultural ties with past traditions and evolving ties to a land and renewable resource base; the indigenous population recognizes that their region, traditions and culture are of interest to the modern tourist; and, most have a limited but evolving infrastructure to cope with increasing tourist numbers. So the Sagarmatha National Park case study offers the following lessons to guide the successful development of alternative forms of tourism in other remote, ecologically and culturally sensitive areas of the world.

Having lacked a tourism development plan, Sagarmatha National Park is now responding in *ad hoc* fashion to counter the undesirable impacts of uncontrolled tourism development. The Sagarmatha experience indicates the necessity of establishing a *priori* a regional tourism development plan which considers the region's natural and social carrying capacities, and which encompasses a clear vision of what constitutes development that is *appropriate* to maintaining an area as a viable alternative tourism destination. Further environmental and cultural change, or the overdevelopment of services and facilities, could sufficiently change the tourism product provided by this region to cause the park to be abandoned as a destination for the true adventure traveller. The growth of adventure tourism in Sagarmatha has in many respects paralleled the stages of Butler's tourist area cycle model. Having passed quickly through the early stages of 'exploration' (few visitors and meagre facilities) and 'involvement' (residents provide services to increasing numbers of visitors), the region appears to be in the stage of 'development' (commercial and national agencies become involved in developing the area, the destination is advertised internationally, and visitor numbers peak). However, should tourism planning (or a lack of it) take the region beyond the 'development' stage, into 'consolidation' (development focuses almost exclusively on tourist services) and 'stagnation' (serious and long-term impacts occur), then Sagarmatha National Park may lose its niche in the international adventure travel market.

The measure of appropriate tourism development ultimately rests in the measure of its sustainability, which is determined by how successfully it protects the region's natural resources and environmental quality, minimizes adverse cultural impacts, and preserves the kind of experience which is important to its visitors. In seeking to achieve these outcomes, a regional tourism plan may regulate visitor ceilings and visitor user fees, set visitor quotas where necessary, authorize tourist access to given areas and guide tourist behaviours/activities, direct the development of infrastructure and services, generate taxation policies to equitably distribute tourism income, and regulate the utilization of' the region's natural resources. Management planning must also be an on going process involving periodic reviews to allow for changing regional objectives and adjustment to existing regulations.

For example, given that volume of tourists is closely tied to regional change, a strong case can be made for reducing tourist numbers in Sagarmatha National Park while increasing their per capita expenditures. The park entry fee (about US$10) and trekking permits (about LJS$5/week) are currently so low as to be inconsequential to the majority of park visitors. Reducing visitors would not necessarily hurt the local economy if trekking fees were increased and the revenues put toward park improvement, or used for local subsidies (for alternative fuels for example) or local community development programmes. Gurung has further suggested that, in order to spread tourists more evenly through Nepal's parks, trekking or park entry fees could be set at different levels with relatively high fees for overcrowded areas and low fees for rarely visited areas.

From this perspective, alternative tourism development would preferably be selective and small in scale, which, while generating only modest economic returns, would better safeguard the local culture and protect natural resources.

Essential to the coordination of regional tourism planning is a protected area authority that has real decision and policymaking clout and adequate funding to service its programmes, Sagarmatha National Park managers have been criticized for focusing their efforts on forest protection at the expense of providing a lack of direction for tourism development, especially with regard to regulating visitor numbers, the proliferation of lodges, overgrazing by packstock, and dealing with waste disposal. In reality, however, the park authorities have been in the difficult position of having quite limited political power and insufficient funding to effectively run conservation or development projects, The park authority is required to run its programmes on whatever budget it is allocated by the government, it has no legal authority to intervene in village affairs, and it has at present minimal jurisdiction over visitors. For example, while the park authorities regard excessive visitations as contributing to substantial environmental degradation, a complex system beyond their influence dictates the level of visitation, with the Department of Immigration issuing all visas and trekking permits, the Nepal Mountaineering Association issuing trekking peak (below 6000 in) permits, and the Ministry of Tourism authorizing expeditions to the higher peaks.

Successful tourism planning requires the expertise of individuals who are familiar with the region's social, cultural and ecological underpinnings, and who share a commitment to maintaining the region's long-term vitality. Protected area managers in the third world are often native to the area or have resided for long periods in the area, and therefore tend to be knowledgeable of the area's successes and problems. Furthermore, since they can also provide the security of long-term planning, park managers should have real decision-making influence when it comes to where, when and what kind of tourism should be permitted when the principal attraction is a protected area.

The experience at Sagarmatha National Park demonstrates that local people can benefit economically from tourism development while maintaining their cultural integrity and major control of their local land and resource base. Although some of the processes that have shaped this balance may be unique to the region, others have wider applicability. The seasonality of tourism has allowed the Sherpas to maintain subsistence agriculture as a major part of their lifestyle and to not become entirely dependent on tourism revenues. Their close-knit society and strong culture have also been helped by distinctly supportive host-client relations. Perhaps of most significance, tourism development in Khumbu has been shaped first and foremost by the Sherpa themselves, with relatively little direction from the national park or local governments. Through their entrepreneurial efforts and support by foreign loans, the Sherpa have been able to dominate lodge ownership and regional tourism employment. The integration of panchayat (village government) in Khumbu has also enhanced community involvement in directing aspects of tourism development, and the reintroduction of the traditional forest guardian system has seemingly led the local people to see the forests again as their resource and responsibility, and has increased their concern for forest protection. Although Sherpa access to forest and grazing resources has been restricted by park regulations, these costs appear relatively minor in comparison to their economic gains from tourism.

While the accomplishments in Sagarmatha National Park may be difficult to realize in other tourism places of the third world, there are valuable lessons to be learned on the involvement of local communities. Since local people must live with the long-term consequences of tourism development, local communities must at the outset be educated to develop an understanding of what tourism means as a concept, and be made aware not only of its potential economic benefits but also of both the positive and negative changes that tourism may bring to their lifestyles and social structures. Tourism must also be developed within the traditions of existing communities, essential to which is the involvement of local communities in decision-making processes that directly influence their lifestyles, affect their community development, or use the locality's natural resources. The more aware local people are made of the potential rewards and pitfalls of tourism, and the more they are involved in and benefit from tourism development, then the greater the likelihood that they will accept the tourism industry and commit to preserve the natural and cultural values upon which tourism is based.

According to Shaw et al., the significance of tourism to the economy of the United Kingdom is, 'considerable and takes a variety of forms ranging from its contribution to the balance of payments through to its role in the creation of jobs'. The economic and political importance of tourism is recognised through the development of ministerial guidelines and tourism growth projects. Interested parties tend to stress tourism's role in terms of the country's balance of payments, its potential as a stimulatory factor, and as an aid to the promotion of regional development.

Because of its economic potential, tourism has traditionally been studied in terms of its economic impact on a region or nation. However, in the late 1970s an increasing awareness developed regarding the potential social, cultural, and environmental impacts of tourism. Studies conducted in the United States, Europe and the United Kingdom focused on residents' perceptions of the impact of tourism on their community. This line of research focused on the notion that the continued support of residents was vital to regional tourism's success.

Although inconclusive, the results of early studies suggested the existence of several relationships. Pizam reported that heavy tourism concentration leads to negative attitudes towards tourism development. Studies conducted by Rothman, and Var et al. found that residents who were employed in the tourism industry saw tourism development more favourably than those who were not. In Santa Marta, Columbia, Belisle and Hoy found that the distance of residence from the central tourist zone was a significant predictor of residents' perceptions of tourism development. It has been suggested that residents' perceptions of tourism's impact are unrelated to resident characteristics. Studies have shown that residents perceive the positive impact of tourism to be related to its potential as an employment generator, Residents of various communities have also been found to associate certain negative impacts with tourism development. These include increased congestion, crowding and noise. It has also been suggested by Sheldon and Var, that length of residence affects residents' sensitivity to the impact of tourism.

Many of the early studies were exploratory in nature and limited their attention to particular environments. Inskeep suggested that attention should be paid to existing tourism destinations 'which are beginning to suffer some environmental or social problems of overdevelopment or unsuitable development'. Most of this research, although interesting at a descriptive level, lacked a theoretical framework to explain residents' perceptions. Recently, the biological concept of carrying capacity has been extended to include social issues. This concept has been recognised as useful in the assessment of the social impacts of tourism. According to Murphy, the measurement of social carrying capacity has proved difficult, but recognition of the concept as a means to explain residents' perceptions may have great potential. D'Amore defined social carrying capacity as 'that point in the growth of tourism where local residents perceive on balance an unacceptable level of social disbenefits from tourism development'.

York is a leading destination in the United Kingdom with an estimated 2 610 000 tourists in 1984. The income received from these visits, excluding accommodation, was estimated at 14.4 million pounds sterling or the US equivalent, 25.5 million dollars.

At a time when the average length of stay in Britain has fallen to an all-time low of 10.8 days there is a great deal of competition between cities attempting to increase visitor levels.

Visitor levels have increased from 1 154 000 in 1970, to 2610000 in 1984. In order to cope with the number of tourists, the number of visitor beds has increased from 1900 in 1970 to 5848 in 1988. Feinstein stated that 'tourism has made a vital contribution to the recent prosperity of the city, and that one of the best prospects for the future must lie in its further growth'. This statement concerning the economic potential of tourism development is a constant and dominant feature within local government tourism development policies, a feature compounded by the authority vested in local government to establish tourism development policies.

Interest in the social aspects of tourism are comparatively recent. According to Cleverdon and

Edwards, academic recognition of the importance of tourism's impact on a society and culture dates from the early 1970s. More recently, Ap conducted a review of four studies, and found that a variety of approaches had been used to gain insight into residents' perceptions of tourism development. Ap suggested five possible strategies to improve the measurement of the social aspects of tourism development. These can be summarised as follows:

I. Research should be based within a conceptual and theoretical framework.
2. More attention should be given to the significant findings to date.
3. More emphasis should be placed on longitudinal research.
4. Reliability and validity measures should be reported and identified.
5. Sampling methodology should be accurately reported and described.

The majority of studies on residents' perceptions of tourism development have taken place in small rural or resort-type destinations. In contrast, the urban environment has been largely ignored. This study attempts to extend the work of Perdue et al. into a large urban area. The authors attempted to develop a greater conceptual and theoretical under standing of residents' perceptions of tourism's impact on their community. With respect to the strategies proposed their model may prove pivotal in establishing a conceptual framework of residents' perceptions of tourism development in relation to their characteristics, perceptions and support for specific 2 policies. Research questions

1. To what extent do residents' characteristics (home ownership, age, whether or not they were born in

York, income, length of residence in York, and distance of residence from the central tourist zone) and economic reliance on the tourism industry (employment in the tourism industry, and the importance of tourism to their occupation) predict positive perceptions of tourism development?

2. To what extent do residents' characteristics and economic reliance on the tourism industry predict negative perceptions of tourism development?
3. To what extent do residents' characteristics, economic reliance on the tourism industry, and positive and negative perceptions of tourism development, predict support for local government control of tourism development?
4. To what extent do residents' characteristics, economic reliance on the tourism industry, and positive and negative perceptions of tourism development, predict support for local tax levies for tourism development?

Hypotheses

1. No differences will be found among the independent variables (residents' characteristics and economic reliance) regarding their ability to predict residents' perceptions of the positive aspects of tourism development.
2. No differences will be found among the independent variables (residents' characteristics and economic reliance) regarding their ability to predict residents' perceptions of the negative aspects of tourism development.
3. No differences will be found among the independent variables (residents' characteristics, economic reliance, and positive and negative perceptions of tourism development) regarding their ability to predict residents' support for local government control of tourism development.

4. No differences will be found among the independent variables (residents' characteristics, economic reliance, and positive and negative perceptions of tourism development) regarding their ability to predict residents' support for local tax levies for tourism development.

The city of York is unlike most other English cities in that the city centre is surrounded by walls, and therefore physically demarcated from its suburbs. In order to ensure that each household within the York area possessed an equal chance of being selected for the study, a circle, with a radius of four miles was placed on the map of York and surrounding area. The location on which the centre of the circle was positioned, was called Parliament Street. This street was selected following discussions with the Chief Executive of the York visitor and Conference Bureau, Paul Wells. Conversation at this meeting centred on the question of, 'How could one define the central tourist zone in the city of York?' It was the opinion of Mr Wells that the central tourist zone was fairly well outlined by the new paving works around the city centre. These works were intended to remove vehicles from the central city. Parliament Street is the centremost street in this area and has been selected for redevelopment at a cost of three million pounds sterling (US: 5.3 million dollars), scheduled for completion in early December 1992. Each grid-referenced square on the map which lay on the peripheral boundary of the circle was included if at least 50% of its total area fell within the outer boundary.

Each grid square which fulfilled the above criterion, was enumerated. With this completed, the total sample area was seen to consist of 131 grid squares. From this sample area, 10 grid squares were selected using a random numbers table. The sampling frame consisted of all residential addresses within the 10 grid squares chosen. The completion of this task was facilitated by the use of the Royal Mail's Postal Address File on Compact Disc. The computer then performed a grid search that produced a list of all the streets and residential addresses, including their post codes, contained within those areas. A booklet was compiled from this information which consisted of 7728 residential addresses. Each address was subsequently enumerated.

After 15 years of research interest in this area, results, on which many recommendations have been made, still appear inconclusive. Low sample response rates, 20%, 21%, 25%, and a fragmented approach to research methodologies (telephone survey, mail questionnaire, personal interviews, hand-delivered and collected questionnaires), while highlighting some important perspectives have only served to raise more questions.

Murphy obtained 283 usable responses, 68 from Windsor, 89 from Torquay, and 126 from York. Again one must wonder about the level of representation achieved by so few responses given the size of the respective populations.

Dillman's Total Design Method was adopted in an attempt to improve the effectiveness of data collection. Dillman recommends the use of three separate mailings. The first includes a letter of introduction and the research instrument. The second takes the form of a postcard reminder, and the third is a follow-up letter to non-respondents with a replacement questionnaire.

A total of 315 usable questionnaires was returned. The final response rate was 58%.

The survey instrument used in this study comprised a subset of items from the Lankford Tourism Impact Assessment Model and a scale developed by Perdue et al.

The instrument consisted of two sections. The first section included 19 closed-style items and required respondents to rate their level of agreement with each item, through indicating their response on a five-point Likert scale which ranged from strongly disagree (1) to strongly agree (5). Each of the items were related to specific aspects of tourism development. Several of them shared an interest in a particular aspect, therefore enabling the creation of subscales. Two scales were developed. The first contained nine items related to positive aspects of tourism development, while the second contained eight items pertaining to negative aspects of tourism development.

An additional two items were also included in the first section. The first concerned residents' support for local government control of tourism development, while the second regarded residents' support for a local tax levy for tourism development).

The second section sought demographic information and is summarised below.

The majority of respondents (32%) were between 31 and 45 years of age. The overall mean age for the sample was 44.4 years (SD 0.94). The actual mean age of adult residents in York was 46 years at the time of the last census in 1981 (Her Majesty' Stationery Office, 1982). Nearly 54% of the sample were born in York, and 68% reported owning their own home. The number of females responding accounted for 53076 of the sample. This figure is representative of the actual number of females living in the York area, which according to the latest census was 52.4%. A large proportion of respondents (71%) had lived in York for over 20 years (*M* = 33.3, *SD* = 1. 15). Nearly 61% of the sample had an annual household income of less than 14 999 pounds sterling. Nine per cent of the sample reported that a member of their family was currently employed in the tourism industry. In addition, 15% felt that the tourism industry was either important, or very important to their occupation.

The independent variables were entered into the equation on the basis of past research and in accordance with Ap's recommendations. Further to this the 'I strongly disagree, 2 = disagree, 3 = neutral, 4 = agree, 5 = strongly agree. 'Scale range= 945. 'Reversed coded item order of variable entry was such that Perdue et al.'s model could be tested.

In the process of testing the research questions, several items from within the blocks of independent variables proved significant in their ability to predict the dependent variable, There was a significant relationship between the importance of tourism to the respondent's occupation and the positive perception of tourism development (Beta = 0.2l, p <0.01). Similarly, those employed in the tourism industry (Beta = 0. 16, p < 0.05) were more likely to perceive the positive aspects of tourism development than those who were not similarly employed. Residents' negative perceptions of tourism development (Beta = 0. 18, p <0.05), were found to be significant predictors of respondents' support for local government control of tourism. The most significant findings of the study appeared during the testing of research question four. Those who owned their home (Beta = 0.16, p < 0.01) were less supportive of local tax levies to support tourism development than those who rented their home. As the respondents' age increased, so too did their support for local tax levies (Beta = 0. 13, p < 0.05). The greater the annual household income (Beta = 0.17, p <0.01) the more agreeable residents were to a local tax levy for tourism development. Finally, the greatest significance was found to exist between respondents' positive perceptions of tourism development (Beta= 36, $p < 0.001$) and their support for a local tax levy for tourism development. This suggests that the more positively respondents perceived the impact of tourism development, the more supportive they were of a local tax levy for tourism development.

The results of the hierarchical regressions rejected all four null hypotheses. The hierarchical regression models used to test research questions one and four were found to be particularly strong. They explained 17% and 30% of the variance in positive perceptions and support for local tax levies for tourism development respectively. In contrast, the hierarchical regression models used to test research questions two and three were more modest in their ability to explain the total variance in the dependent variables. The second regression using residents' negative perceptions of tourism development as the dependent variable explained 10% of the variance. The third regression using residents' support for local government control of tourism development as the dependent variable explained only 8% of the variance.

The four main findings resulting from the data analysis are summarised. First residents' characteristics were able to predict a significant amount of the explained variance in residents' positive perceptions of tourism development. Secondly, residents' characteristics also contributed significantly to residents' support for a local tax levy for tourism development. Third, residents' economic reliance on the tourism industry made a significant contribution to the explained variance in residents' positive perceptions of tourism development. Finally, residents' positive perceptions of tourism development was a significant predictor of residents' support for local tax levy for tourism development.

The finding that residents' characteristics predicted

both residents' positive perceptions of tourism development and their support for a local tax levy contradicts earlier research which suggested that residents' characteristics had little effect on residents' perceptions and attitudes concerning tourism development. The implication that emerges from these findings is that researchers and planners alike should not ignore the potential of residents' characteristics to predict a community's positive perceptions of tourism development and their support for specific tourism policies in large, relatively stable urban populations.

A positive relationship was found to exist between residents' positive perceptions of tourism development and their economic reliance on the tourism industry. This finding is consistent with the results reported in earlier research.

Finally, residents' positive perceptions of tourism development were found to predict their support for a local tax levy which would be used to assist additional tourism development. Inasmuch as this represents their support for additional development, this finding agrees with that of Perdue et al., that support for additional development was positively related to residents' positive perceptions of tourism development. This finding is especially interesting because it suggests that educating ,he local community to recognise the potential benefits of tourism development will increase the likelihood of their supporting additional tourism development. This, according to Murphy, is essential to the development of destinations in countries with strong traditions of local politics and public participation.

This research was somewhat exploratory in that it examined residents of a large urban community in which tourism has been present for an extended period of time. Further research is required in other large urban areas to validate and improve the results of this study. Further to this it is noted that no research has appeared in the literature suggesting that researchers have returned to the original communities on which they based their study. Without such follow-up or longitudinal research, how can we truly appreciate the perceived changes which may occur as a result of tourism's impact on the host community.

This study examined residents' perceptions of tourism development within the theoretical framework of social capacity. Previous research suggested that the seasonal nature of tourism may be responsible for varying levels of friction between residents and tourists. In order to address this question, further research into residents' perceptions of tourism development is required during the shoulder, or quiet tourist season. In York, this is between November and February based on bed occupancy levels. In addition to this, the suggestion that residents adopt coping strategies in response to tourism's impact may add a further dimension to the nature of resident perception research.

Similarly to those of Perdue *et al,* and the research conclusions of Keogh, the results of this study suggested that public relations programmes aimed at improving tourism's image with the local residents could offer a viable means of increasing local support for tourism. It was Keogh's belief that a major reason for residents' lack of appreciation of tourism is their lack of knowledge regarding the benefits of tourism to the community. People who are not economically reliant on the tourism industry, and therefore do not perceive any direct benefit from tourism development, should be among the groups targeted. By identifying the interest groups, the information needs of residents can be assessed and public participation programmes developed to assist in the effective and sensitive development of tourism in York.

Prentice has noted that contentious matters in tourism development should be expected to cause a divide within the community according to whether or not its members perceive themselves as benefiting from developments. This was seen as offering an opportunity to pre-identify potential conflicts of interest as well as creating a potential weakness, for there is no guarantee that differences of opinion can be resolved.

It has been said that 'resident responsive tourism is the watchword for tomorrow: community demands for active participation in the setting of the tourism agenda and its priorities for tourism development and management cannot be ignored'. It becomes increasingly difficult to merely pay lip service to the need for public relations exercises and tourism education programmes. As Mathieson and Wall have noted, 'The consequences of tourism have become increasingly complex and contradictory ... (and) are manifested in subtle and often unexpected ways'. It may be suggested therefore that we must continue to expand our understanding of residents' perceptions of tourism development if we are to fulfil our task, which in the present context 'is to establish a framework and a process by which to provide leadership to a community, a region or a country in its efforts to formulate a vision as to what it can or should seek to become as a tourism destination'.

5

Commercial Short Holiday Breaks

Short breaks in hotels have grown rapidly in size, value and sophistication since the 1960s. They are now a valuable market to Scottish tourism in terms of contribution to hotel fixed costs, reduced seasonality, and high supplementary spend, accounting for £87.5 million in 1990, 70% of all short holiday spend. This chapter explores the nature and development of commercial short holiday breaks (CSHBs) within Scottish tourism, highlighting the range of marketing strategies employed by major operating companies, and through an understanding of the highly segmented market conditions forms a base for allowing further analysis of corporate performance relative to market and industry dynamics.

The research concentrates on commercially-centred activities. CSHBs are therefore defined as 'hotel packages of one to three nights which for a single price together with accommodation include one or more of the following: meals; transport; entertainment; or a programme of activities'. This definition allows use of secondary sources for Scottish market background, and primary sources for more detail of supplier provision and performance. As hotels account for 78% of all spend in the CSHB market compared to other forms of accommodation, the definition is suitable for the purposes of this chapter.

A review of CSHB literature was undertaken and revealed little systematic study on the subject. Most coverage was in the form of newspaper and trade press articles, conference papers, government publications, and industrial research documents. A computerised database containing the 30 largest hotel groups in Scotland (by room capacity) was therefore constructed from primary data drawn from company literature, group brochures, and company accounts. To compensate for differing demand patterns and operating environments, and to allow comparative analysis of performance, CSHB provision, regions, and market segments, the database was split into seven regions of Scotland, with boundaries determined by area tourist board boundaries.

To determine the relationship between market structure, competitive advantage and performance, a strategic framework was developed, based upon Scherer's structure conduct performance approach to industrial economics. This framework was applied to the CSHB market using data of a competitive and strategic nature, obtained via structured telephone interviews with key personnel of 23 CSHB providers. These interviews were later supplemented by further interviews directed towards financial and nonfinancial performance. The samples accounted for 74% of the database room stock and 76% of the estimated CSHB revenue generated by the corporate sample.

The chapter examines the key areas of Scherer's approach relative to the CSHB market supply, establishing the evolution of CSHBs, market structure, market conduct and market performance, and concluding with a suggested model of market performance.

Evolution of short breaks

To determine the relationship between market structure, competitive advantage, and performance, it is necessary to establish how CSHBs have evolved and the effect this has had upon the nature of the CSHB market. Full appreciation of CSHB evolution requires examination of developments from both supply and demand perspectives.

The CSHB concept devolved from off-peak marketing efforts of hotel groups and associated intermediaries during periods of low demand where premium rates for accommodation and service could not be achieved, with the philosophy that any room sold during off-peak periods was contributing to fixed costs, emphasising the importance of marginal pricing as a strategy to boost occupancy and increase profitability.

As the market matured, the off-peak concept developed into a market in its own right, companies actively attempting to compensate for low-season trade by offering short breaks to effectively extend their operating season.

Such developments continued throughout the 1970s and into the later 1980s, when it became evident that a combination of economic boom, international crisis, and the tendency to holiday two or three times a year, had resulted in major growth in the UK short holiday market, which by the end of 1989 accounted for up to 90% of the UK holiday demand of UK Hotel Groups Plc. Suppliers were putting more effort into differentiating their product, seeking new markets and deliberately altering the off-peak image associated with short holiday breaks. As the market further matured so too did the means of marketing and distributing the concept. Thus suppliers have not only extended the variety and season of short breaks but have also increased the spread of market level and location, and used a greater variety of distribution channels to raise awareness of their efforts.

The increased availability of CSHBs in number, variety, and perceived quality, combined with the increased levels of consumption and the experience of package holidays abroad, makes it reasonable to assume that customer knowledge would increase through experience, fuelling maturation of the market as consumers become more aware of alternatives, holiday more frequently, and demand new, value-for-money experiences.

The resulting effect of demand and supply developments has been the gradual evolution of a CSHB concept, away from the traditional off-peak image and representing a growth market in its own right. In more recent years, a greater degree of market segmentation has arisen incorporating more sophisticated marketing strategies and selective use of distribution channels, resulting in a highly varied and competitive market.

Short break market structure—a supply approach

This section examines the nature of CSHB supply by establishing the dominance of hotel groups followed by a market structure analysis based on Porter's 'industry structure' model. It concludes with a summary of the key elements of CSHB market structure.

While demand is important in terms of understanding market conditions, this chapter focuses on strategic and competitive dimensions of supply and therefore deems the evolution of demand and related conclusions as an adequate demand perspective to the study.

The following supply sources have been highlighted by the research as the main areas of CSHB provision.

- Corporate hotel group/chain: large, often publicly quoted hotel companies, who issue specialist brochures for CSHBs.

- Short break operator: specialist intermediaries, not owning hotels but obtaining revenue by brochure inclusion fees and commission; often used by hotel groups to supplement distribution.
- Hotel consortia: organisations often used by small privately owned hotels to gain marketing and purchasing economies. Gains revenue via membership fees and commission.
- Destination marketing: organisation designed to market a particular location area, thus providing valuable spin-off benefits for all local trade, and direct marketing for members.

From the identified supply base, corporate hotel suppliers in Scotland account for approximately 77% of CSHB revenue share from only 6% of unit share.

Hotel groups dominate revenue market share, pressurising smaller operators and causing many CSHB market features to reflect their own characteristics, including: market level of three/four star; density of location in major cities; tariffs based on accommodation with add-ons at cost; all-year availability, seven days a week; usually offering breaks via a corporate brochure, with 21 companies offering 24 brochures, 86 different packages and eight core segment themes 1991/2. Such results have been an evolutionary result of competitive and strategic activities and warrant investigation via a market/industry structure analysis.

CSHB industry structure

The purpose of this section is to determine the nature of competitive rivalry and form a grounding for determining competitive advantage. Each of the four forces acting on competitive rivalry are analysed in turn, establishing barriers to entry and level of threat or bargaining power.

Potential entrants

There are two forms of potential entrant, the entrant challenging physical provision and the entrant challenging distribution, the former being capital-intensive and marginal-contribution-based, the latter, more market-driven and commission-based. Physical provision, in this case the 'hotel', can be challenged from a number of sources, the main of which are other hotel groups, independent unaffiliated hotels, and consortia.

Distribution is an area where, in the past, a number of operators have attempted to enter the market, some successfully, e.g. Goldenrail, Superbreaks, P&O, others not successfully—Stardust, and Camelot. These agents work for commission and include short break operators, travel and transport companies, and handling agents. While the basic concept of a CSHB is easily replicated by any hotel-based organisation the viability and levels of awareness generated by such organisations is highly dependent upon the size, or critical mass, the organisation can achieve, as such corporate hotel groups are in the ideal position to enter the market, while unaffiliated independents are less able to enter the market in a feasible or recognisable manner, and as such turn to consortia to gain the mass required. These characteristics have helped fuel the distribution entrants who, once established, are able to operate in a more cost-effective, less labour-intensive manner, spending a majority of expenditure on promoting and distributing brand concepts, and attempting to raise barriers to entry and hinder new entrants attempting to overcome start-up cost.

Barriers to entry. In the previous section, 'Evolution of short breaks', CSHB was established as potentially very lucrative, providing not only an additional market in a maturing holiday industry but also compensating for markets lost or lagging. To gain additional, and protect existing market share, operators create and raise barriers entry. In the CSHB market these barriers are clearly evident, often forming the basis of suppliers' competitive strategy. The most evident barriers to emerge since the 1980s are location, market level, facilities/differentiation, and size, acting as barriers for both physical providers and distributors, These barriers are essentially the key competitive strategies of the 1960s to 1980s, suggesting that perhaps the strategies of the 1980s and 1990s may become the barriers to entry of the future.

Substitutes

Substitutes are evident in the 'prime functions' of CSHB provision: accommodation, location, activity, and reservations.

Accommodation: in substituting accommodation, a number of alternatives to hotels exist, including caravans, VFR, and campsites. In addition, the level of accommodation can be changed, i.e. trading down. These threats of substitution are very high, however, as CSHB demand shifts more to cities and fully serviced accommodation packages are promoted, barriers to entry are raised.

Location: as hotels are fixed in location they are under considerable threat if consumers substitute location, e.g. city/resort, national/international.

Activity base: activities can be substituted, i.e. local attractions offering what may have been part of a commissionable hotel package at a cheaper price, or customers taking advantage of the basic hotel B&B package and making their own entertainment.

Holiday type: trends and disposable income are the key instigators in substituting holiday type, with consumers deciding to try different types of holiday or fewer longer holidays.

Booking method: booking methods are closely linked to distribution and commission. Methods include via travel agents, direct with hotels, through consortia, and through short break operators. With commission ranging from 0% to 30% this can be a costly area of substitution.

Substitutes can therefore be related to the physical properties of the hotel or are representative of the consumer/producer interface (distribution).

Barriers to entry. Barriers to entry vary considerably from company to company and segment to segment; main barriers are similar to new entrants, with the addition of specific strategies directed towards market share, expected standards, and group size, including brand loyalty, relocating breaks from resorts to cities, packaging, and introducing 'flexible breaks'. The type of barrier and the effectiveness of such barriers is dependent upon how well the organisation is able to monitor and adapt to the environment, resulting in groups using environmental complexity created via segmentation to deter entrants and substitutes (see the following section, 'Short break market conduct').

Suppliers take a number of forms, essentially constituting the component parts of any hotel or CSHB product. As hotels are reliant in varying degrees upon the provision of food and beverages, accommodation and support services, suppliers to hotels in these areas will have varying market powers. As CSHB markets are targeted emphasis is placed on different forms of supply, exposing areas of reliance on each type.

In addition to hotel suppliers, CSHB markets require additional categories of supply such as finance, entertainment/activities, and communications, e.g. booking methods. The former combine to constitute the supply of a CSHB segment(s), displaying differing market characteristics and determining the suppliers' bargaining power in the market.

CSHB consumers are 'buyers' which, while predominantly domestic/pleasure based, do have elements of international inbound demand, differences in price sensitivity/elasticity, and basic requirements by segment.

The four forces identified act upon the market, creating competitive rivalry; such rivalry is clearly identified in the type of strategies used by hotel companies to gain competitive advantage and forms the basis of the market conduct analysed later.

The market structure analysis reveals key elements relative to CSHB market structure and competitive rivalry.

- The market is increasingly mature, with suppliers adopting sophisticated marketing strategies to gain market share.
- CSHB growth is in terms of market share of total hotel markets.
- Hotel groups dominate CSHB supply.
- As competitive rivalry intensifies, market complexity increases, resulting in a greater need for groups to inform and segment customers, often through branded packages.

The next section focuses on competitive rivalry and the means of gaining competitive advantage, through an analysis of market conduct.

Short break market conduct

An analysis of the main CSHB competitors and strategies adopted, indicates where and how competitive advantage is gained and sustained in the market. This section firstly establishes the main market CSHB competitors, before focusing on competitive advantage.

It was established that competition takes a number of forms: hotel groups, independent hotels; other forms of accommodation; intermediaries; and locations. Figure 40.6 provides a breakdown of competition, emphasising the main CSHB suppliers. Hotel groups are the main form of competition, probably owing to their width of market coverage and predominantly high-profile supply base.

The four main intermediates, Goldenrail, Superbreaks, Rainbow, and High-life, are seen as major competitors, implying that smaller independent operators will find it difficult to compete, as the market further matures and begins to show tendencies of monopolistic competition, emphasised by the minimal representation of consortia.

Competitive advantage

This subsection is in three parts: competitive advantage explained; strategic activity; and value chain linkages—which when combined comprise the means by which groups gain and sustain competitive advantage.

Competitive advantage

'Porter argues that firm profitability is a function of industry attractiveness and the firm's relative position within it. Strong relative positions imply that the firm has a competitive advantage that can be sustained against attacks by competitors and evolution of the industry. Competitive advantage comes from creating value for buyers that exceeds the costs of generating it'. Competitive advantage is therefore the edge created by an organisation to outperform competitors. To build competitive advantage is not enough; it must be sustained.

Strategic activity

As hotel groups dominate market share this section focuses on hotel group methods of competing, determining and categorising CSHB market strategies. Hotel groups compete against intermediaries and unaffiliated hotels for market share via distinct competitive routes: broadly categorised into strategies that 'defend' market share, acting as barriers to market entry, and 'predator' strategies that expand market share by attracting or shifting market segments.

Defensive strategies

Defensive strategies are adopted by companies to help sustain market share. There are two key types: pricing and differentiation strategies.

Pricing

Pricing appears relatively unstructured based primarily on location and market level, often at package cost plus margin. Essentially smaller operators are unable to compete on price, owing to the lack of flexibility for marginal contribution; thus groups are not forced to offer very low prices, as long as the customer is receiving perceived value for money.

Differentiation

Differentiation occurs in three forms, all raising perceived value, increasing market complexity (comprehension of the operating environment), and preventing new entrants/substitutes by setting basic standards and raising start-up costs.

Differentiation is by market level (setting standards, raising values/expectations), by location (i.e. city centre or resort), or by facilities (e.g. offering leisure facilities). These forms maintain basic price command and create barriers to entry causing non-price-based competition and therefore raising profitability.

Predatorial strategies are categorised under three headings: distribution, segmentation, and promotion. Their prime function is to gain market share.

Distribution

Distribution strategies are used to reach target segments as effectively or efficiently as possible; each form of distribution can be used in isolation, or more commonly in combination. Figure 40.8 shows distribution channels used.

Individual hotel activity. Independent actions of individual hotel units, including special offers, leaflet distribution, and press advertising, Cost is variable and therefore widely utilised by smaller units.

Corporate activity: hotel group. Used by hotel groups to present a corporate image or brand, essentially in the form of CSHB brochures distributed by mail via the CRS and head office.

Corporate activity: consortia. Small operators are limited to the consortia brochures, often racked in travel agents. Utilised in much the same way as hotel groups, to gain additional exposure, scale economies, and to present a group identity.

Destination marketing. This distribution benefits both independent operators and hotel groups. There are a number of forms, ranging from area tourist boards to local authorities. The aim of the organisation is to market an area, through the use of local facilities, including hotels, resulting in many direct and indirect benefits.

Operator brand. This refers to short break operator brochures used almost entirely by hotel groups, because of the commission, and associated charges. They have good travel agent racking, and brand by operator name, e.g. Superbreaks.

The importance and usage of distribution methods by hotel groups is shown in Figure 40.9. It can be seen that rankings one (hotel group brochure) and two (individual hotel activity) are very close, while ranking three (SBO) is almost half their importance, perhaps because of high associated costs, e.g. commission. Destination marketing is of less importance (four), with consortia used least, probably as they are essentially designed for and used by small operators. It therefore appears that hotel groups use the top three distribution methods most, while the lower ranking channels are used by independent, small hotels.

Segmentation

Predatorial strategies include segmentation, not only acting to segment the market, reducing or increasing complexity, but also raising the customers' perceived value of CSHBs by (a) raising the ease of purchase, (b) disguising contributions to fixed costs and enhancing product synergy through packaging, and (c) creating identifiable and interchangeable target markets, with a variety of price and activity brackets while maintaining a degree of flexibility. Figure 40.10 shows the range of market segments targeted by various groups and their associated brand names.

A key method of achieving segmentation is via packaging, ranging in style, number, and components, an essential strategy adopted by many groups. Packages take two forms, (a) pure and (b) mixed. Pure packaging relates to a bundle of components offered as a single product, not added to or broken down, e.g. a coach touring break. In mixed packages a basic theme is offered, and the consumer is allowed to pick and mix various 'extras' to add to the theme, e.g. DBB with the option of golf. Mixed packages are most evident in the CSHB market with 16 groups producing 63 packages under 22 brands. Key themes are special interest and DBB breaks; the most important package components, identified as being essential, are evening meals and child discounts.

In addition to pure and mixed packages, groups can utilise add-ons, additions to the perceived value of the break, not directly related to the principal theme. They increase the perceived value/price ratio at no apparent cost to the customer, e.g. toiletries, chocolates.

Promotion

Promotional strategies are based on brochure production, advertising, and branding and are closely interlinked. Brochure production as the main media for distribution plays a differing role for groups.

Advertising is becoming more widespread among hotel groups in attempts at non-price competition, establishing brand loyalty and therefore gaining market share. Branding is product-based, reflecting segments and brochures, and is used to reduce consumer decision complexity while maintaining supplier complexity.

It can be seen that lower-order defensive strategies are used to sustain and protect market share, essentially raising market complexity and reducing initial attractiveness, while the higher-order predatory strategies are used to gain market share by managing complexity and maximising achievable marginal contributions. Table 40.1 summarises key strategies adopted by various groups operating in the CSHB market.

Value chain linkages

Examining the 'functional' aspects of gaining and sustaining competitive advantage via a value chain analysis exposes areas of linkage occurring within or between organisation functions, allowing strategically important activities to be identified. Figure 40.13 shows the key value chain linkages within groups. Central reservation systems (CRS) are the most common linkage, followed by travel agents, and sport/activity, where the centre circle represents the CSHB market and the outer circle the hotel company linkages, represented by blocks to the market. CRS has become the most common linkage through companies raising the environmental complexity by segmentation (to reduce new entrants), then attempting to raise, reduce, or manage the complexity within their organisation to gain market share.

Strategies adopted by major companies vary between market segments, they appear relatively primitive, the packaging component being the most developed. While pricing, and differentiation exist, these seem to act more as barriers to entry, with value chain linkages creating cost economies essentially in the area of CRS for widening/targeting markets and reducing commission payable; packaging is used to gain additional market share.

CSHB strategies are adopted by a wide range of companies, all with differing levels of ownership, cost structure, location, market level, and tariff; yet some companies perform significantly better in the market than others.

Short break market performance

This section examines the performance of hotel companies operating in the CSHB market in terms of (i) financial and (ii) nonfinancial performance, examining an industry and competitor/concentration approach before relating strategy to identified performance.

Financial performance

Industry financial performance of hotel companies operating in the CSHB market, is examined before focusing on CSHB performance in concentration terms.

After completing the financial appraisal, nonfinancial performance is assessed in a similar manner before determining links between performance and competitive advantage.

Industry performance

The 16 groups established in the previous section with identified strategies are examined in terms of general industry performance. Performance is assessed using prime indicators of: revenue; profits; return on capital; gearing; and liquidity. Based on these indicators.

Having established basic performance indicators, the groups can be divided into performance categories. The criteria for these divisions is fully explained in the conference presentation, where each individual group is categorised into a single performance category, ranging from A (top performers) to D (lesser performers). While these measures are subject to environmental and scale issues, they form a basis for comparison at industrial level.

The next subsection establishes the performance categories of the groups, in the same way, when based on market concentration ratios in the CSHB market, after which nonfinancial performance categories are established and a summary of all performance categories provided.

CSHB market: concentration performance

This section determines group performance in the CSHB market, in terms of CSHB revenue concentration ratios.

With groups having been classified into financial performance categories, the next subsection establishes nonfinancial performance categories based upon two measures: portfolio concentration (rooms and units), and level of competitive identity.

It was established in the earlier section, 'Short break market structure—a supply approach', that greater market and strategic power is gained by larger hotel groups.

Competitive identity

An indicator of nonfinancial performance can be seen to be the perceived level of threat that the company imposes on other companies within the market. This is identified in terms of whom companies see as their main form of competition.The larger hotel groups, as may be expected, are identified as most competition, with Forte (59%), Stakis (55%), and Mount Charlotte Thistle (50%). When these results are tabulated with most competition (higher performance) at category A, a ranking of competition performance of the sample companies is achieved. Note that 'other' has been removed and groups not mentioned are categorised D.

Strategy, competitive advantage and performance

This section identifies areas of linkage between established general strategy categories, more specific competitive advantage and level of performance achieved, first in financial, then nonfinancial terms, before concluding with a model of strategy and performance.

Financial performance related

Using measures of financial performance and relating them to strategy establishes the potential industry effect of offering CSHBs on corporate performance, before focusing on CSHB market concentration performance and specific competitive advantage/strategies.

Corporate performance links

There are three areas in this subsection, linkages between volume of CSHB business as a percentage of total revenue and identified performance, type of strategy adopted, and specific category of CSHB strategy adopted linked to performance.

Percentage short break revenue

When CSHB percentage of total revenue is compared to performance, the higher the percentage of revenue attributable to CSHBs the better the corporate financial performance. While this may be due to a number of reasons, e.g. higher supplementary spend, more consistent markets, etc., the fact remains that groups with higher CSHB revenue percentage are better corporate financial performers.

- *General strategies*: In terms of general strategies of predator and defender, Figure 40.17 shows that all the groups in higher corporate performance brackets A/B adopt predator strategies while those adopting defender strategies are in the C performance bracket.
- *Specific strategic categories*: More focused, Figure 40.18 shows specific strategic categories adopted. The vast majority of high performers use distribution and promotion strategies while lower performers appear to rely upon segmentation and pricing strategies. (Note that companies will adopt a number of strategies; the key strategy is their main focus.)
- *Corporate (financial) performance summary*: While it is recognised that most of the corporate high performers (A) are groups with low total ownership, there also appears to be strong indications of linkages between CSHB provision and performance, with groups that utilise promotional and segmentation strategies generally performing better.

The next section focuses on the CSHB market performance linked to specific strategies, number and type of competitive advantage areas, and organisation linkages.

Market (financial) performance links

- *Strategy category*: This section determines linkages between the strategic categories (promotion, segmentation, distribution, pricing) and market performance. From Figure 40.19, market performers (A) use mainly promotional strategies, followed by segmentation strategies, while the poorest performers (D) use distribution strategies. This may indicate the effects of commission, however; in an attempt to establish why such strategies are adopted, it is useful to relate performance to the number of sources of advantage and then link strategies adopted to the number of sources of advantage.
- Number of sources of advantage: The relationship between performance and the number of areas of competitive advantage. Category A performers are of two types, those with many areas (sources) of competitive advantage and those with few. Closer analysis reveals that the A performers with many areas of competitive advantage use segmentation strategies, while those with few use promotion strategies. The D performers can be seen to have few areas of competitive advantage but adopt a distribution strategy, perhaps attempting to gain scale economies and critical mass; these groups should perhaps focus on developing promotional-based strategies to aid market performance. Combining the areas of competitive advantage and the strategic categories, a number of distinct characteristics are evident.

Groups adopting promotional strategies and pricing strategies have few sources of competitive advantage, while distribution strategies have medium to few sources, and segmentation many sources—resulting in the former strategies being more focused and the latter more broad and innovative, essentially driving and steering market development.

- *Main type of advantage*: Companies with enhanced performance (A) tend to identify image as their main competitive advantage. While A performers have main advantage of image, D performers main advantage is location.

Further analysis of advantage type relative to strategy reveals that companies adopting distribution strategies identified location as their main advantage, while those adopting promotion and segmentation strategies have the advantage of image.

- *Organisational linkages*: Organisational linkages appear to be secondary to strategies adopted. What appears to be the case is that performance in the market at corporate level is not greatly affected by linkages. In some cases, however, where strategies are similar but performance is different, linkages appear to enhance (financial) market performance, e.g. Milton and Principal Hotels; both adopt pricing strategies with few areas of competitive advantage yet Principal has considerably better market performance. This may be due to the fact that Principal identified many areas of organisation linkages while Milton identified few areas of organisation linkages.
- *Market (financial) performance summary:* It appears that the number of areas of competitive advantage determines strategies adopted, which in turn can be linked to financial market performance and the key form of competitive advantage. For example: a group with few areas of competitive advantage would essentially adopt promotional or pricing strategies; adopting promotional strategies (given the ability) would lead to enhanced performance and a concentration of efforts on image as the key competitive advantage.

In addition, as indicated by the Milton/Principal scenario, organisational linkages can enhance performance of certain strategies adopted; this is most likely to occur at the unit level and will form the basis of further study into unit/market-based performance.

Nonfinancial performance

While financial measures are often used to determine performance, alternative measures, i.e. nonfinancial, allow a more qualitative assessment of performance. This section examines portfolio performance (market presence of groups) and competitive identity (perceived threat in the market) relative to identified CSHB strategies in nonfinancial terms.

Competitive identity

High performers are characterised by identifying image and marketing as the main competitive advantage. These are also characteristics of A to D performers.

However, where performance appears to be enhanced, i.e. the difference between Forte, Stakis (A) and Holiday Inn, Scottish Highland (C), it is in the number of organisational linkages.

It can be seen that higher performing companies with similar identified competitive advantages are better performers owing to their higher number of organisational linkages; so while the previous subsection established linkages as playing a minor role in terms of market (financial) performance, they would appear to adopt a more important role when achieving nonfinancial performance.

6

Greening of the Hospitality Industry

Tourism both depends upon, and affects the quality of, the natural and cultural environment. The tourism industry has awakened to some new realities. Like other businesses whose operations affect the environment, it is being held to close scrutiny and accountability for the effect of its activities on the environment. The paradox is !hat for many years it has proclaimed its awareness and sensitivity to the environment, but actions have not always corresponded to those assertions. Environmental issues are not fading, and we will continue to live with them as we move past the 1990s and into the new millennium. Tourism represents a potentially valuable instrument for sustainable development, and the industry has much to gain from promoting and applying this concept combining economic opportunities with environmental conservation and enhancement activities.

The hospitality industry, comprising commercial food and accommodation services, is an enabler, rather than a primary motivator, for tourists. However, it can play a major role in assisting consumer awareness as well as contributing to resource conservation, while at the same time deriving specific economic benefits from these activities. The greening of the hospitality industry and of tourism—positioning the industry to respond to the environmental challenge—represents a pivotal issue for the 1990s and beyond.

A number of trends have emerged which have begun to influence lifestyles and leisure and tourism choices. One of the most evident of these is the growth of the 'green' movement and general concern about the impact of modern industry, including tourism development, on the physical and social environment. Public and tourist concern over the environment is not just a passing fad.

More and more, tourists are demanding environmentally friendly products and services. Environment is becoming a competitive issue, for the whole industry. A survey conducted by the WTO confirms that not only are tourists becoming more environmentally conscious, but the behaviour of the travel trade has also been affected.

In tourism, many of the concerns related to the environment have dealt with the relationship of the tourism industry to the 'external' environment (both natural and cultural). For example, special reports on tourism and the environment by the Economist Intelligence Unit in 1989 and 1992 dealt virtually exclusively with the external environment, as did the 'World Travel and Tourism Review'.

However, the 'internal' environment of' any tourism operation also plays a part in conservation. The hospitality industry is a microcosm of the external environment, in terms of attitudes to, and use of, resources. An establishment's organizational, management and operational system should reflect a holistic approach to the environment and to sustainability.

The hospitality industry is a major generator of solid wastes, and is an inefficient consumer of water and fossil fuels. It uses large quantities of paper, not to mention environmentally unfriendly products such as disposable plastics, non-recyclable containers, cleaning fluids and other supplies. The new generation of conservation conscious traveller is increasingly sensitive to the onslaught of advertising flyers in hotel rooms, the use of unrecyclable and biodegradable products, and other wasteful practices.

In Italy, hoteliers in the Veneto region are discovering that 'going green' may be a way to lure back dissatisfied customers. The region makes up 10% of Italy's hospitality industry, yet it saw a slowdown of demand in 1992 despite an excellent year in 1991. Its Northern European guests were dissatisfied with the region's attitude to the environment. The region created a consortium which provides free environmental consultation, to demonstrate the important coexistence between hotels and their habitat, and to send a strong positive message to tourists. The first hotel to apply this approach, the Hotel Ariston in Milan, increased its occupancy by 15%, while the Milan hotel, occupancy is down 25%.

The greening of the hospitality industry makes good business sense and is applauded by guests, who are willing to accept changes to better the environment. At the Boston Park Plaza Hotel, which established a four-star conservation programme, business increased $750000 in 1992 from groups that want to align themselves with a hotel that is committed to the environment.

The Swedish Hotels and Restaurants Association (SHR) is involved in comprehensive initiatives, which range from focusing on environmental matters at conferences to information sharing, contracting research, and developing networks, 'Hotel and restaurant enterprises, like most of us, have come to realise how they themselves affect the environment'.

The International Hotels Environment Initiative, (IHEI) has an operational manual which guides individual hotel managers in what changes to make, whether to the laundry or to the lighting system. It enlisted the support of 11 of the world's leading chains, which between them control more than one million hotel rooms worldwide. This initiative smashes the myth, that sound environmental awareness is at odds with hotel profitability, and is aimed at promoting and supporting good environmental practice within the hotel industry.

Internal environmental programmes

Almost one-half of the waste generated in North America may be recyclable. Leaders in the hospitality industry have discovered that the benefits of recycling are too great to ignore. These include reduced landfill fees, increased local legislation requiring recycling, and public demand for recycling. However, other benefits can include a sense of team spirit among employees, as well as the contribution to conservation of the environment. In some hotels, savings are going back to the hotel operation, in others, they are going to local charities.

The hotel chain that initiated the first comprehensive 'green' programme, was Canadian Pacific Hotels & Resorts (CP). According to their research, the average guest generates a Pound of' solid waste a day, and two pounds on checkouts day. With 20000 checkouts a day, the waste is considerable.

The Canadian Restaurant and Foodservices Association (CRFA) mainly comprises small, independently owned outlets. Because of relatively narrow profit margins, members are most likely to undertake only those environmental initiatives which lead to reduced costs and/or increased sales, thus the CRFA has focused its efforts on waste reduction and reuse. As part of a members' education and action programme, the CRFA has published a booklet 'Going green without seeing red'. This is causing an 'environmental ripple' across the entire food services industry.

Reduction of garbage can be achieved in numerous areas: rejecting over-wrapped produce such as bananas or oranges; buying beverages in returnable containers; eliminating throwaway cups or cutlery; and not buying or selling 'tetrapack' containers or blister-plastic packaging. The purchase of bathroom amenities without elaborate packaging can reduce costs by up to 10%. At the Wait Disney World Dolphin, guests stay an average of four nights, so the hotel's goal is one 2-oz. container of each product per stay. With more than 400 000 room nights per year, this can add up to a significant saving. The Saunders Hotel Group's Boston Park Plaza is part of a property-wide conservation programme. It has introduced a 24-oz. pump dispenser for liquid soap, mouthwash, shampoo and hair conditioner. These replace the more than two million individual packages annually which previously became garbage.

A number of organizations routinely reuse everything possible, from storing food in reusable plastic containers to sending surplus foods to food banks or soup kitchens, and selling organic kitchen scraps for animal feed, or composting kitchen and yard wastes.

In Thailand, the Amari Hotels in Pattaya offer guests the option of having their sheets changed every other day instead of every day, thus saving water, cutting detergent use, and reducing operating costs. About 40% of guests accept this option. This is similar to CP's practice, as well as that of hotels in Sweden and Germany. The Swiss Hotel Association, too, asks members to encourage guests to reuse bathroom linen.

The Marriott has had properties involved in recycling since at least 1988. One property, when first starting, reduced 35% of its garbage going to the dump in just one month. By simply removing glass from its waste stream, the Marriott in Schumburg, Illinois, has cut its tonnage by almost 30%. The Hyatt Regency, Chicago, has a recycling programme run by a subsidiary company. The hotel produces an average of 70000 pounds of trash each month. This includes almost 500 pounds of glass nightly, and 10 tons of cardboard every 6 days, The recycling centre on the premises had a capital cost of $25 000, but that cost was recovered in less than a year. The hotel was recycling 40% to 50% of its waste within a year, with over 50% reduction in its waste bill—about $60 000 savings in 1990.

The IHEI suggests that companies list every product they use, and for each product, check whether it should be reduced, reused, recycled or replaced, as a means of evaluating impact and determining proper disposal methods.

To many people, saving energy or water means some sacrifice of personal comfort, to others, it is a way to cut costs. In the hospitality industry, it has appeared contradictory to think of maintaining guest comfort, while increasing conservation. However, by applying energy-efficient management and low-energy design not only to new-built projects, but also to existing schemes, a huge annual savings may be realized. Some facilities can consume up to 10 times more energy than others. This variation is due to building design, design of services, and occupant's behaviour. Oreszczyn estimates that improvements in any of these can result in halving a building's energy consumption, and that, of these, 20% of energy is wasted through inefficient management.

In the last few years there has been a revolution in lighting technology, which has provided many choices for retrofits and new installations. The potential for savings in energy use and cost is significant. Some existing lighting systems can, be retrofitted to provide the same amount of light with only 20% of the electricity previously used. Also, the new lamps will operate up to 10 times longer than the equipment being replaced.

In Ontario, Kenora's Inn of the Woods Lakeside Hotel has achieved an annual $14 000 energy cost savings, by converting 278 incandescent bulbs to compact fluorescents. The savings were exactly as originally projected, and the $11000 conversion was paid back in about eight months. The planning of the retrofit involved Ontario Hydro, so qualifies for a $4200 rebate under their Energy Efficient Lighting Program. An additional advantage is that the new equipment needs far less maintenance.

At the Royal Connaught Hotel in Hamilton, more than 1000 lights were replaced with compact fluorescents. The total cost of the project was just over $35 000 and saved 63 kilowatts of power. This represents a saving of $33 113 on the hotel's annual hydro bill. In addition, Ontario Hydro provided a $16 875 incentive.

The biggest user of energy in hotels is the heating, ventilation and air conditioning (HVAC) system (22%), followed by the guest rooms (19%) and the kitchens (12%). Energy cost for HVAC can range from 25% to 50% of the total energy cost—the lower figure related to smaller, unsophisticated hotels in moderate climes, and the higher figure to luxury hotels in subtropical and tropical countries. Opportunities for energy efficiency is very high.

CP's Prince Edward Hotel in Charlottetown, PEI, has reduced consumption of 97 000 litres of fuel in one year through the use of a water source heat pump. This transfers heat from an overhot room into a water loop which traverses the building, and heats coot rooms. The more balanced the load, the more efficiently it runs. The extra heat is used to preheat hot water, and to heat the swimming pool. This has meant that the hotel, which used to run two 75 h.p. boilers now needs only one, thus cutting electrical, maintenance, and chemical costs.

The Ritz Hotel, London, has recently upgraded its energy management system. The three large boilers installed 20 years ago were replaced with four high efficiency gas-fired units. A cooling system was installed in the hotel restaurant and a computer-controlled energy management system (EMS) was implemented to control and monitor energy consumption. Also, when the old boilers were removed, 7000 sq. ft were freed and converted to more bedrooms.

Water savings alone may contribute considerable dollar savings. Companies now offer electronic sensors to control water flow (for toilets, urinals, showers and sinks) which not only reduces water consumption but also reduces vandalism because there are no knobs or handles to break, and water cannot be left running.

In Boston, the Saunders Hotel Company was faced with stiff increases in water and sewer bills so it refitted its Lenox Hotel. Showers had flow resistors and heads, reducing flow to from 6-7 to 3 g.p.m. (at a cost of only $20 per head). Water faucet aerators reduced flow from 4 to 1.5 g.p.m, and there was no noticeable flow difference to guests, Similarly, 1.6 gal/flush toilets replaced the 67 gal/flush toilets. The results were dramatic: for the first quarter of 1989 the sewer and water use was 1.88 million gallons, down almost 75% from the previous year. Total payback was less than two years.

Water and energy use are often linked. The food services industry is examining the efficiency of its operations and cutting wasteful practices, According to Ontario Hydro, sanitizing and dishwashing account for 18% of costs of an establishment, requiring considerable water, power, labour and detergent, also service and maintenance. Waste heat recovery saves on both water and power by recycling rinse water to the next load's wash. Other features are being built into new macnines: reuse of machine-generated steam; gas-heated machines for use in northern locations where power costs are high; water-saving machines using up to 59% less water; and greater insulation of machines. 'The incentive to choose a high-efficiency dishwasher is going to be the bottom line: to save money. The bonus is energy is saved through efficiency'.

Certain retrofits may he costly, but effective. The Sheraton purchased two laundry-water reuse systems for hotels in Seattle and Long Beach, at $71000 each. However, the systems, which treat and rinse the final rinse water of the preceding wash for the next wash cycle, save about $39 000 a year. The net effect of this is that the system pays for itself in less than two years.

Air emissions from the hospitality industry contribute to pollution from CFCs, burning of fossil fuels, exhausts, etc. The industry should aim to reduce emissions at source, reduce consumption, and switch to less harmful products. There have been great improvements in maintenance products: sprays without ozone-destroying materials, odour-free products, and biodegradable or refillable containers. Now manufacturers of air conditioners and heating units are offering products which save money and eliminate the need for chemical deodorizers.

Near Vail, Colorado, Beaver Creek ski resort has no above-ground parking, and the amount of dust and other airborne particles is measured continuously. Each commercial and residential fireplace in the resort has an attached red light. If the air is polluted by vehicles or chimneys, fires must be doused immediately, benefiting both internal and external air quality.

While nonsmoking rooms are common in the hotel

business, 'green rooms' which contain water and air filtration systems are the newest element in amenities for the industry. These rooms are designed to appeal to those with allergies, health-and-fitness enthusiasts and environmentally conscious travellers. More and more hotels are buying their own equipment as the demand for these rooms increases. The cost of converting to 'green rooms' is about $500 per room for the Sheraton Grand at Dallas/Fort Worth, with a surcharge of $5 to the guest, this is a payback period of only 100 occupied nights. These rooms achieve higher than average occupancy rates, and have directly related repeat business.

Purchasing decisions can make a great contribution to environmental protection, and are a key element of environmental protection in the hospitality industry. At the worldwide level, the hospitality industry may have a significant impact on supply industries. At the local level, it can benefit the economy if products are bought locally, which also reduces transportation costs. A key concept is 'pre-cycling', where purchase decisions support responsible products and packaging, assist recycling, and reduce waste. This becomes very significant where landfills are scarce or costly.

Most companies that are committed to the principles of recycling and waste reduction have not paid higher prices only to support the public interest. Rather, they have instituted new purchase policies that offer additional business benefits. The Westin's company policy is to use recycled paper products for its stationery, paper towels and toilet paper. By using recycled paper, for the Westin letterhead alone, they saved $10 000. In addition, certain Westin hotels (such as the Bayshore Hotel in Vancouver) discourage suppliers from overpackaging. The Bayshore refuses to discard items such as waxed box containers, and insists that suppliers pick them up for reuse themselves.

At the Hotel Inter-Continental, LA, liquid amenities are packaged in 100% PET-G resin recycled from soft drink bottles; soap ingredients are vegetable-based; tinting and colouring agents are food-grade suitable; animal testing is avoided; only recycled fibres are used in packaging; and all papers are acid-free and water-based with vegetable-based inks used in printing.

The Sheraton Senggigi Beach Resort in Lombok, Indonesia, had a very limited supply and variety of local vegetables. Instead of importing, the chef and the local farmers experimented with a wide range of vegetable seeds to determine what crops grow well locally. Now the farmers have a new source of income which is more profitable than the traditional rice crop, the hotel has a regular supply of fresh vegetables, and the Sheraton Group has an enhanced image through developing an alternative, mutually beneficial approach.

The SHR provides its members and associates with educational information to influence product purchase, and is networking with all others in the industry, from farmers to suppliers. All companies should be using their positions as purchasers to work with suppliers to improve environmental performance. Implementing a product purchase plan involves: auditing all products and services, and assessing their environmental impact; determining availability of environmentally friendly alternatives; prioritizing actions; and educating suppliers about better alternatives.

External environmental programmes

The environmental activities of the hotel sector, as demonstrated in such leadership documents as CP's 'Green partnership guide' or in the IHEI's *Environmental Management for Hotels,* are focused on internal operations related to resource use and conservation. A number of ad hoc initiatives do exist, which recognize he relationship of the hospitality industry to the external environment; however, a systematic approach is needed.

Marshall advocates that the hospitality industry provide hospitality to the nation's hungry. Apparently, fear of lawsuits is commonly cited as justification for food dumping. But Good Samaritan Food Donor Acts can protect from legal liability for good-faith donations of prepared food. An increasing number of convention managers are requesting that excess food be donated to a charity.

At the Days Inn in Baltimore, goods that would have otherwise been thrown away (e.g. sheets, bedspreads, soap and food) are given to a local ministry that assists the homeless. CP's 1992 audit showed that 9(016 of all soap, 76% of shampoo and conditioner, and 80% of body lotion remaining after checkout was redirected to local and third-world charities. The Renaissance Hotel in Edmonton, Alberta, is donating partially used soap and shampoo containers to local youth shelters. In Seattle, the Stouffer Madison Hotel donates partially used containers of conditioners, shampoos and lotions, and partial toilet-tissue rolls to an organization that channels supplies to homeless shelters. Thus the hotel cuts down its waste while saving the external organizations part of their cost of buying products.

In 1989, Best Western hotels joined with the American Society of Interior Designers (ASID) to launch a national community service project to aid homeless shelters. The hotels are encouraged to contribute furniture, fixtures and equipment to designated shelters, and ASID members work with the shelters to develop and implement design plans using the donations. Within a year, four projects had been completed, and it was typical for Best Western to donate 25 rooms of furniture and equipment. In the UK, Forte Plc has programmes oriented toward the communities in which it operates. In association with the Conservation Foundation, it launched a 'Community Chest' scheme in the 1980s to provide monthly grants to aid local environmental programmes. This has helped create school gardens, plant trees and reseed village greens. It also has Colonel Sanders Environmental Awards aimed at encouraging community tidiness and litter reduction.

In his inaugural address, the president of the American Hotel and Motel Association asked the lodging industry to take steps against illiteracy, pointing out that educational deficiencies cost businesses about $30 billion annually. Best Western International donated 50 000 surplus road atlases and hotel travel guides to Chicago's public schools for use in classrooms. It is also getting on board city-wide traffic-reduction efforts in Phoenix, where the company is based. To encourage car-pooling, Best Western offers its corporate employees preferential parking and other considerations, which may include flexible work hours.

As the Indonesian Minister of tourism recently commented, 'people don't come to certain places for their hotels, but for their natural beauty, attractive culture and interesting tourist objects'. But the hospitality industry has been slow to recognize this fact.

The Ramada International not only has significant *internal* conservation programmes, but has an especially high profile with respect to *external* environmental conservation. It offers a joint programme with American Express, where Ramada automatically contributes to The Nature Conservancy when guests pay by American Express. Its 'Hotels of the New Wave' programme is a grassroots effort, in which the company allows each property's staff to initiate and implement its own ideas.

Ramada encourages individual hotels to work with local environmental groups to promote community causes and contribute to major environmental groups.

The Jupiter Beach Hilton in Florida developed a 'Turtle Watch' programme. It organizes evening lectures and has established an incubation pen if eggs are laid too close to the heavy beach traffic. Resort naturalists monitor the nests and guide guests along the beach to watch turtles lay eggs in June and July. This has proved to be a successful conservation and awareness programme. It had the additional benefit of earning wide recognition when presented with a special Judges Award by the Travel Industry Association of' America.

In Asia, Hong Kong's major hotels use the twin concerns of environmental preservation and heritage conservation as part of their marketing programmes. Initially, they introduced menus on recycled paper, as a small contribution to conservation. However, early in the 1980s Singapore launched a multimillion dollar restoration programme and repositioned itself as a 'Green Dream' destination. Hong Kong has now become a catalyst for the regional hotel industry to clean up the environment in order to sustain tourism over the long term, Major hotel chains have joined this effort: the Hilton, in conjunction with the World Wildlife Fund, is emphasizing a 'Healthy Oceans Campaign' focusing on city children; the Shangri-La Group, with Asian resorts, has strict guidelines related to building heights, lighting systems and sewage treatment plants: and the Mandarin Oriental Group has introduced a glass-recycling programme for Hong Kong properties, and managed cleanup campaigns for local beaches.

Partnerships, or strategic alliances (with government, public institutions, or other companies) may help split initial high costs of some conservation measures. A number of utilities have programmes where incentives are directed toward energy savings. Ontario Hydro's Savings By Design programme is intended to promote any project that reduces electrical demand (kW) or energy (kW.h) through improved electrical efficiency, whether new projects or retrofits, Funding assistance of $500/kW of demand reduced is available. The Royal York Hotel in Toronto replaced some older motors in its main air supply, makeup and exhaust air fans. It saved more than 708 000 kW.h, representing $42 500 annually. In addition, the $40 000 grant from Ontario Hydro meant that the project paid for itself in a year.

There are a number of programmes through which operators may obtain advice about energy efficiencies. In the UK, the Energy Efficiency Office helps managers assess if their buildings are using excessive energy, and provides grants to help organizations with such consultancy costs.

The US Water Alliances for Voluntary Energy Efficiency (WAVE) is a non-regulatory programme that offers mostly technology-based solutions. Hotels and motels are encouraged to install and implement water saving techniques and equipment. Owing to the fact that laundries can be significant water-users, a hotel or motel can reduce its water use by 15% to 30% or more by changing to water-efficient equipment, with payback periods of one to four years. WAVE has served as a stimulator to intensify energy-conserving laundry practices.

Industry partnerships can assist where costs are high. For example, recycling can present problems of inadequate space for storage of materials to be recycled. However, in Vancouver, a group of maintenance and housekeeping management personnel from downtown properties have discussed sharing the cost of the daily pickup service to make that option more economical. Strategic alliances and partnerships make good economic and environmental sense.

Corporate commitment

Much of CP's Green Plan success is due to its senior personnel. CP's president and CEO launched the green programme, and said, 'either protect the environment that is the basis of your industry, or have no industry to worry about'. A top-down approach can provide vision. While employees are enthusiastic about recycling in theory, in practice they may not be systematic unless recycling is brought in as an official policy initiative.

Corporate commitment may also attract and keep workers. In initial surveys, more than 80% of CP's employees said they would feel better about working for a company with an environmental policy.

Employee involvement

One of the surest ways to enlist the cooperation of employees is to make them a part of the solution. When the Opryland Hotel in Morgantown, West Virginia, began looking into recycling in late 1989, one of its first tasks was finding out how workers at all levels felt about the idea. Surveys found high enthusiasm and uncovered ideas that management had not even considered (e.g. recycling office and computer paper, motor oil, batteries, and kitchen fats and oils). This employee input also increased programme acceptance.

CP, in beginning its greening activities, surveyed each of the company's 10 000 employees. More than 90% of respondents favoured the programme. It conducted a detailed environmental audit of its hotels, and its 12-step Green Plan is directly based on staff input. This approach is comprehensive, produces support, and improves corporate image. Idealism and enthusiasm alone are not enough to make green programmes a way of life in the hospitality industry. CP admit that their biggest problems are their managers at the individual property level, in terms of implementing the plan. However, the firm which assisted CP in its green plan, warned that any audit and subsequent environmental education must stress cooperative benefits as opposed to a 'policing' approach. This is particularly important in the context of existing infrastructures, and established procedures.

Inter Continental Hotels & Resorts tackle the problem at various levels and have a quarterly eco-newsletter, The *Daily Planet*, geared toward sharing success stories, and fostering consistency among hotels. They developed a 200-page environmental manual which mandates the 3 Rs, and at each hotel, the manager's bonus depends on compliance and accomplishment. They are producing their manual in a number of languages, to assist in meeting targets.

Guest and industry education

At the Star Hotel, Sollentuna, Sweden, all personnel are given information on the hotel's environmental programme, and there are regular meetings of an environmental group representing all departments to increase staff awareness and provide information. It has a similar education programme for guests. There is information on the Star's environmental programme in each room, with an invitation for guests to participate, or example, by turning out lights, or by using towels several times.

Guests like a company that is environmentally sensitive. CP's programme already has lured some business the hotel may not otherwise have booked. Similarly, the Hyatt Regency in Chicago's recycling programme has been used as a marketing tool to attract conventions.

Education of staff at all levels has proved to be invaluable at Inter-Continental and CP. Similarly, guests need and welcome education. Radisson Hotels International has had occasional guest complaints about in-room occupancy sensors which control the HVAC. Guests feel they should be able to leave the air conditioning on full blast when they're not in the room, unlike their attitudes when they leave their own homes. Although they seem to have a double standard regarding their hotel room, one wonders what is being done to educate guests about this device, and its benefits.

Today's hotel guests do seem willing to accept conservation measures such as bulk amenity dispensers, water-saving devices, and the replacement of non recyclable items with recyclable ones, if they know the benefits. At the Holiday Inn in Leicester, UK, a letter is left in each room, explaining environmental programmes to guests, and requesting comments. In the three years of the programme, no adverse comments have ever been received.

One of the biggest challenges in the hospitality industry is to implement conservation measures, while still meeting guest perception. Guests need to be educated and asked for their opinion. To increase acceptance of a hotel's environmental programme, guests should feel like they are doing a good deed. Translate savings into meaningful language (e.g. reinterpret paper reduction in terms of trees saved), and promote the hotel's good environmental record. Encourage guests to feel that they are participants in a programme that is morally and ethically right. If they don't know the problems, they are unlikely to want to be part of the solutions.

At the employee level, recognition assists in maintaining enthusiasm and generating ideas. Ramada evaluates the best ideas from each property and the best earn a Chairman's Award at the annual convention, and cash incentives. Any incentive helps, even publicity in a staff newsletter.

At the industry-wide level, there are a now numerous environmental awards given by local, national and international organisations. These all assist in promoting environmental stewardship.

The Thai Wah Group has won the International Hotel Association's 1992 Environmental Award, It rescued a polluted and unreclaimed mining property, and turned it into a resort. It was their thorough commitment to the environment which gave their Laguna Beach Resort the edge. They considered all aspects, from construction materials, aesthetics, and xeriscaping (landscaping using species of plants and trees, often indigenous, which require little watering), to water and energy efficient designs and programmes, traditional craftsmanship, minimal impact on local way of fife, and incorporation of traditional economic activities. Celebration of success is a vital role, and can be expanded to the local community.

The dean of Florida International University's Hospitality Management School rather overstates the case for green marketing: 'It is time for hotels to hop on the environmental bandwagon. It saves money and planet Earth, too.,.. Taking steps to save energy and reuse waste saves money while saving the Earth. So don't turn red at the suggestion for making your hotels more environmentally sensitive; turn green—all the way to the bank. Conservation pays'. Yet Knipp maintains that most tourism representatives discount possible short-term gains in occupancy levels from environmental action, stressing that it strengthens ties with the local community and eventually improves the image of a hotel company in the eyes of both guests and staff. However, sincere environmental action can be a useful tool in a marketing programme. It is the strong green sell of a business with no equivalent environmental actions which is not legitimate or sustainable.

In a WTO survey, one-third of all travel trade respondents claimed to have already taken environmentally friendly action or initiatives in marketing and promotions, and a further 22% said they intended to do so. These actions ranged from using recycled paper in brochures, to making contributions to environmental charities, to giving clients environmental guidelines or codes of conduct. It is conceivable that in the near future, companies will list their environmental activities in an official green 'report card' which will detail the energy a company has saved, the pollution it has reduced through buying recycled products and developing new manufacturing technologies, etc.

Future directions

Solar power is a possible application in the hospitality industry (e.g. to heat shower water in guestrooms or heat dishwashers in hotel restaurants) but has a longer pay back period. Cogeneration produces savings from the simultaneous production of electricity and use of free heat energy which would otherwise have been lost. The Hotel del Coronado in San Diego has used a solar gas turbine engine for cogeneration since 1983. This 800-kW engine provides 350%, of the hotel's electrical need; the steam from its waste heat provides up to 95% of the hotel's heat in summer and 70% in winter.

Heating problems often relate to the high cost of heating, and draughts. A Canadian system provides an alternative to conventional heating systems which expend most energy by blowing hot air throughout a given room or lobby. Co-Ray-Vac uses its energy to heat objects in that room (e.g. carpets, appliances). The advantages are that it eliminates draughts and chills because the system creates no air currents, and in saving the energy of blowing air, it cuts heating costs by as much as 50%. It is ideal for hotel lobbies, back rooms, open-air restaurants and pubs. New technologies are continually evolving to address problems, and their costs are decreasing.

Many companies are establishing internal 'codes of conduct' as a means for encouraging ethical behaviour for their organizations. The tourism industry is seeing this in the realm of environmental codes. A number of tourism organizations (ministries, associations and operators) have recently developed codes of ethics, or guidelines, but these vary in usefulness. Many codes of practice do not provide the specific guidance expected in a code of practice.

Canada has developed a comprehensive 'Code of Ethics and Guidelines for Sustainable Tourism'. Specific practices are recommended for each tourism subsector, such as: energy conservation related to all areas, including heating, air conditioning and lighting; waste minimization through reduction, reuse and recycling; water conservation; minimizing pollution; selection of energy conserving modes of transportation; purchase policies related to 'green' products and packaging, and environmentally sensitive suppliers; and periodic audits.

We can no longer place the responsibility for the environment elsewhere. At both personal and professional levels, we have to take responsibility for actions. Our notions of ethics must consider impact beyond our immediate horizons. However, good environmental management is fully compatible with good business practice. These should be viewed as the 'double bottom line' (balancing ecological and fiscal considerations) and in the long term are essential for business survival. Ethical codes and practical guidelines are an excellent step in achieving this.

Thailand has actual pollution problems (air, water, litter, and loud traffic) exacerbated by high visibility (on beaches and commercial areas). This presents an image problem and occupancy rates recently plummeted to 20%-30%, with better hotels struggling to keep rates above 50%. The Thai Hotel Association launched an environmental code, which calls for improved waste management, developing recycling programmes, offering information, raising environmental consciousness of guests, staff and the community, improved hotel facilities and equipment, and monitoring environmental quality. In 1994, a green leaves symbol will designate hotels which have qualified to the environmental standards. Although there are only 27 members of this group so far, they represent 7000 of the 27 000-plus rooms.

The Danish Hotels and Restaurants Organization has a similar programme. Although environmental initiatives are at a preliminary stage, there is now increasing realisation that guests are more environmentally aware, and that a number of environmental investments are actually profitable. A working group has been set up to develop standards and minimum environmental criteria required for the right to use their 'Green Key Sign'.

In 1989, Inter-Continental Hotels mandated the greening of the hotel chain. They also penalize managers who fail to meet environmental standards. For example, in 1991, the company released an environmental manual to its 103 hotels in 48 countries around the world. It includes a checklist of more than 130 targets, and general managers must meet 95% of the company's goals or their bonus pay suffers. The company has twice-yearly internal audits which prevent 'faking it'. So far, Inter

Continental's North American properties lead in meeting their goals. Corporations may increasingly take such a standards oriented approach.

One of the most compelling reasons to become more environmentally responsible, is the threat of government regulation. If the lodging industry doesn't clean up its own act, regulators will. Thus, environmental efforts at the corporate or association level may spare business regulatory burdens.

At present, there is little or no comprehensive. environmental auditing in the hospitality industry. The IHEI Industry Guide mentions only energy audits. However, a comprehensive environmental audit is desirable, and can yield financial as well as environmental and other benefits. These are being undertaken by only a few leaders in the hospitality industry. Advantages are that staff can contribute, they provide a database for preliminary decisions, and can be used for performance measurement and monitoring.

Around the world, business is recognizing that it must increasingly move 'beyond compliance'. In the field of corporate accounting and reporting, this means that companies must ensure they comply with fiscal reporting and begin to report on a growing range of environmental performance indicators.

Agenda 21, the 1992 UNCED report, calls on business and industry to 'report annually on their environmental records, as well as on their use of energy and natural resources. Companies will likely move from zero environmental performance reports, to incorporating environmental reporting in annual reports, to free standing environmental reports'. This will be driven by corporate citizenship, but competitive advantage will be the main motivator.

7

Planning, Staffing and Evaluation

There are five key phases which will need careful attention to ensure that an event has the best possible chance of success:

1. The pre-feasibility phase.
2. The feasibility study.
3. The planning phase.
4. The event itself.
5. The evaluation phase.

The pre-feasibility phase

This is the point at which an individual or an organisation has an idea for an event, which may or may not prove viable. Many of the people who work in leisure and tourism are very good at formulating ideas for new events which they believe can't fail to attract visitors in huge numbers. The aim of the pre-feasibility phase is to look objectively at any proposal to see if the event really has the potential to be a winner. In many respects, the pre-feasibility phase is the most important of all; the decision to commit staff, time and money to a full feasibility study will be taken at this stage. The sorts of questions that will need careful attention are:

- Why stage the event?
- Does it meet the organisation's mission or objectives?
- When will it take place?

- Is there a suitable location?
- Can staff be made available or extra people employed?
- Does it have the backing of senior management?
- Will funding be made available?
- Does the organisation have the confidence to stage the event?

It is important at this stage to take soundings from people within the organisation and from respected individuals and organisations outside, remembering always that a degree of confidentiality will be necessary. Their views and concerns will help to answer the question is the idea a good one?'. Depending on the scale and nature of the proposed event, it may be felt necessary to seek the views of national governing bodies, professional organisations and local or regional groups.

If reactions to the idea are positive and those canvassed consider it worthy of further investigation, it will be necessary to begin to 'put flesh on the bones' by carrying out a feasibility study.

The feasibility study

The aim of the feasibility study will be to evaluate the idea as objectively as possible and to determine whether it is practical in an operational and financial sense to stage the event. The written study should include information on:

— The aims and objectives of the event.

— Details of the nature of the event.

— The benefits to the organisers.

— How the event fits into the overall mission of the organisation.

— The resource implications finance, staff, time, premises, equipment, administration, etc.

— The 'track record' of those proposing the event.
— Possible problems and their solutions.
— The time-scale for planning the event.

The feasibility study should be circulated to key decision makers for their comments. If they are convinced by the study that the proposed event is viable and will bring benefits to the organisation, then the real work can begin! The commitment from senior management is crucial and should preferably be in the form of a written response to the feasibility study. An endorsement in writing will signal the go-ahead for the event and the detailed planning can begin. If senior personnel are not convinced that the event has potential, it is better that it is stated at this point rather than half way through the planning phase. They may either think that it is a nonstarter altogether or may consider that with a little fine-tuning it could be made to work. Far better that any doubts are raised at this point in order to save valuable time and money later.

The planning phase

Having received the approval to proceed, the detailed planning to ensure that the event is a success can begin in earnest. The key stages in the planning process are:

— Make the decision to go ahead widely known.
— Appoint a coordinator.
— Assemble a committee or steering group.
— Create an organisational structure.
— Clarify objectives.
— Set timescale targets and deadlines.
— Set budgets.
— Devise contingency plans.

Make the decision widely known

It is important to publicise the fact that the event is to go ahead for a number of reasons. First, making it generally known when and where your event will take place should ensure that other organisers don't choose the same date and venue; in reality, it is practically impossible not to clash with other events taking place on the same day, but it should be possible to avoid events of the same kind on the same day, thus ensuring a good attendance. A second reason for publicising the event at this stage is to create interest from the general public and, if it is a sports event for example, to give them the opportunity to start training. A third reason is to signal to those who may be interested in helping the event in some way, to get in touch.

If there are a number of options as to when the event could take place, it is important to give some thought as to the most appropriate date, bearing in mind who it is you are trying to attract. Knowing the dates of school holidays is important if the event is aimed at families; it is also a good idea to avoid meal times for the same reason. It may be important to bear in mind the dates when British Summer Time begins and ends, if the planned event is to be staged close to either of these two dates.

We have already mentioned that one of the reasons for publicising the fact that the event is going ahead is to avoid other events occurring on the same day. Equally important is the need to be aware of any other international, national or local events already planned to take place. It would be disastrous if the sponsored walk for the local soccer team was inadvertently organised on the same day as the World Cup Final! Thankfully, the dates of major events are set well in advance. It is interesting to note the power that television is having over the staging of major events, particularly sporting events. The timing of events often has to be planned so as to fit in with TV schedules. One of the disadvantages Sydney faced in its bid to host the Olympic Games in the year 2000 was the fact that many of the events would be taking place in the middle of the night European time, because of the time difference between Europe and Australia. As things turned out, Sydney was successful in its bid and will be liaising closely with TV companies to ensure maximum coverage of events to satisfy sponsors and those paying to advertise on television.

Getting the right person to coordinate the planning of the event is crucial. Time taken at this stage in drawing up a list of qualities that the ideal co-ordinator should have, and then finding somebody who matches most closely these qualities, will pay dividends in the long run. An ineffective coordinator can be a liability in the quest for success in the planning of the event. Although every event is unique, there are basic skills and qualities that any good coordinator should have:

— Excellent leadership qualities.
— An excellent communicator.
— A good organiser.
— The ability to delegate.
— Somebody not afraid of hard work.
— A motivator.
— Somebody with creativity and flair.
— A persuasive negotiator.

The event coordinator should be appointed with the full confidence of the senior management of the organisation, and should be given the necessary resources, authority and support to do the job properly. All those involved in the planning of the event need to be clear where the power and responsibility lie. There should be delegation downwards whenever possible so that paid staff and volunteers feel involved in making the decisions that will ensure that the event is a success. However good the event coordinator, he or she will not want to operate in isolation, but will want to be involved in the selection of individuals who will collectively take the detailed decisions on planning the event: the committee.

Assemble a committee or steering group

Although it is feasible for a single person to organise an event, particularly if it is small and local, most events will be organised through a committee. For very large events, it may be useful to agree a constitution, the rules by which the committee will operate; this is often carried out for events that happen every year or have national or international significance.

The committee will have a number of functions:

— To oversee the smooth planning of the event (together with the coordinator).
— To divide the necessary work amongst individuals and subgroups.
— To free the coordinator from routine tasks.
— To take executive decisions on matters relating to the event.
— To agree an organisational structure for the event.
— To ensure that finances are managed appropriately.
— To ensure that the necessary permissions to stage the event are obtained.
— To develop a promotional plan for the event.

The membership of the committee is important. The event coordinator should ideally be the chairperson and be involved in deciding who is invited to sit on the committee, which will be made up of key people who are willing to give the time and effort to the job in hand. If the event is part of the activities of an existing leisure and tourism organisation, whether in the public, private or voluntary sector, the committee will include staff from within the organisation and, depending on the event's size and importance, people from outside as well. It is often prudent to invite on to the committee, individuals from professional bodies, sponsors, local authorities and the like, whose support for the event is seen as vital to its success. Depending on the size and type of event, it may be necessary to form subcommittees to deal with particular aspects of the planning of the event.

Every event committee will need a chairperson, treasurer and secretary plus others with special responsibilities peculiar to the particular event being organised. These could include individuals with responsibility for:

— Promotion and marketing.

— Fund-raising and sponsorship.

— Staffing and staff training.

— Entertainment.

— Catering.

— Equipment.

If it is thought that the committee is becoming too large and unwieldy, an executive committee may be set up to take decisions in the absence of all committee members. The executive committee will be made up of a small group of key individuals, including the coordinator, who should be present at every meeting.

The event organiser will need to use all his or her skills of persuasion and negotiation to ensure that the organising committee doesn't become just a talking shop but takes on the role of a working group. Committees are all about fairness and democracy in decision making, but the process can be painfully slow at times. The committee will need to meet regularly to review progress, but members should not be afraid to cancel a planned meeting if there is little to discuss at that particular time; holding a meeting just because a date has been set is time wasting and can lead to frustration in committee members. Specialists can be co-opted on to the committee from time to time to help with particular aspects of the planning of the event. It is sometimes thought to be a good idea to invite a well-known person to be a figurehead by appointing him or her as president of the committee. This patronage can help promote the event and lend a welcome degree of credibility to proceedings.

The event coordinator, in conjunction with the organising committee, must now begin the task of developing a structure that will ensure that all aspects of the planning of the event are carried out meticulously. One of the first jobs will be to identify 'unit' areas, which are broad areas of work, each of which will have a set of tasks associated with it. For example, an event such as a farm open day, will have the unit areas and tasks. Once the unit areas have been identified, the next job of the coordinating committee is to assign an individual or team to develop the detailed tasks associated with the unit and accept the responsibility for making sure that the work in this area is correctly planned. The size, nature and significance of the event will determine whether an individual or team approach is needed. Those assigned to this work will report to the event organiser and organising committee.

At this stage it may be useful to draw up an organisation chart showing the linkages between the different unit groups and how they relate to the event organiser and the organising committee. By putting the structure on paper, the lines of communication and flow of responsibilities are made clear. It will help to resolve any problems or areas of overlap between individual unit areas. For major national and international events, it is often necessary to produce an organisational handbook, incorporating an organisation chart, to explain in detail the process by which the event is being organised.

Clarify objectives

Now that the event coordinator, coordinating committee and unit leaders are in place, it is as well to clarify exactly what it is the whole team is trying to achieve. This will be a two-stage affair, concentrating first on the overall objectives of the event, as explained in the feasibility study, followed by the specific objectives for each unit leader and his or her team. This is best achieved by the event coordinator calling a meeting of all event personnel and setting the scene before the work in earnest begins. The work of the unit teams will concentrate on:

- — Establishing the tasks within their particular unit area.
- — Setting the dates and deadlines by which each of their tasks must be completed.
- — Setting expenditure limits (and income targets, if applicable) for each task in their unit.
- — Establishing what level and type of staffing they will need.

Set time-scale targets and deadlines

The coordinator will need to ensure that all unit leaders set their timetables and deadlines within an overall event timescale plan, which will need constant monitoring and refining in response to unforeseen circumstances. It is very helpful to have a flowchart or critical path analysis detailing the unit areas with key time targets and deadlines incorporated for each one. It is usual practice to work back from the day of the event when deciding on time deadlines. It is as well for event personnel to remember that things often take longer than expected to happen, so it is a good idea to allow extra time for 'contingencies'. It is also sound advice to allow plenty of time at the initial planning stage, so that the systems and procedures adopted can be implemented with as few changes as possible. Event organisers invariably work from checklists, either ones they have developed themselves or adapted from a reference source (there are a number of good books on event management which give example checklists). The detailed planning process for the event coordinator will involve matching the items on his or her checklist with the deadlines being developed by the unit groups, to produce an overall event planner giving the full picture of unit areas, tasks and deadlines for completion.

Set budgets

It is important to be as specific as possible when estimating the likely income and expenditure for the event, and the budgets (if any) needed by the different unit groups. Accounting for income and expenditure is particularly important when funds from external sources are being used, for example in the form of sponsorship or a grant from a local authority or voluntary trust. They will want assurances, and evidence, that their investment is being prudently managed. Unit leaders will need to account for their particular expenditure, while the responsibility for overall budgeting and finance lies with the event coordinator and the treasurer on the coordinating committee.

Different events will have different financial objectives. The main reason for a local authority staging an event is not likely to be to make a profit, but perhaps to make its leisure and tourism facilities and services better known to the local population; an event put on by a commercial organisation, however, may well be expected to create a healthy profit. While public sector events may well be subsidised by the local authority, it will none the less be made clear to the organisers that they should aim to minimise expenditure, maximise income and, hopefully, at least break even financially on the event. It is important that the event organiser and the organising committee know what the financial objectives are for their particular event; are they permitted to make a loss, and if so, how much? Should they aim to break even? Are they expected to make a surplus, and if so, how much? Without knowing the financial aims within which they must work, planning the finances for the event will be impossible.

Whether or not the event being planned is a moneymaking venture or has a non-profit objective, the importance of carefully setting expenditure limits for each unit area and methodically recording what is actually spent is just the same. Even small events in the local community will have costs associated with them and the idea that local authority events are 'free' is far from the truth. Local people will have contributed to the cost of organising the events through their local and national taxes. Income generated by the event can be from a variety of sources, such as:

— Donations.
— Grants.
— Low interest loans.
— Sponsorship.
— Sale of advertising space.
— Ticket sales.
— Raffles and other competitions.
— Car parking fees.
— Income from concessions (businesses given the authority to trade at the event)

— Income from television or radio companies
— Sale of merchandise.
— Sale of food and drink.

Income targets for each unit area should be realistic and agreed by the unit leader and his or her team from the outset. Estimating income is notoriously difficult, particularly when an outdoor event is at the mercy of the weather, and any event is competing with other leisure and tourism activities for customers. Murphy's Law applies just as much to events as it does to other leisure and tourism facilities and services, so 'if anything can go wrong it will!'. Some things that happen to test the nerve of even the best-prepared event organiser can truly be said to be unforeseen, but many can be predicted and contingencies or alternatives devised. In Britain, the weather must be one of the least predictable factors surrounding any event, be it in summer or winter. Organisers can reassure the public that an outdoor event will go ahead 'whatever the weather by publicising this fact from the outset and giving an alternative venue should the worst happen. A cold spell or sudden downpour can also affect attendances at indoor events, with people choosing to stay in the comfort of their own homes rather than venturing out.

Other occurrences that will need contingency plans include:

— Failure of power supplies.
— Non-arrival of key staff or personalities (have 'extras' on hand).
— Heavy traffic.
— A major accident.
— Parts of the site waterlogged.

There are occasions when an event will have to be called off altogether, often for reasons outside the control of the organisers. Although very disappointing for both organising staff and the visitors, the same degree of professionalism that was in evidence for the planning of the event must be maintained to deal with this situation. The organiser will need to make the decision to either cancel or postpone until a future date. Whatever is decided must be communicated as quickly as possible to the general public; an excellent way of doing this is by contacting the local radio station, which will gladly broadcast regular information so as to let as many people as possible know. There must be a method by which any advance payments can be returned in the event of cancellation, or tickets can be reused if the event is only postponed. Those responsible for press and public relations will need to handle the situation sensitively and have their own contingency plan for dealing with any adverse publicity.

Assuming that all the prior planning has gone smoothly, the day of the event itself should be as enjoyable for those who have been involved in its organisation as for the visitors who support it. It is a good idea to hold an eve of event briefing session to go over the final details, iron out any last minute hitches and confirm any alterations to schedules. It may be that some parts of the event, perhaps the opening and closing ceremonies, will need a final rehearsal. Regardless of the size of the event, there are one or two important points that should be remembered:

— *Give the coordinator a 'roving brief'* he or she should not be given specific tasks to carry out on the day itself, except perhaps welcoming and entertaining VIPs, but should be allowed to circulate around the event helping with any difficult situations that may arise and generally maintaining a positive and professional approach.

— *Stress the importance of customer care* whether the event is free or customers have paid to enter, it is important that all staff involved in any way with it are mindful of the need to give customers the attention they need so that they can enjoy the event to the full. Visitors with special needs will warrant particular attention.

— *Keep to any published times* there is *nothing more* frustrating for visitors than to turn up at a particular point to see something that doesn't happen. If changes to the schedule have to be made, make sure the message is conveyed to those attending the event.

If these points are remembered, and all the prior planning has achieved its objectives, then the event should be a memorable celebration for all concerned.

The evaluation phase

It is true to say that we all learn from our mistakes and experiences; there is invariably something we would have done in a different way if we had the chance again. The process of looking back and evaluating is just as important in event management as in any other sector of the leisure and tourism industry. Any evaluation of an event should try to answer the following questions:

— Did the event achieve its objectives, both financially and operationally?

— Was the organisational structure workable?

— Were all eventualities covered?

— Were the sponsors happy with the outcome?

— Were the customers satisfied with the event?

— What changes would be made if the event was to be staged again?

The event organiser and the organising committee should hold a debriefing session with staff, at which the above points should be considered while still fresh in their minds, before a final report on the event is prepared for distribution to interested individuals and organisations, with one copy being retained for future reference. If the event takes place over a number of days, is very large, or is split into discrete activities, more than one debriefing session may be needed.

Information that may be helpful during the evaluation phase of an event can come from a number of different sources, including:

— *Records any* information or data about the event which has been recorded will help in the evaluation. Items such as financial accounts, attendance figures, ticket sales, receipts, photographs, video clips and media coverage can be used to reflect on the event and draw conclusions.

— *Customer feedback this* can be both formal and informal. Formal feedback can be from surveys carried out during, and sometimes immediately after, the event. As well as information on the profile of customers attending the event, the organisers can use visitor surveys to discover attitudes and opinions. All staff should be trained to register informal feedback, in the form of comments, complaints and suggestions from customers, since this is often as valuable as the formal data.

— *Comments from observers the* organisers of larger events often appoint observers whose role is to look at how the event has been organised and, more importantly, observe how the event comes across 'on the day'. It is useful to have the views of respected individuals who lie outside the organisational framework of the event, and whose comments can help the evaluation process. *Comments from staff whether* staff are paid or are working in a voluntary capacity, they will have useful ideas of their own as to how their particular role could have been improved. The event organiser should take the time and trouble to interview key staff and feed their comments into the evaluation process.

Probably the best question to ask at the evaluation stage is, 'was the event worth all the hard work, money, time and effort that went into its planning and staging?'. If all concerned can answer yes to this, then the event can truly be said to have been a success.

Launched in 1985 as a contribution to the World Conservation Strategy, the Mid Wales Festival of the Countryside has grown into a pioneering model of responsible rural tourism. The Festival is a series of events (some that have been in existence for some time, some new) which take place in the countryside, towns and villages of Mid Wales from June to December. Its aim is to show that informed concern and respect for the environment can go hand in hand with economic development, in an area of Britain which is working hard to attract inward investment, create new jobs and improve the social fabric for the local people. Spearheading this work is the Development Board for Rural Wales (DBRW), a government-funded quango, which considers that high quality tourism can play a significant role in the economic development of the region.

The DBRW is one of the major sponsors of the Festival of the Countryside, along with the Countryside Council for Wales and all eight local authorities in the area. It is staffed by a part-time director, two full-time assistant directors, and associates brought in for specific functions including research and compiling the Festival's annual magazine. An avid supporter of the Festival of the Countryside is leading environmentalist David Bellamy, who visits Mid Wales every year to take part in events. He said of the Festival recently,

The Festival, with its base in Newtown in the heart of Mid Wales, acts as an umbrella' organisation for marketing purposes and as a catalyst for the development of events, linking with individuals, voluntary groups and the private sector. The aims of the Festival of the Countryside are:

1. Environmental education to convey, in an interesting and coherent way, the messages of the countryside and conservation.
2. Enjoyment of the countryside to help satisfy the varied recreational demands of residents and tourists.
3. Socio-economic development to stimulate the rural economy, support providers of rural attractions and to involve the local community in culturally-acceptable ways.

In seeking to achieve these aims, the Festival has had notable success and is now spreading its message through links with rural areas in Europe and beyond. Training for event organisers has been provided through periodic information seminars and local group work, as well as a residential business development course held in 1992. A handbook of good practice in responsible rural tourism has been prepared for use throughout Europe.

Staffing an event

Success or failure in planning and staging an event often hinges on the quality of the personnel given the responsibility of completing the task. Depending on the size and nature of the event, personnel will fall into one of the following categories:

— *Senior management these* are the people responsible for setting the framework and policy within which the event will be developed. In the case of the Olympic Games, this function is carried out by the IOC (International Olympic Committee) with representatives of all the competing nations. An event of national or regional significance, such as the Great North Run, will normally have an organising committee working with an individual event coordinator to oversee the planning work. The management of small, local events is sometimes left to a single individual who will make all the necessary decisions, 'A more usual practice, however, is to form a committee or steering group to ensure fairness and democracy in decisionmaking; often this is made up of only a chairperson, secretary and treasurer.

— *Middle management working* to the policy set by the senior management team will be 'middle managers' who will take on responsibility for specific functions of the staging of the event, for example publicity, staff training or health and safety matters. This unit that most events will be divided into unit areas, and unit leaders appointed to coordinate the staff working in the unit and carry out the necessary tasks associated with the unit.

— *Employees and helpers* once the fact that an event is going to take place is publicised, there will be many people and organisations willing to get involved and help in whatever way they can. Existing employees may be 'seconded' from their normal duties to help plan or stage the event. Extra staff may need to be employed, particularly if the event is very large. Volunteers may be needed regardless of the size of the event; the NutraSweet London Marathon, for example, uses 5,000 volunteers to help on the day.

— *Support staff* as well as the staff under the direct control of the event organisers, other support and ancillary staff may be associated with the event, for example security personnel, concessionaires, volunteer medical backup, creche workers and maintenance staff.

Recruitment and selection of staff

Organisers of local events may not have the necessary resources to be able to pay staff, and may have to plan the whole thing from start to finish with the help of volunteers. Where an event is of national, regional or even international significance, key staff will need to be appointed and offered an attractive remuneration package; the more significant the event the more attractive the package will need to be. As we saw in the last section, finding the right person to take on the role of event organiser is crucial. To be considered for the job of an organiser for a major event, the individual is likely to have a good 'track record' in events management and considerable experience of the leisure and tourism industry. An organiser may well be 'head-hunted', i.e. approached by an organisation to see if he or she is interested in the position, rather than making an application themselves.

Staff for events can be found in a number of ways:

- By advertising in the appropriate newspapers and magazines.
- By contacting voluntary organisations.
- By sending press releases to newspapers and magazines.
- By 'word of mouth'; local councils, youth groups, colleges and voluntary groups may well know of people willing to get involved.

If organisers are in the fortunate position of having more applications than there are positions to be filled, then a standard recruitment and selection procedure should be operated involving members of the organising committee. Particular attention should be paid to the employment of staff who will be working with children. There are published guidelines on this matter and the advice of the local Social Services Department should be sought at an early stage. It may also be able to help with the recruitment of staff with experience of dealing with disabled visitors and those with other special needs.

Staff training

Where staff are paid to take on a specific role in the organisation of an event, taking part in the necessary training can be incorporated into their job specification. When using volunteers, however, it may not be feasible to expect them to give up time, over and above their involvement in the event itself, to attend training sessions. In practice, therefore, tasks that involve a large amount of training will normally be given to paid employees, e.g. health and safety procedures. Volunteers can be issued with written notes related to their particular tasks.

The organiser and organising committee will need to get across to all staff involved in the planning and staging of the event the importance of working as part of a team to achieve the objectives of the event. Larger events may be able to consider separate training sessions in team-building and teamwork. Briefing sessions will be an important part of the training element of an event and should be made available to all staff. It may be possible to obtain funding for staff training through a local college or TEC (Training and Enterprise Council) if the event can be seen to be contributing to the economic or social wellbeing of the area.

All staff must be made to feel a valued part of the organisation that has taken on the job of setting up the event. This is when the event coordinator and unit leaders have a vital role to play in managing the staff under their control. The particular circumstances of volunteers will need careful and supportive action; pushed too far, they may well lose interest in the event.

Important ways in which organisers can help staff feel more involved include:

— Listening to their ideas and suggestions.
— Thanking them for their help and support throughout the event.
— Paying them a fair rate for the job.
— Giving volunteers a 'reward' for their efforts, e.g. a small gift or contribution towards their travelling expenses.
— Having clear communication channels.
— Having clear health, safety and security procedures in place.
— Giving adequate training and briefing.
— Providing refreshments and a rest area.
— Holding a social event for all staff.

Teamwork in leisure and tourism is a means to an end, rather than an end in itself. It is a process, not a one-off event. Too many teams fail not because their initial planning and development lacks direction, but because they commit little, if any, time to review their effectiveness and to ensure that the gains, agreements and decisions made by the team are being implemented. Any evaluation of team performance will be trying to answer some or all of the following questions:

— Did the team as a whole achieve its objectives?
— Was the team leader effective?
— Did individual team members perform to the best of their ability?
— Were any weaknesses identified?
— Were measures put in place to rectify weaknesses?
— What were the strengths of the team and its members?

— Were there examples of outstanding performance?
— Was good performance commended or rewarded?
— Did the team identify any new directions for future work?
— Were the channels of communication effective?

The precise methods of evaluating team performance and the personnel involved in the process will differ from one organisation to another. It is, however, generally agreed that the people who should not be left out of any evaluation are the team members themselves. They will have the most knowledge about how the team operated and will be aware of its successes and failures. Their perception of how the team performed will, of course, be subjective, i.e. their conclusions will be from their own viewpoint as members of the team. None the less, their views are critical to obtaining a valid evaluation of performance. To arrive at a more objective view of the team's performance, the team leader may carry out an appraisal of the relative performance of each member of the team. A member of the senior management of the organisation may be allocated the job of appraising the team leader, individual team members or the team as a whole (see Unit 9 on human resource management for more details of staff appraisal). This same senior manager may be given the task of reviewing the team's performance against its objectives to see if it has, for example, achieved any financial targets it was set or reached any quotas on use by particular members of the local community, e.g. disabled people.

An observer is sometimes used to further increase the objectivity of the exercise. Usually from outside the organisation, this person will view the team's progress from the outset and be able to comment on performance and development issues. Consultants, staff from leisure and tourism departments at Colleges and Universities, local authority personnel and staff from professional bodies can be called upon to take on the role of observer to a leisure and tourism team.

Evaluation methods and techniques

Team review and evaluation

As soon as possible after the team has finished its work, or at pre-planned stages of its development, the team should carry out a review and evaluation exercise. This is likely to take the form of a meeting of all team members and will include both informal and formal feedback. Informal feedback from the team members will include their personal views and comments on their own performance and the effectiveness of the whole team, including the team leader. While informal feedback is a very useful tool for identifying broad areas of success and failure, a more formal reporting mechanism will be needed to measure team effectiveness. It is likely that the team will have identified its objectives at the start of its work. The more precise the objectives, and any associated performance criteria, the easier it will be for the team to measure its effectiveness in meeting its targets. For example, a member of a team that has been set up to introduce a new customer care programme into a museum may have been set performance criteria that could include:

- — Record every complaint on an official complaint form.
- — Write a letter to each person who complained apologising on behalf of the organisation and keep a copy for reference.

It will be a relatively straightforward matter to check whether these tasks have been carried out and so reach a conclusion on this element of the person's work performance. Other recorded information that could be useful in measuring the team's performance includes customer feedback questionnaires, sales returns, ideas in suggestion boxes, wastage rates, repeat orders, numbers of returning customers, etc.

Staff performance review

Individual team members may be interviewed by either their line manager or the team leader, who may in fact be the same person, to formally assess an individual's performance in the team. This may be part of a wider staff appraisal exercise that links pay to performance. The interview will seek to identify good performance by the team member and areas where performance needs to be enhanced, perhaps by a particular type of staff development activity, e.g. going on a course that improves decision making. The outcome of the performance review should be a written development plan, agreed by both the reviewer and member of the team, which should list personal development objectives and the activities needed to meet the objectives.

Self-appraisal

Team members may be asked to formally evaluate their own performance against objectives and performance criteria by carrying out a self-appraisal, which, if undertaken in as objective a way as possible, can produce useful feedback both for the individual and his or her line manager. Such an appraisal can be fed into any wider staff appraisal exercise the organisation may undertake.

Peer appraisal

Peer appraisal involves the evaluation of a member of the team by his or her peers, i.e. the other members of the team. Formal rather than informal peer appraisal is more useful, since it can prevent the exercise becoming too personal. If managed effectively by the team leader, however, it can be very enlightening and can help to identify strengths and weaknesses in individual team members, who can use the outcomes to identify any remedial measures that may be necessary.

Planning a customer care programme

The term customer care' is on the lips of so many professionals in the leisure and tourism industry today that we might be persuaded that it is a concept that is totally new to the industry. This is far from the truth as any study of the high standards expected by travellers in the heyday of Victorian Britain would quickly show. What is new is the almost universal acceptance that customer care is an integral part of any successful leisure and tourism organisation.

Customer care is a vital element of any customer service strategy since it focuses on the crucial interaction between customer and member of staff, and, if planned and executed effectively, will help the organisation. Achieve its overall objective. There are, however, a number of 'ground rules' that need to be explained before any customer care programme can be implemented.

Ground rules in customer care

There are many considerations an organisation will need to take into account before embarking on a customer care programme for its staff. Some of the more important, which we will look at in more detail, include:

- Always start at the top!
- Involve all staff.
- Have clear aims and objectives.
- Be realistic as to what can be achieved.
- Put yourself in your customers' shoes!
- Integrate customer care with other marketing efforts.

— Be prepared to invest time and money.
— Monitor the programme and measure results.

Every individual in the organisation must be committed to carrying out a customer care programme if it is to succeed. This means starting With the highest levels of management, whether it be the chairman of the board, the chief executive, the head of personnel or the director of leisure services. Without their enthusiasm and support the programme will be doomed to failure. Some senior managers sometimes need convincing of the benefits of a customer care programme before they commit resources to it, and this is where an individual from outside the organisation can sometimes play an important role in presenting an objective view of the situation.

Involve all staff

It is no good putting just 'front line' staff through a customer care training programme with the hope of saving a little time and money. This piecemeal approach will not achieve the aim of promoting a customer-centred approach throughout the organisation. All staff, whether on reception or in the plant room, will need some training in customer care and their role in helping to give the customer excellence in service. It is important also to involve staff in the planning and design of the programme, recognising that they have valuable experience and expertise to offer. Any programme that is seen to be 'imposed from above' will create hostility and not help staff to relate to the benefits of good customer service.

Have clear aims and objectives

Any leisure and tourism organisation should be asking itself the questions, 'why are we planning a customer care programme and what do we hope to get out of it?'.

Unless management is clear on its aims and objectives for the programme, it will be difficult to measure whether anything has actually been achieved. The aims of the customer care programme will vary between organisations and even between different departments of the same organisation. Private sector leisure and tourism companies will equate customer care with increased profitability while the public and voluntary sector providers will invest in customer care to provide enhanced levels of service to their customers.

Be realistic as to what can be achieved

Management will need to be aware of not setting unrealistic targets for the customer care programme, since staff will feel they have 'failed' if the aims are not met. Management should be in the best position to know what resources of time, money and equipment the organisation can devote to the programme and any limitations or constraints that may exist. Outcomes should be framed within any limiting factors and should be planned over a reasonable time-scale; it is always better to have achievable aims that staff will feel good about having met, rather than unrealistic outcomes that could lead to demoralised employees.

Put yourself in your customers' shoes!

Taking the time to look at your organisation from the customers' perspective will pay dividends in helping to develop a customer care programme that is truly customer focused. Managers and staff can become complacent and overlook problems that may be obvious when looked at from the customers' viewpoint. All customers have particular needs, including:

— *Attention—customers* do not like being ignored or being given only partial attention.

— Control—they like to feel in control of the situation

and feel good about themselves and what they are doing.

— *Understanding—customers* value friendliness and acknowledgement.

— *Fairness—they* want to feel they are being treated with fairness and honesty.

Integrate customer care with other marketing efforts

Customer care should not be seen by staff and management as a 'bolt on' to other marketing and promotional work being carried out in the organisation. Rather it should be viewed as an important part of the total marketing plan. Staff who are striving to achieve excellence in customer care should be confident that:

— Effective market research has been carried out to determine customer needs.

— The products and services offered by the organisation reflect these customer demands.

— The products and services are effectively promoted to their intended audience.

Only when customer care is integrated with all marketing activity will it achieve its full potential for the organisation.

Be prepared to invest time and money

Planning and implementing a customer care programme will have financial implications both in the long and short term. Short-term costs will revolve around releasing staff from their normal duties in order to be able to attend training sessions, and employing a trainer to see the programme through. The trainer need not necessarily be a consultant employed on a contract basis from outside the organisation; an existing employee with the right skills and attitude could be asked to do the job. However, many institutions that have used 'in-house' staff have found that their knowledge of employees and procedures within the organisation sometimes acts as a barrier to fully achieving the objectives of the customer care programme.

The organisation may well be faced with longer-term financial costs, since the customer care programme may highlight procedures, systems or equipment that may need to be changed in order for the staff to fully implement what they have learnt as part of the programme.

Financial help and advice for implementing customer care programmes may be available from such sources as the Department of Trade and Industry (DTI), under its 'Marketing Initiative' scheme, and the Employment Department.

Monitor the programme and measure results

All the effort and expense of seeing through a customer care programme will have been wasted if measures are not put in place to measure its effectiveness. This is why it is important to have specific objectives and outcomes against which to measure success. Techniques for receiving feedback from customers must be maintained to check whether there are measurable gains from the programme, such as the expected increase in sales or the predicted rise in positive customer response shown in a questionnaire survey.

Establishing a customer care programme

Having investigated the ground rules underlying the introduction of a customer care programme, we must now turn to the detail of the programme itself and the stages that must be gone through in order to ensure success. Figure 3.4 shows the principal stages in carrying through a customer care programme.

Organisational policy

One of the ground rules we looked at was making sure that the commitment to the customer care programme started at the top of the organisation, in other words it must be embedded into its policy. All organisations nowadays seem to spend a great deal of time developing mission statements setting out the reason for their very existence. This trend seems to be evident in all sectors of leisure and tourism, whether private, public or voluntary sector.

Mission statements are important in that they give an indication of what an organisation is trying to achieve; the mission is often followed by specific objectives that will detail how it is to be achieved. Any leisure and tourism organisation committed to excellence in its customer relations should say so in its mission statement and associated objectives. In this way, staff at all levels within the organisation will be sent a clear message on the importance of positive customer relations, and customers will know what to expect.

It is not enough just to develop a mission statement and then forget about it. The mission is a clear public statement that should be used as the basis for future activities by the organisation. It is also essential that the mission is communicated to all staff and that they understand what the organisation is trying to achieve.

Market research

Once the leisure and tourism organisation has developed a mission statement that clarifies its commitment to excellence in customer care, the next stage of the customer care programme, namely market research, can be put into action. It is essential to identify customer needs if we wish to provide them with a high level of customer care. Without market research, management will not have a clear and unbiased view of who its customers are and what it is they are wanting. Identifying customer needs and the techniques that can be used to collect the data. The collection of information on customers invariably involves a survey of some sort, which will collect both factual data (age, sex, employment status, etc.) and customer opinions on the facilities and services they use. Some organisations may wish to know why people do not use their services and may carry out themselves or commission a non-user survey. This may reveal interesting information on why people choose to use rival facilities and services and may prompt management into making changes to its own activities.

It is important to spend time and money on getting the right information on customers; using inaccurate or incorrect information at this early stage of the customer care programme will put into jeopardy all that takes place from this point on.

Employee perceptions

Market research on customers will generate very useful information on their needs, habits and opinions. Just as important to any leisure and tourism organisation striving for excellence in customer care is to know what its own staff think about the organisation and their place within it. If staff feel undervalued and overlooked in their job, it will be difficult to inspire them in any activity aimed at improving customer relations. Depending on the size of the organisation, there are different approaches that can be adopted to discover staff perceptions. A large company or public sector organisation will probably carry out an employee attitude survey This will often be filled in anonymously so that staff can express their feelings freely without threat of reprisal. A smaller organisation may wish to interview all staff about their work attitudes or conduct a small-scale survey. Employee attitude surveys should not be filled in just by 'front line' staff but by management as well. A survey may reveal that although the majority of staff are very keen on the idea of improving customer care systems and practices, some senior managers may not be convinced of the merits of the idea. This may highlight the need for changes in management style, which will need to be implemented if the whole drive towards a customer-centred organisation is going to be a success.

Customer care training for managers

Whether or not the surveys of staff attitudes have indicated a need for changes in management style, all managers will need to be trained in their role in implementing a customer care philosophy. Once the initial programme has finished, it will be the job of management to inspire the staff and ensure that the initiative is a success. Although there will undoubtedly be delegation of tasks, they will also be responsible for the monitoring of the programme and its constant refinement. Management will need updating in leadership qualities and teambuilding techniques to ensure that the customer care programme is a success. The manager will need to be comfortable with people in their work-places, be a good listener, trusting, open and fair. Management must keep staff fully informed of what is happening and why, which can be done through a combination of short meetings, newsletters and social events.

Customer care training for staff

We have mentioned earlier in this unit that it is a mistake to train only 'front line' staff in customer care improvement; all employees need to feel part of the drive for excellence. There are likely to be two main aims of the customer care staff training in leisure and tourism organisations. The first aim will be to focus all staff on the new company attitude towards its customers, and the second will be to equip staff with the appropriate skills in dealing with customers. The latter will include such things as:

— Communication skills.
— Listening skills.
— Dealing with difficult situations.
— Telephone technique.
— Body-language.
— Dealing with customers with special needs.

The training should deal with both internal and external customers and should not be a 'one-off' event; it is important that training in customer care is seen as a continual process. Some organisations use a technique known as 'cascading', with senior management being trained first, then middle management who are in turn responsible for passing on the training to junior managers and staff.

Alterations to systems

All leisure and tourism organisations will have systems in place to handle the day-to-day management issues. A commitment to improving customer relations and the establishment of a customer care programme may expose weaknesses in existing systems which will need amendment. The systems will need to be customer-orientated and not developed solely because they bring benefits to the organisation. Looking at how customers are dealt with from their point of view, will help the management put in place systems that are far more likely to succeed.

It is at this stage in the customer care programme that management may consider pursuing external certification of its systems by going for BS5750/IS09000 or 'Investors in People'. Having these certificates may give the organisation a 'marketing edge' over the competition, but they require a great deal of dedication, hard work and money to put in place. The British Standard BS5750, for example, will involve the organisation in extensive auditing and documentation of procedures, practices, processes and personnel related to any aspect of quality within the organisation. Some leisure and tourism organisations, regardless of whether they wish to apply for full certification or not, use relevant parts of the BS5750 guidelines when developing customer care systems.

Developing customer-orientated systems for a leisure and tourism organisation can only be totally successful when whoever is doing the development work has an in-depth understanding of the organisation, its mission and its customers. It is only when considerable time has been spent on these three points that the actual development of the systems can take place. Once developed, the systems will need embedding in the organisation and constantly updating to take account of internal changes and improvements.

Monitoring and measuring

Once the customer care programme is up and running, it will need careful monitoring to ensure that a customer focus is being maintained. Left to its own devices, any programme will wither and die. Part of the development of systems mentioned above should be the means to measure the tangible benefits that the programme has generated, e.g. increase in profits, improvement in customer attitude, etc. The whole subject of the monitoring and evaluation of customer care programmes.

Evaluating a customer care programme

There is always the danger when a leisure and tourism organisation is implementing a customer care programme that the staff will think their work is over when the programme is finally put in place. In reality, this is far from the case and is likely to be when the hard work really begins! If the staff (and management) see the customer care programme as just another campaign, it will start to falter from day one, and another campaign will need to be launched at a later date.

All those involved with the programme must realise that it is not a 'one-off 'but is part of the process of creating a different culture within the organisation, one that has customers as its focus. A customer care programme is not a 'quick fix' that will sweep away all the organisation's problems overnight. Rather it is a process that will take time to achieve its objective of excellence in customer service.

Customers needs and expectations are constantly changing in the leisure and tourism business, so that any customer care programme must be flexible enough to meet the requirements of an increasingly discerning public.

All of these factors point to the need for constant monitoring and evaluation of the customer care programme to ensure that it is meeting the aims set by the organisation. Monitoring and evaluation is the last link in the chain of customer care, which begins with setting objectives, investigating customer needs, moves through training of staff and managers, and looks at alterations to existing systems. Monitoring is concerned with looking at how the customer care programme is operating in the organisation, where evaluation means measuring its effectiveness. Evaluation is important because: 'If you can't measure it, you can't manage it!'.

Why bother with monitoring and evaluation?

For the leisure and tourism professionals who take

quality to their hearts, customer care can become a way of life, even a crusade. Following the route to excellence in customer service may change not only the way they operate at work, but also their whole attitude to life in general, with a greater degree of openness and fairness. Sadly, not all staff within a leisure and tourism organisation may share this same zeal. For example:

— Pressures on senior management may force it to move its commitment away from customer care to some other function.

— Staff may become sceptical about the benefits of a customer-orientated approach.

— There may be breakdowns in communications within the organisation.

It is because of these sorts of problems, which arise when a customer care programme is put into place, that it is essential to monitor and evaluate its effectiveness. Measuring effectiveness allows an organisation to do a number of things:

— Estimate where it stands according to certain criteria.

— Identify strengths and weaknesses.

— Focus efforts.

— Develop training.

— Monitor progress.

— Quantify achievements.

— Reward staff accordingly.

In practice, most organisations, use monitoring and evaluation to achieve a mixture of the above points.

The type of questions that should be asked include:

— Are the original objectives of the programme still valid?

— How does performance to date measure against the established criteria?
— What are the successes of the customer care programme?
— How can the organisation build on these successes?
— What are the weaknesses of the programme?
— Have the customers' expectations of service quality changed?
— In which areas do improvements need to be made?
— What are the major priorities for action to put things right?

How is a programme evaluated?

There are three main elements to the evaluation of any customer care programme:

1. Setting performance standards/criteria.
2. Measuring to see if the standards are being met.
3. Putting in place measures to rectify any shortcomings.

Setting performance standards

When leisure and tourism organisations strive for excellence in customer care, it soon becomes clear that it is not enough simply to encourage staff to 'treat the customers well'. There comes a point when the management has to define just what 'well' means. Employees need to know the standards against which their performance will be measured. Staff will need both a clear job description and a set of performance standards or performance criteria for each of the tasks they are responsible for.

Many organisations talk at great length about their excellent customer service, but few are prepared to put in place the necessary performance standards to measure objectively just how good their service really is.

Devising and implementing performance standards is a very time-consuming task and one which, if done properly, will call for an investment of financial resources from the organisation. Large leisure and tourism organisations, with extensive personnel and training departments, may well carry out the task themselves. Smaller organisations are likely to appoint a consultant to devise the standards on their behalf or use criteria already available through professional bodies and other industry organisations.

The following example of typical performance standards that could be used in a restaurant, hotel or any catering outlet, show the detail needed for the exercise to be a success.

Superimposed above any detailed performance standards for specific job tasks will be the overall objectives of the customer care programme, which again must be specific and detailed. Examples of objectives of customer care programmes in leisure and tourism could be:

— To achieve a 5 per cent increase in memberships sold for a golf club.

— For a hotel to achieve a 10 per cent increase in bednights sold to customers.

— For a leisure centre to achieve a 10 per cent reduction in the number of complaints.

— To achieve a 10 per cent increase in the 'excellent' category for responses to a customer satisfaction survey.

Using the objectives of the customer care programme and specific performance indicators as the yardsticks against which the effectiveness of the programme can be measured, the organisation is now in a position to consider the most appropriate ways in which the measurement can take place.

Measuring to see if the standards are being met

Leisure and tourism is very much a service industry. Whereas a company in the manufacturing sector can reasonably easily set standards for the quality of its products, and measure to see if the standards are being met, this process is much more difficult in an industry so heavily dependent on customer service. However, although a difficult task, it is essential that any leisure and tourism organisation committed to improving customer care must develop systems and procedures to measure the effectiveness of its activities.

Some of the main techniques for measuring to see if standards are being met are:

— Surveys.
— Observation.
— Recording informal feedback.
— Checking financial figures.
— Analysing customer data.

Surveys

Surveys are the most common method of monitoring levels of performance in customer care. An organisation will use a survey as part of a customer care programme to see if the targets it set itself are being achieved in reality. A survey provides a 'snapshot' of an organisation's health at a particular point in time. Surveys are important to management since they measure the satisfaction levels within the organisation and provide crucial information on which decisions can be made.

Surveys as part of a customer care programme can be directed at:

— *Customers*—a survey of visitors at a tourist attraction or a customer satisfaction survey at a leisure centre will provide valuable information about how the customer perceives their leisure experience; how they feel about the standard of service, the attitude of the staff, how any queries have been dealt with, etc.

— *Staff*—it is important to continually seek and act on the views of staff at the 'sharp end' of customer care. Without their continuing support, the programme will not succeed. An employee attitude survey will give them the chance to have their ideas and concerns formally noted. Management will be able to see if particular concerns are being expressed by more than one individual and act accordingly.

— *'Internal customers'—we* have seen that all staff in an organisation have 'customers', whether or not they deal with the public face to face. Internal customers are colleagues in the same organisation, who may be in a different department, but whose cooperation and support is vital if the move towards excellence in customer care is to be successful. Surveys can be a useful way of establishing whether all departments are happy with the progress of the customer care programme.

— *Management—the* managers in the organisation should be surveyed routinely to see if they are clear on their role in achieving total customer satisfaction. If the management are unclear or unhappy about the culture of the organisation, these fears may be transmitted to other staff and even customers.

— *Non users—it* may be useful to find out why people are not using your facilities but are choosing to spend their money on competitor products and services, Such a survey, which is normally carried out in the street or door to door, may highlight aspects of poor customer service that could be put right.

Observation

Observing what people do and say, whether they are customers, managers or staff, can provide useful feedback on the effectiveness of any customer care programme. It is common for an employee, who has been given clear performance standards to achieve, to be observed in the work-place by his or her line manager. Indeed part of the evaluation process of the programme may be a manager observing his or her staff and recording their progress over a period of time. Staff in certain leisure and tourism organisations may also be tested from time to time by management on such matters as pricing and product knowledge.

Customers may be observed as well as surveyed in order to get a fuller picture of their satisfaction levels. Staff may be given the task of 'mingling' with customers to listen to their views; people are often more open with their comments if they know their answers or reactions are not going to be recorded on a questionnaire. The sectors of the industry where observation of customers is a particularly useful technique include visitor attractions, restaurants and cafes, museums and art galleries.

Recording informal feedback

Any leisure and tourism organisation striving to improve its customer care will go out of its way to seek customers' views in a variety of ways. To give the whole programme credibility in the eyes of the customer, it is vital that their views are listened to and acted upon. There are many occasions in the course of a normal day when staff in leisure and tourism will have the opportunity to receive informal comments from guests, clients and visitors. It is important that staff have the chance to 'pool' this feedback since it can be an invaluable management aid. It may be that staff discussion groups could be held once a week when the informal feedback could be discussed and perhaps recorded. Alternatively, customer feedback sheets could be issued to all staff for them to record the information as it happens.

Checking financial figures

If one objective of the customer care programme is financial, e.g. for a hotel to achieve a 5 per cent increase in conference business within 12 months, measuring to see if this has happened should be a relatively straightforward affair. A check on sales figures should provide the evidence.

Analysing customer data

Data on customers, such as the volume of repeat business, frequency of bookings, satisfaction levels, customer spend, etc., is available both from surveys and internal records. Analysing such information, either manually or with the help of a computer-based system, will allow managers to see if performance standards and specific objectives of the customer care programme are being met.

Putting in place measures to rectify any shortcomings

If the process of measuring actual performance against the performance standards shows that targets are not being met, measures to rectify the situation will need to be implemented as soon as possible to maintain the impetus of the customer care programme. The measurement exercise may highlight the need for more training for staff or management, or perhaps alterations to systems in order to improve matters. Once the measures have been put in place, the process of monitoring and evaluation will continue using a mixture of the techniques described above.

Maintaining the momentum

We have seen that the planning, implementation and

evaluation of a customer care programme in leisure and tourism is a very complex and time-consuming process. Any faltering on the part of management or staff could lead to the whole exercise failing to meet its objectives. One of the most important tasks for management is to make sure that the momentum of the programme is maintained throughout. Some managers adopt a 'campaign' approach to this by involving staff in devising slogans, having T-shirts, posters and pens printed with the slogans, and arranging extra social and sporting activities within the organisation. Such an approach is particularly useful in the early stages of the customer care programme to build staff loyalty to the scheme.

Managers and staff should not be afraid of publicising achievements within the programme; perhaps a performance standard has not only been met but exceeded. Newsletters and notice-boards should be used to communicate such examples to all staff to help maintain the momentum.

Above all, managers should appreciate what their staff are doing to achieve excellence in customer care and reward them accordingly.

The many promotional techniques available to the leisure and tourism professional to stimulate demand for products and facilities. Rather than using any single promotional tool, an organisation is likely to develop a 'promotional mix' that includes elements of all the techniques described. The exact proportions of each in the mix will vary over time and in response to internal and external influences.

Planning promotional campaigns and putting them into action are two important stages in the process of stimulating customer demand. However, without a third crucial element, namely evaluation of the promotional activity, a marketing professional may say that the whole process has been a waste of time and money. The results of any promotional work must be capable of being measured; only then can the organisation say with any degree of certainty that the time and money invested in the promotional activity was worthwhile.

Promotional objectives

Before being able to measure whether a particular promotional campaign has been successful or not, the organisation must ask itself the question 'what were we hoping to achieve from the promotion. In other words, promotional objectives will need to have been developed and it is against these aims that success, or the lack of it, is measured. Such objectives should be:

1. *Specific it* is pointless having vague objectives as this will make the task of deciding success or failure all the more difficult. For example, an objective such as 'the promotional work should increase the number of guests staying at the hotel' is not specific enough. Will just one extra guest mean that the promotion has been a success? A much better objective might be 'the promotional work should result in a 5 per cent increase in the number of guests staying at the hotel'. Some managers shy away from setting such specific objectives since they may not feel comfortable about achieving them.
2. *Time constrained all* objectives should be set within a particular time span so as to determine whether they have been achieved. Using the hotel example in 1, the objective may be developed into 'the promotional work should result in a 5 per cent increase in the number of guests staying at the hotel within the next 12 months'.
3. *Realistic all* objectives must be realistic and capable of being achieved by the organisation and the staff working within it. Setting wildly unrealistic aims and

targets is counter-productive and wasteful of resources. Going back to our hotel example, it would be pointless to set a target of, for example, achieving a 50 per cent increase in the number of guests within a three-month period. When the target was not met, staff would feel demoralised and the future success of the hotel would be put in doubt.

The promotional objectives are likely to reflect the overall objectives of the organisation, which, are many and varied, depending on which sector of the leisure and tourism industry is being studied.

Measuring the effectiveness of promotion

— Advertising in the local press.
— Mailing of leaflets to local districts.
— Press releases to local newspapers and local radio.
— Local radio advertising.
— Promotional items such as pens, badges, carrier bags, T-shirts, etc.
— Free demonstrations of fitness facilities.
— Discounts for squash club membership.
— Incentive bonuses for staff to encourage sales of memberships.

As you can see, the centre has used the five main types of promotional activity, namely:

— Advertising.
— Public relations.
— Direct marketing.
— Sales promotion.
— Personal selling.

While the management may be quite happy with the overall promotional plan, certain elements of the plan may not have been successful and money may have been wasted on these. Unless there are systems in place to monitor the effectiveness of each activity, management may be unaware of any weaknesses. If the information is readily available, funds can be taken away from the weak activity and channelled into more effective promotion.

How can the effectiveness of promotion be measured?

Measuring promotional effectiveness is harder in some activities than in others.

1. Advertising effectiveness is relatively easy to measure, especially press advertising, which can include a coupon with a particular code written on it denoting which newspaper or magazine it is in. Television and radio advertising are a little more difficult to measure, and are often used for image-building purposes anyway, i.e. to create or sustain a product's image in the minds of the viewer or listener.
2. The effectiveness of public relations activity can be very difficult to measure. PR too is about image-building, and attributing success to any particular part of a PR campaign is not easy. One area that is relatively easy to measure, however, is editorial coverage, i.e. articles and features in newspapers and magazines. The editorial usually stems from either a press release or complete article sent out by the leisure and tourism organisation or a visit by the journalist, sometimes referred to as a familiarisation trip. Such visits are common in leisure and tourism, particularly in the travel sector. The coverage, either in column inches in the case of press articles or 'air time' if the feature is on radio or TV, can be easily measured and a calculation as to how much the same coverage would have cost in paid advertising can be made.

3. The effectiveness of direct marketing is fairly easy to measure because of its very targeted nature. Mailings to households can include coded coupons or tickets that can be traced to see which particular district a customer lives in. Telephone selling can be carried out in a very structured fashion with the salesperson logging customer details.
4. Personal selling skills should be relatively easy to measure, particularly if individual staff members are given targets to reach. Incentives can be introduced to increase sales effort and reward the high achievers. Training can be introduced for those staff not yet meeting their targets.
5. Because of their very temporary and short-term nature, sales promotion activities are generally easy to measure. They often demand a firm commitment from the customer in return for which a discount, free gift or similar incentive can be gained.

Techniques for measuring effectiveness

Techniques that can be used to measure the effectiveness of certain promotional activities. All promotional objectives are necessarily concerned with increasing profits. Certainly in the public and voluntary sectors of leisure and tourism, promotional activities may be put in place to increase the participation of a particular section of the community. Even in the private sector, a company may wish to change its customer profile by perhaps going 'up market', which may not always involve increased numbers of visitors to a facility and sometimes quite the reverse.

8
Pricing and Marketing Strategy

We find leisure centres and fitness centres offering similar services at vastly different prices. It has been said that an, airline running a jumbo jet carrying 350 passengers will charge 350 different prices. Newspapers have been waging a price war that have dragged prices below production costs. Some shops have as many sale and offer days as normal trading days. This chapter investigates how", prices are determined in the real world.

Pricing in the private sector

Private sector organizations which seek to maximize Profits will attempt to minimize their costs and maximize their revenue. Revenue is composed of price multiplied by quantity sold, and the price that an organization can charge to, its product depends largely on the type of market within which it is operating. At one extreme, economic *theory* describes the model of perfect competition, Here firms have to accept market price, since any attempt to increase their own price over and above market price will lead to consumers purchasing identical goods or services from competitor firms.

What do firms get for their labours in such markets? They get normal profits defined as that level of return which is just sufficient incentive for a firm to remain in its present business. Any excess profits will lead new firms into the industry and this extra supply will drive prices down to the level where normal profits are restored.

However, whilst free market Prices and normal profits are good for, maximizing producers will aim to increase protect profits. Thus there are few examples the real world of price takers', and if firms are not in the fortunate position of being price makers they will generally take steps to become price shapers.

Price makers

At the other extreme from perfect competition, some firms exist in conditions of monopoly or near monopoly and thus have considerable control over prices.

Monopoly pricing

A monopoly is literally defined as one selller, and monopoly power is maintained by barriers to entry in to the industry. Therefore he firm's demand curve is the same as the industry demand curve. Because of this, the monopolist is in a position to be a price maker. There are examples of near-monopolies in the leisure and tourism sector. For example, there are only two car ferry services to the Isle of Wight and these operate on different routes, thus giving each operator some control over price. Unique tourist attractions also have some degree of monopoly power.

The price that maximizes total revenue for this organization is one of £5 when a total revenue of £250 per hour is generated. This is illustrated in Figure 1. In Figure 1(a), D represents the firm's demand curve, whilst in Figure 1(b), TR represents the firm's total revenue curve, found by multiplying quantity sold at each price, Price £5 generates total revenue of £250 per hour, whilst a higher price of £8 or a lower price of £2 causes total revenue to fall to £160.

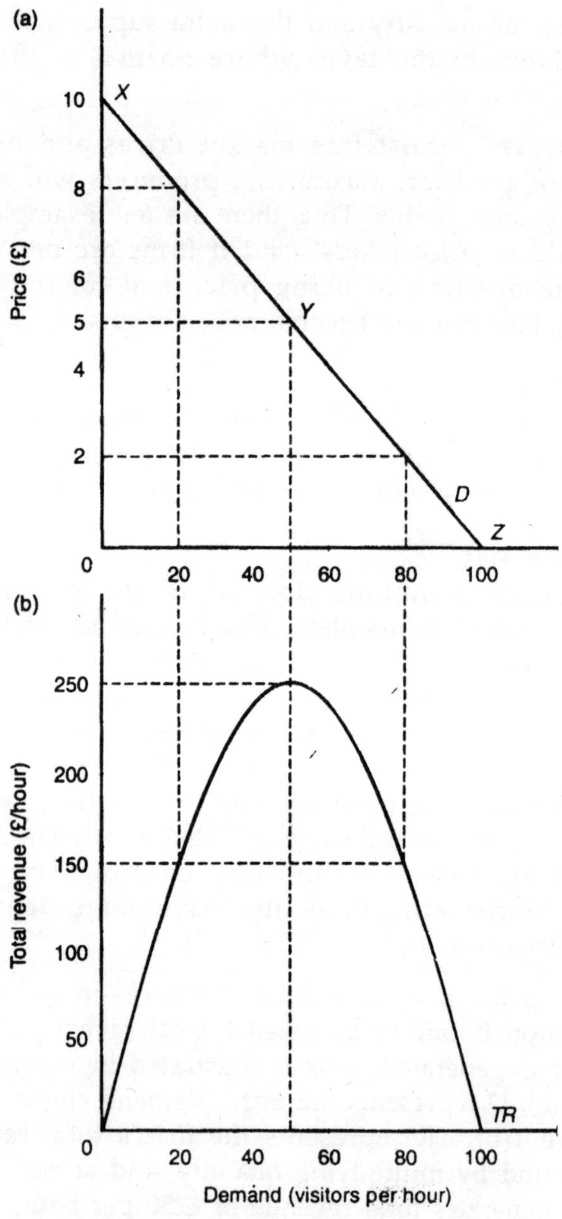

Figure 1: (a) Demand and (b) revenue maximising price for monopolist

This confirms the relationship between changes in price changes in total revenue *and* elasticity of demand discussed. Where demand is inelastic a rise in price will cause an increase in total revenue. Where demand is elastic, a fall in price will cause an increase in total revenue, Profit maximization therefore occurs where demand elasticity is (—)I. In Figure 1 the demand curve is elastic in the range X to Y, inelastic in the range Y to Z and has unit elasticity at point Y.

To summarize, monopolists can choose a price resulting in high profits, without fear of loss of market share to competitors. The actual price chosen will reflect both demand conditions and the firm's cost conditions.

BAA, the airports operator, is asking the government for authority to increase airline charges at Heathrow and impose restrictions on which aircraft may use the airport. BAA has proposed that it be allowed to 'premium price' at Heathrow to reflect its position as the world's busiest international airport. BAA announced a near 50 per cent increase in pre-tax profits last year to £285m.

Price discriminating monopolist/yield management

Some firms sell the same good or service at different prices to different group of people. For example BA return fares from London to NewYork are £4026, £2208 (Super APEX), £84.40 (Staff 10per cent standby) and £0 (staff yearly free standby/holders of airmiles or frequent flyer miles. In fact BA is not a monopolist since there is much competition on this route, but most fares are subject to International Air Transport Association (IATA) regulation and thus many firms are able to act as monopolists. It should also be recognized that the fare differential for club and firstclass passengers is not strictly price discrimination. Since these represent different services with different costs. But since all economy-class passengers receive an identical service,

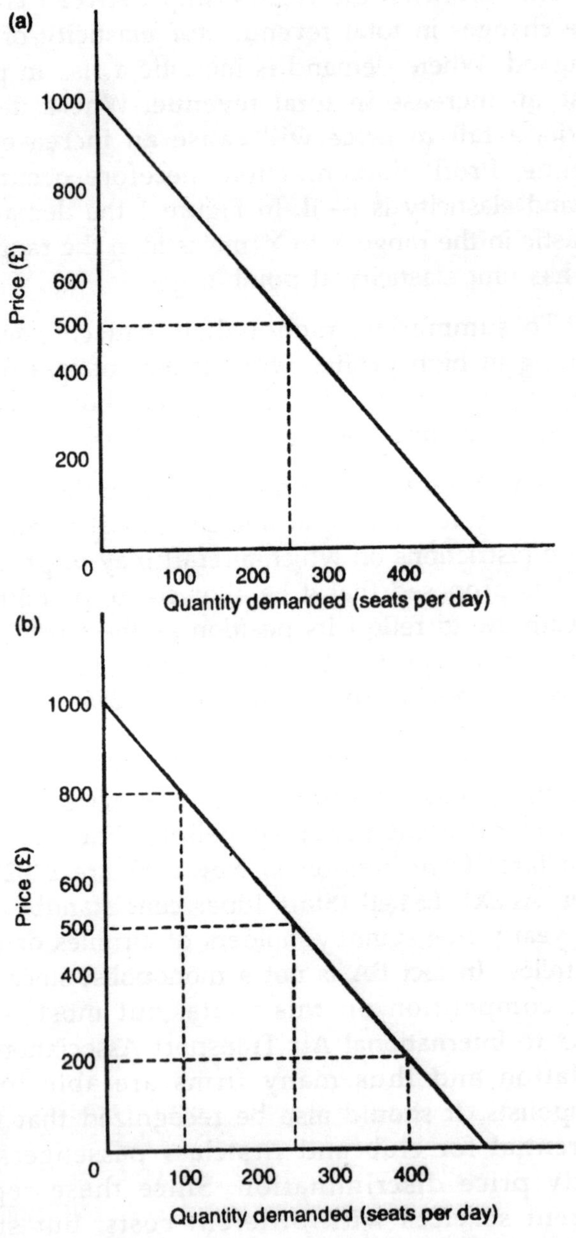

Figure 2: (a) Single price and (b) price discrimination

why should BA charge different prices and why do passenger's accept different prices?

The conditions for price discrimination to take place are:

- The product cannot be resold. If this were not the case, customers buying at the low price would sell to custorners at the high price and the system would break down. Services therefore provide good conditions for price discrimination,
- There must be market imperfections
- The seller must be able to identify different market segments with different elasticities.

If a single price of £500 is charged as in Figure 2(a), then 250 seats are sold and total revenue is £125000. Figure shows a situation in which three prices are, charged. One hundred seats are sold at £800, the next 150 seats are sold at £500 and the next 150 seats are sold at £200, producing a total revenue of £185 000, an increase of £60000 over the single-price situation.

Airlines must consider the behaviour of costs when price-discriminating. Once the decision has, been taken to run a scheduled service, marginal costs are low up until the aircraft capacity, when there is a sudden large jump. Airlines are able to discriminate by applying travel restrictions differently priced tickets. So, for example, full fare economy tickets are fully refundable and. Flights may be changed at no cost. Cheaper tickets are non-refundable and have advance purchase and travel duration restrictions.

Special report on business travel

The fare shown on a ticket for the 8000-mile round trip between Gatwick and Atlanta USA is, £818 but over £600 was saved by buying it through a agent. And not a dodgy backstreet operation-£211 to Thomas Cook. If BA had not been prepared to discount so heavily, a dozen other carriers *would* been prepared to sell a ticket for much less than the official fare.

Yield management is a sophisticated form of price discrimination. Computer technology, is able to identify patterns of demand for a particular, product with its supply. A request for hotel reservation or an airline ticket will system suggesting a price that will maximize the yield for a particular flight or day's reservations.

Price shapers

Whilst firms operating under condition of perfect competition are price takers and those operating under conditions of monopoly are Price makers, firms operating in markets between these two extremes can exert some influence on price.

The two main market types which will be examined are,

- oligopoly
- monopolistic competition

Oligopoly pricing

An oligopoly is a market dominated by a few large firms. An example of this of this is the cross-channel travel market. Oligopoly makes pricing policy more difficult to analyse since firms are interdependent, but not to the extent as in the perfectly competitive model. The actions of firm A may cause reaction by firms B and C, leading firm A to reassess its pricing policy and thus perpetuating a chain of action and reaction. For these reasons firms operating in oligopolistic markets often face a kinked demand curve (figure 3).

Consider the demand curve D, which might illustrate the demand curve for a cross-channel car ferry firm. The prevailing price is P0. Notice that the demand curve is elastic in the range X to Y. This is because, if a firm decides to increase its price, for example from P0 to

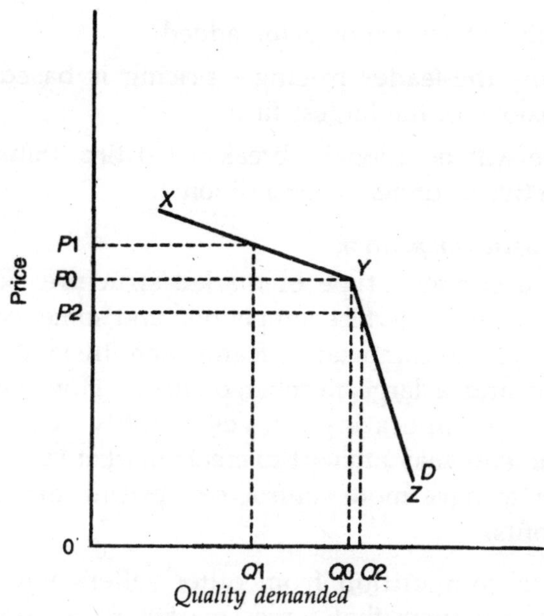

Quality demanded

The kinked demand curve

P1, it will lose customers to its competitors and demand will fall sharply from Q0 to Q1 and the firm will suffer a fall in total revenue, On other hand, if it should decide to reduce its price from P0 to P1, it is likely that its competitors will match the reduction in price to, protect their market share and there will be only a small increase in demand from Q0 to Q2, resulting in a fall in the firm's revenue. Thus the demand curve *is* inelastic in the range Y to Z, and the demand curve is kinked at point Y. In this situation it *is* clearly not in the interests of individual firms to cut prices, and thus such markets tend to be characterized by price rigidities.

Marketing and competition under oligopoly conditions are often based around:

— advertising
— free gifts and offers

— quality of service or value added,
— follow-the-leader pricing - pricing is based on the decisions of the largest firm
— price was occasionally break out if firm thinks it can effectively, undercut opposition

Monopolistic competition

This is a common type of market structure exhibiting some features of perfect competition and some features of monopoly. The competative features are freedom of entry and exit and a large number of firms. However, firms which are operating in essentially competitive environments may attempt to create market imperfections in order to have more control *over* pricing market share and profits.

It is competition from other sellers with homogeneous products that forces market Prices down and thus firms will often concentrate on these two issues in order to exert the market power. The more inelastic a firm is able to make its demand curve, the more influence it will have on price, and thus will attempt to minimize competition by:

— product differentiation
— acquisitions and mergers
— cost and price leadership

Product differentiation

The rationale for product differentiation is to make demand for a good or service less elastic giving the producer more scope to increase prices and/or sales and profits, There are a number of routes to product differentiation.

The first is by advertising, One of the aims of persuasive advertising is to create and increase brand loyalty even if there are no major differnces between a firm's product and that of its competitors. The second route to product differentiation is through adding value to a good or service, This may include, for example, making improvements to a good or service or adding value some where along the value chain. The value chain can be thought of as all the interconnecting activities that make up the whole consumer experience of a good or service.

The point of adding value and differentiating product is that it enables firms to charge a premium price but still retain customers.

Acquisitions and mergers

These are discussed but they are an important consideration in pricing strategy as they can:

— reduce competition (and thus reduce downward pressure on prices)
— lead to economies of scale (which can underpin price leadership strategies)

Cost and price leadership

Another key strategic move to increase market share and profitability is through cost and price leadership. Cost leadership involves cutting costs through the supply chain squeezing margins from suppliers, and economizing where possible in the production of goods or provision of services by stripping out unnecessary frills. The aim of cost leadership may be to increase margins but this is unlikely to be achieved since consumers are likely to resist lower quality of goods or services without any compensation in price.

Equally it is difficult to maintain cost leadership since other firms will attempt to achieve similar cost reductions. However, where cost leadership is translated into low prices it may be possible to increase market share. This can then lead to the creation of a virtuous circle where increased market share leads to economies of scale which enable lower costs and thus lower prices to be maintained ahead of rival firms.

Thomson promises to remain cheapest until 21st century
Thomson has sent out a clear warning to nearest rivals such as Airtours that it will never be beaten on price over the next decade. Although not specifically mentioning closest rival Airtours, managing director Mr Newbold said: 'To those competitors which think that Thomson's low prices in 1994 are just a short term *measure and* the umbrella of high prices will return, think again. Thomson's low prices are here to stay. We intend to be the number one choice well into the 21st century'.

Price war pays off as Compaq doubles sales
New York Compaq Computer emerged as one of the few victors from the price wars raging in the personal computer industry yesterday, reporting sharply higher second-quarter profits on sales that were double their year ago turnover. The Houston-based manufacturer earned $102m, or $1.21 a share, compared with $29m, or 35 cents a share, for the same period in 1992.

Compaq started the price war almost two years ago, aggressively cutting its own production costs in a bid for greater market share. Yesterday it reiterated its goal of becoming the world's Number One PC manufacturer. 'The PC industry continues to be highly competitive, but clearly Compaq's business strategy has positioned the company to be a winner in the current industry consolidation,' Eckhard Pfeiffer, chief executive, said in a *statement.*

Pricing in the public sector
Prices of public sector goods and services will depend upon the market situation which prevails in a particular

industry as well as the objectives set for a particular organization. These might be:

— profit maximization

— break-even pricing

— social cost/benefit pricing

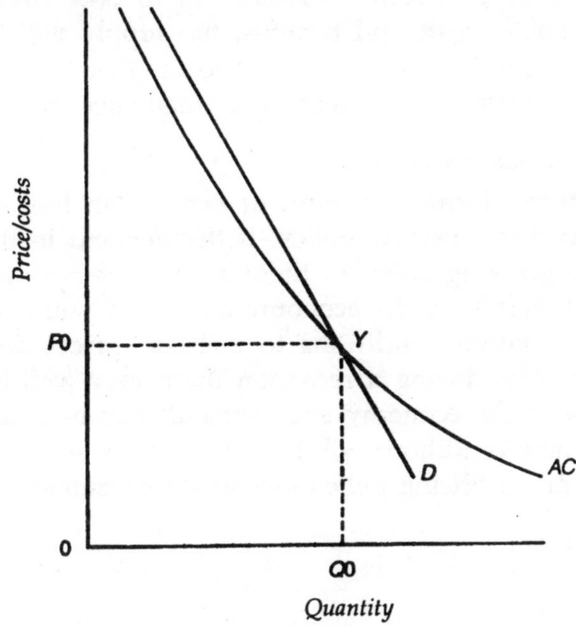

Figure 4: Break-even pricing

Profit maximization

In the case of profit-maximizing aims, an organization's pricing policy will follow the pattern set out earlier in this chapter.

Break-even pricing

Break-even pricing aims at a price which is just Sufficient to cover production costs rather than one which might take advantage of market imperfections and maximize profit. Figure 4 illustrates a firm with average costs of AC and a demand curve D. At price P0 total revenue is 0-

P0x0- Q0, and total cost is 0-P0x0- Q0and thus the firm is breaking even. Any price higher than P0 would result in extra profit and àny price below P0 would result in losses.

Social cost/benefit pricing

Where the aim of public provision is to take fuller account of public costs and benefits, the supply will be subsidized to produce a price either lower than market price (partial subsidy) or at zero price (total subsidy).

Pricing and the macroeconomy

The condition of the economy at large also has an influence on firms' pricing policy. If the demand in the economy is growing quickly, there may be temporary shortages of supply in the economy and firms will take advantage of boom conditions to increase prices and profits. Similarly, during a recession there may well be overcapacity in the economy and demand may be static or falling. These conditions will force firms to have much more competitive pricing policies to attract consumers.

9

Excellence in Customer Services

The UK leisure and tourism industry has experienced dramatic changes over the last 1015 years, from the boom days of the early 1980s to the recession of the late 1980s and early 1990s. The high levels of investment in new facilities and services seen in the 1980s have all but dried up. CCT has forced local authorities to examine the facilities they offer to their increasingly discerning visitors. The English Tourist Board has seen its government funding severely cut, putting into question the whole concept of a 'national' tourist organisation.

It is against this background that we will look at the importance of customer service in the leisure and tourism industry. It is fair to say that the expansion of facilities and services mentioned above was not matched by investment in the human resources of the industry its staff. Except for some notable exceptions, the message that customer service and customer care are vital to the very survival of leisure and tourism has not been widely practised within the industry. It is true that many organisations have nailed their colours firmly to a 'putting customers first' strategy, but in times of financial cutbacks the resources needed for customer service training have often been sadly lacking. Many people would argue that investing in a customer service approach is more important in times of recession since competition for customers and their reduced disposable income is even fiercer. A leisure and tourism organisation that excellence advocates customer service is sure to survive a recession better than one that gives the subject little attention. Many organisations that are striving to improve customer service use statements similar to the following to answer this question:

What is a customers?

— Are the most important people to our organisation.

— Are not dependent on us we are dependent on them.

— Are not an interruption of our work they are the purpose of it.

— Are not people to argue with or match wits against.

— Are not statistics but human beings with feelings and emotions.

— Are the people who bring us their needs. It is our job to handle these profitably for them and for ourselves.

— Are always right!

This simple definition shows that without customers there would be no business. It is only when organisations begin to put the customer at the centre of all activity, that a true customer service approach has begun. The key issues to be addressed by any organisation committed to a positive approach to customer service include:

1. *Identifying customer needs* knowing what your customers want is fundamental to the success of any business. It is important to remember that the gathering of data is often relatively easy; what is often more difficult is putting into action the recommendations the information suggests.
2. *Developing the right products and services* having found out what its customers' needs are, the organisation can begin to develop products that match these requirements to make sure they are offered at the

right price, in the right place, at the right time and at a profit.

3. *Measuring customer satisfaction customer* service is a constant process to strive to be as successful as possible in satisfying customer needs. The products and services will need careful monitoring and adjusting to meet any changes demanded by the customers.
4. *Developing internal systems customer* service isn't just about satisfying the customers 'on the other side of the counter'. Many leisure and tourism organisations, particularly large employers, will need to give attention to the needs of the 'internal customer', i.e. the staff working within the organisation. Mechanisms to improve internal communications, including regular meetings, social events and internal newsletters, are all part of improving the overall level of customer service.
5. *Staff training*—training in customer service handling and attitude is vital for all staff in leisure and tourism organisations, not just those whose work brings them into daily contact with customers. Staff working 'behind the scenes', perhaps in kitchens or on maintenance duties, need to appreciate also that they have an important role to play in customer service.

Developing a customer service approach is all about creating the right culture within the organisation. Sometimes referred to as a quality culture, TQM (total quality management) culture or customer culture, the end result should be the same; customers who enjoy their experience, come back again and tell their friends! Some names commonly used to identify customer service approaches include:

- — Putting customers first
- — Quality pays.
- — Profit through service.
- — Caring for customers.
- — Service first.
- — Excellence in service

The factors that have led to a customer service approach

There may be many reasons why a leisure and tourism organisation decides to strive for excellence in its customer service strategy. As the British Airways case study above shows, the factors that drive a customer-centred approach are either external or internal to the organisation.

External factors

Changing customer expectations

Customers in Britain today have far greater expectations of service quality than was the case even 1015 years ago. In leisure and tourism today it is very much a 'buyers market', where organisations have to compete not only on price but also on quality of service in order to win their share of customer spend. Service is no longer seen as peripheral as was the case in the recent past. There is considerable evidence to show that customers, although not always willing to complain openly about poor standards of service, will take action to show their disapproval. The US Office of Consumer Affairs, for example, quotes the following:

- — 96 per cent of dissatisfied customers never complain.
- — But 90 per cent of them will not return in the future.
- — One unhappy customer will tell at least nine others.
- — 13 per cent of unhappy customers will tell at least 20 others.

Changes in customer expectations have been brought about by such influences as:

— Exposure to life-styles from around the world via TV and other mass media.

— More foreign travel with exposure to foreign customer service standards.

— Changing eating patterns and food choices.

— Increased educational opportunities.

— Greater mobility.

— Changing work patterns.

The outcome of these influences is a new breed of customer who, in leisure and tourism, is demanding improvement in both product quality and the level and standard of customer service; customers who are looking for *en suite* facilities in their hotels, who want to be able to play a game of squash at 9.30 in the evening, who want a particular newspaper with their freshly-ground coffee at breakfast, who want to party until the early hours of the morning and who want to see the latest movies in plush surroundings. In a word, customers who want service excellence.

Competition

Leisure and tourism is a fiercely competitive business. Organisations survive and prosper by having a competitive edge over the opposition and by winning customers from the competition. Because leisure and tourism is such a diverse industry, there is competition within sectors as well as between companies in the same marketplace. Competition within sectors means that the money an individual spends on leisure could be spent on any number of different leisure activities or products, e.g. a person could go to the cinema, an amusement arcade, go swimming, go to the pub or put the money towards a week's holiday in Greece. Competition between companies is common-place with, for example, travel agents, tour operators, health and fitness clubs, theatres, etc. In such a competitive environment, excellence in customer service is vital for the survival of many organisations.

Some leisure and tourism organisations have realised that they cannot compete on price alone. A number of tour operators, for example, have seen their profit margins reduced to such a level that their long-term survival is put in serious jeopardy. Many have decided to develop superior customer service strategies to, help single them out from the masses. The race to attract and retain business customers in the airline industry has led to emphasis being placed on such factors as in-flight catering and personal service.

The rise in consumerism

Following hard on the heels of customers across the Atlantic, British consumers are becoming more vocal in their opinions of product and service quality (indeed many British people will have picked up the habit of speaking their mind in such places as the USA where customer complaints are not frowned on but used as a form of market research to be built upon). The introduction of television and radio programmes devoted to the cause of consumerism, e.g. 'That's Life' and 'You and Yours', is evidence that people are no longer willing to accept poor service and will 'vote with their feet'.

The rise in consumerism has accelerated the emergence of customers who place quality of service, in its widest sense, above all other factors when making purchasing decisions in leisure and tourism. People are, of course, still sensitive to the price of the products they are buying. There is, however, a growing belief that customers will pay a higher price for a higher quality product, delivered with the highest levels of customer service.

Changes in the economy

We have experienced in the UK a shift from a manufacturing economy to one based on service industries, such as banking, insurance, financial services, and leisure and tourism. It is estimated that about half of the country's GNP comes from the service sector. By the turn of the century, economists estimate that three out of every four jobs in Britain will be in service industries. These fundamental changes have brought about a climate in which customers are dealing with staff in the service sector, either in person, over the telephone or in writing, on a much more regular basis than was the case in the past. This has led in turn to organisations having to respond to higher levels of customer expectation in the area of quality of service.

Privatisation, the moving of previously state-controlled industries into the private sector was heavily promoted in the 1980s under the Conservative government. This too has led customers to demand a higher standard of customer service from the newly privatised companies.

Benefits to the organisation

The benefits are part of a cyclical process starting with increased management effectiveness, which in turn will lead to a more motivated work-force. The positive attitude of the staff will ensure that customers are happy with the service they are receiving and will hopefully tell others. This will lead to increased sales or use, depending on whether the organisation is in the private, public or voluntary sector. This will help the organisation. To achieve its particular objectives, be it profit maximisation or providing a service for the local community.

Other tangible benefits of introducing excellence in customer service are likely to include:

— Fewer complaints.
— Improved cooperation between departments.
— Reduced absenteeism by staff.
— Lower turnover of staff.
— Improved security.
— Less waste.
— Improved quality in other aspects of the organisation's work.
— Reduction in marketing budget.

Most of all, the carrying through of a customer-centred service approach will ensure that the organisation will achieve its objectives and that all who have a stake in the business, whether they be shareholders or council-tax payers, will benefit.

Obstacles to good customer service

Customer service, in all its forms, is a highly skilled task. It requires effort, motivation, commitment and support from both management and work-force. Introducing a customer service philosophy into an organisation will inevitably involve change; in attitude, change in work practices and change in the way that staff are rewarded. The majority of human beings are resistant to change and feel threatened when it happens to them in the work-place. By adopting a positive customer service approach, leisure and tourism organisations must be mindful of these fears on the part of their staff and may have to deal sensitively with a number of obstacles that can hinder the successful implementation of the strategy

Lack of commitment

We are all familiar with the 'take it or leave it' attitude that is still evident in certain sectors of the leisure and tourism industry today; the restaurant waiter who gives the impression that he would rather be at home watching the TV or the sports centre attendant who is less than helpful when you try to hire some equipment. Thankfully, this negative attitude is being tackled in many organisations through management and staff training. It is the job of management to:

— Discover any underlying problems that are causing the lack of commitment.
— Put in place measures to deal with the problems, perhaps via staff training.
— Provide a supportive environment in which staff can flourish.
— Involve all staff in customer service improvement.

Lack of knowledge

Some staff, particularly those new to their job, will take time to settle into their role and gain the knowledge and experience necessary to carry it out to the full. Induction training followed by detailed training on the services, products and systems of the organisation should give these staff the confidence needed to sustain a high level of customer service and feel a valued member of the team.

Product knowledge is vital within any leisure and tourism organisation since it can help staff to:

— Inform customers of prices and features.
— Suggest alternatives if the client's first choice is not available.
— Give detailed information of particular services; in leisure and tourism it is often 'the little things' that either make or break the total experience for the customer.
— Raise the general level of awareness of other services and facilities that the organisation can offer.

Poor communication

Lack of communication is often the biggest single barrier to implementing a Successful customer service strategy. It causes resentment among staff, frustrates managers and is often picked up by customers who are sometimes put in embarrassing situations. Managers can help to break this vicious circle by:

— Briefing all staff fully on their respective roles.

— Using simple language and communications methods that everybody can understand.

— 'Walking the job', i.e. taking the time and trouble to talk to staff about their jobs and concerns.

An organisation which looks after its staff is likely to be one that looks after its customers as well.

Lack of cooperation

We saw at the beginning of this section that everybody working in a leisure and tourism organisation has 'customers whether or not they deal face to face with the general public. 'Internal customers' are people working in the same organisation, e.g. clerical staff, maintenance staff, receptionists, etc., who you come across in the normal daily course of events and on whom you rely for services and support. Good customer service requires a team approach and a recognition that it is not just the customers 'on the other side of the counter' who need respect and consideration, but that colleagues within the organisation need to be dealt with in the same supportive manner.

Good and bad service

Defining what is 'good' and 'bad' service is not an easy matter. One person's idea of good service in a restaurant, for example, may be thought of by somebody else as poor. Whether a person is happy or unhappy with their service is essentially a personal experience; no two people have the same perception of what good or bad service means to them. The very personal nature of the customer service experience needs to be accepted by staff working in leisure and tourism organisations; right from the outset. If customers are not treated as individuals, they will become disenchanted with the service they are getting and may choose to take their business elsewhere.

Although it is not always easy to define exactly what constitutes good service, we are all familiar with circumstances when the level of service we have received is either very good or very bad. In leisure and tourism, the following examples give a flavour of what a good customer service approach is all about:

— *In a restaurant an* example of good service would be when the management remembers that an evening booking is for a couple's first wedding anniversary and provides a complimentary bottle of champagne. Bad service is when you telephone in advance to make a booking, only to find when you arrive that the waiter has no record of the booking and all the tables are full.

— *In a hotel good* service would be when the receptionist remembers the name of a guest's child and the hotel provides a box of toys for her to play with. Bad service would be not attending to a broken shower in a guest's room immediately.

— *In a leisure centre an* example of good service would be providing free use of armbands for all the under fives in the swimming pool. Bad service would be the temporary receptionist telling a telephone caller that he is not sure of the cost of hiring the indoor bowls hall for the day as he is new to the job and only comes in on Saturdays.

Dealing with difficult situations

From time to time, even the best trained and most

professional members of staff will find themselves having to deal with awkward situations involving customers; two of the most common are handling complaints and dealing with 'difficult' customers.

Handling complaints: In general, British people are rather reluctant to complain. When they do, however, staff in leisure and tourism organisations must know how to handle the situation and even turn the complaint to positive advantage. Handled correctly, complaints can be thought of as another type of feedback that gives the organisation a second chance to put things right and satisfy the customer.

All people are individuals and so the reasons why they complain are many and varied. Some of the most common reasons can be broadly categorised into:

— *Bad products or service—to* the customer there is a strong link between quality of products and quality of service. If he or she has poor service in getting advice on buying, for example, a set of golf clubs, the quality of the product itself tends to be put in doubt. Poor service, whether it be in person, on the telephone or in writing, is one of the main reasons why people complain.

— *Waiting—people* hate waiting around for attention and wasting their valuable time. The longer the wait the more likely customers are to complain. Mechanisms can be put in place to reduce conflict when a certain amount of waiting or queuing is unavoidable; entertainers are sometimes employed to keep the crowds happy outside London theatres and TV/video screens or the use of music can sometimes have a positive effect.

— *Being patronised* nothing is guaranteed to turn frustration into fury quicker than a patronising tone of voice on the part of the member of staff dealing with a customer. It is wise to assume that the customer has some knowledge of the product or service being bought and staff should be trained not to take a 'we know best' attitude.

Specific examples of situations in leisure and tourism when customers are prone to complain include:

— Having the time of the flight changed on their package holiday at the last minute.
— Not being able to get through to the information department of a tourist board as the line is constantly engaged.
— Finding that a hotel room has not been properly prepared for new guests.
— Not be able to find a parking space in a leisure centre car park.
— Being served a meal that has gone cold by the time it reaches the table.
— Being served cloudy beer in a nightclub or pub.
— Booking a window seat on a coach tour only to find that all the window seats are taken when you get on the coach.

What to do when people complain

1. Listen attentively so that you get the whole story first time.
2. Thank the customer for bringing the problem to your attention.
3. Apologise in general terms for the inconvenience but do not grovel.
4. Provide support for the customer by saying that the matter will be fully investigated and matters put right immediately.
5. Sympathise with the customer and try to see the situation from their point of view.

6. Don't justify the circumstances that led up to the complaint and go on the defensive.
7. Ask questions if you are not clear on any points of the customer's complaint.
8. Find a solution to the problem.
9. Agree the solution with the customer.
10. Follow through to make sure that what you promised has been done.
11. In future, try and anticipate complaints before they happen.

'Difficult' customers

One step on from somebody who has a justifiable complaint is the customer who is intent on 'causing a scene'. Just like handling complaints, there are tried and tested ways of dealing with these 'awkward' individuals:

1. Try not to let them get you down or get under your skin; the fact that they wish to cause a fuss may be a sign of their own insecurity.
2. Never argue with them. It can often get the member of staff into deeper trouble.
3. Never be rude to the customer, however rude they are being to you!
4. Try not to take any remarks personally. You may have had nothing to do with the alleged incident but are simply the nearest member of staff.
5. Let the customer do the talking and listen to what they have to say.
6. If in any doubt, seek help from another member of staff or senior management.

The importance of keeping the customers you already have

Many leisure and tourism organisations, talk about 'increasing market share' and 'targeting new customers but sometimes overlook the importance of providing a quality service to the customers they already have. While new customers are always welcome in any organisation, existing clientele provide a higher profit contribution and provide a much firmer base from which to develop further business.

If an organisation in leisure and tourism can develop repeat and multiple business relationships with its existing customers, it is more able to maximise its resources and achieve its ultimate objective. Creating excellence in customer service is obviously a crucial element in retaining loyal and valued customers.

Over and above developing a positive customer service attitude, there are many ways in which leisure and tourism organisations try to hang on to the customers they already have, including:

— Giving existing clients first choice of bookings before being launched to the general public.
— Offering preferential rates for products and services to existing customers.
— Offering incentives to existing customers to do repeat business, e.g. frequent flyer programmes in the airline industry.
— Hosting events that are only open to existing customers.

It is usual for customers to be categorised according to their volume of business with the organisation, with those at the top receiving maximum incentives to remain loyal.

The figure demonstrates the power that existing customers can have on the success or otherwise of any leisure and tourism organisation. It shows that existing customers generate repeat business and can attract new customers to help the organisation to flourish. When linked to a planned programme of improving customer service, reputation is enhanced and all customers reap the benefits of an organisation determined to give excellence in customer service.

10

Choice, Elasticity and Forecasting

Consumer theory

Consumer theory attempts to explain consumer behaviour, and investigates consumer choice in consuming goods and services. It assumes first that consumers have limited income, second that consumers act in a rational manner, and third that consumers aim to maximize their total satisfaction, subject to the constraint of limited income. Consumer equilibrium will occur when purchases are arranged so as to maximize a consumer's total satisfaction. In other words a consumer cannot rearrange purchases and be better off. Thus in order to analyse consumer equilibrium, the idea of satisfaction needs to be investigated.

Marginal utility theory

Utility is the term economists use to measure a person's satisfaction from consuming a good or service. In fact it is not possible to measure utility precisely, but predictions can be made about how utility changes with consumption. Marginal utility theory can be used to explain consumer choice in a simple model.

Assume a person has a monthly income of £60, and spends all of it on two services visits to a fitness centre which cost £6 each and visits to the theatre which cost £12 each. To see how this person will divide income between the two services the concept of total utility must first be considered.

Total utility

Total utility is defined as the total benefit or satisfaction a person gets from the consumption of goods and services. Generally a person's total utility increases the more of a good or service they consume shows the total utility associated with different levels of consumption of fitness centre and theatre visits.

Notice that where consumption is zero no utility is derived, but as consumption of each service increases, so does total utility. However, closer examination of the data reveals that total utility does not rise at a uniform rate, and this can be revealed by studying marginal utility. Marginal utility is defined as the utility gained from consuming one extra unit of a good or service. This can be calculated from the total utility data: for example, two visits to the fitness centre resulted in a total utility of 44 units and three visits resulted in 60 units, so the marginal utility of the third visit is 16 units.

The information shows that marginal utility falls as consumption rises. This is known as the principle of diminishing marginal utility. The extra satisfaction consumers derive from successive consumption of a good or service tends to diminish. The freshness or novelty of a good or service wears off a little the more of it is consumed.

Maximizing utility

In the above example, a person has a monthly income of £60 which is spent on consuming two services, Table 4.2 shows the various combinations of theatre and fitness centre visits that can be obtained from this income. In addition it shows the total utility obtained from each of the possible combinations of theatre and fitness centre visits. The consumer will be in equilibrium when total utility is maximized. This occurs with a combination of six visits to the fitness centre (total utility = 96) and two visits to the theatre per month (total utility = 57), giving a combined total utility of 153. The consumer cannot rearrange purchases and be better off.

Maximizing utility

It is also possible to find the combination which maximizes utility by calculating and comparing the marginal utility per pound spent on different goods and services. The consumer can again be seen to be maximizing satisfaction by purchasing six visits to the fitness centre and two visits to the theatre, since this is where the marginal utility per pound spent is equal for each (MU/£ = 1. 67). This can be seen to be maximizing satisfaction by looking at other possible choices.

Consider a choice with less fitness centre and more theatre visits. Four fitness centre visits (MU/£ = 2.33) and three theatre visits (MU/£ = 2.33) could be purchased. However, since the fitness centre visits are giving more marginal utility per pound spent than theatre visits, the consumer can increase satisfaction by switching spending away from theatre towards fitness. Similarly, eight fitness centre visits (MU/£ = 1. 17) and one theatre visit (MU/£ = 3.08) could be purchased. However, since the fitness centre visits are giving less marginal utility per pound spent than theatre visits, the consumer can increase satisfaction by switching spending away from fitness towards theatre. Thus it is only where the consumer equates the marginal utility per pound spent for each good and service consumed that utility is maximized. This can be expressed for more general cases as:

Consumer equilibrium = $MUa/Pa = MUb/Pb = MUn/Pn$.

where: MU = marginal utility; P = price; and a, b, n = individual goods and services.

Free goods and maximizing utility

Some goods and services are provided free to consumers. People will consume such goods and services to the point where their marginal utility equals zero. This is because consuming extra units has no cost in terms of other goods which could have been bought with limited income, but will add to total satisfaction as long as marginal utility is positive. This point has important implications for providers of such 'free' goods and services as national parks. There is considerable scope for extra consumption of these services since existing levels of consumption do not take many users to the point where MU = 0. Consumers of free services using quantity OQ1 derive positive marginal utility of OMU1 from this level of usage. However they may extend their usage to OQ2 and up to OQ3 at no extra cost to themselves whilst adding to their total satisfaction, since the marginal utility of using the service is positive throughout this range.

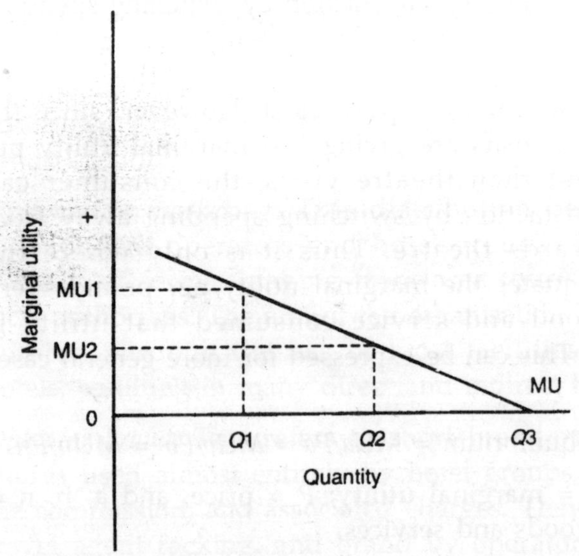

Marginal utility (MU) and demand for free goods/services.
Q = Quantity

Utility: a postscript

The term utility raises many questions in considering consumer behaviour: what factors generate utility in a good or service for consumers? The answers to these questions may be found by using analysis from other disciplines, particularly psychology and sociology. Psychology, for example, investigates personal motivation in consumption, and considerable research has taken place in motivation of tourists.

Derivation of demand curve

Marginal utility theory confirms that demand curves slope downwards to the right and that as price falls demand rises. At the price of £12 per visit to a theatre, the consumer in our example will demand two visits per month. What happens if the price falls to £6 per visit? Examination of the new calculations of marginal utility per pound spent reveals that the consumer will maximize utility at the point of five theatre visits and five visits to the fitness centre since this is where the marginal utility per pound spent is equal for each (MU/£ = 2.00). Thus there are now two points that can be used to construct a demand curve for this consumer for theatre visits: at seat price £12, demand equals two seats per month and at seat prices £6, demand equals five seats per month.

Market demand

A market demand curve is found by adding together the individual demand curves for a particular good or service.

The demand for leisure

Leisure time represents an element in the choice set available to consumers, and maximization of consumer utility will therefore also involve choice about how much leisure time to take. Just as when choosing between other goods and services, consumers will consider the extra utility or satisfaction they derive from leisure time against the price or cost of leisure time. Consumers face the problem of limited time. There are only 24 hours in a day, and thus the most fundamental choice that consumers face is whether to devote their limited time to leisure or work.

We can consider the cost or price of leisure time as its opportunity cost - what has to be given up in order to enjoy leisure time? The opportunity cost of leisure time is clearly earnings that are lost through not working. What will happen to the trade-off between work and leisure when prices change? The key 'price' in this case is wages, and if wages increase there are two potential effects on the demand for leisure time. First, an increase in wages means an increase in the price of leisure time, in terms of loss of earnings. Therefore consumers will tend to demand less leisure time as its price has increased. This is a substitution effect. Consumers will tend to substitute work for leisure to reflect their new relative prices. But the increase in wages will also lead consumers to have more income and spending power. Leisure can be classed as a 'normal service', and in common with other 'normal' goods and services, as income increases more will be demanded. This is called the income effect. There are clearly a complex set of forces which will determine whether the income or substitution effect is greater. One consideration is that as income increases, consumers have the ability to get more satisfaction out of their leisure time, thus resulting in a strong income effect. The utility derived from labour is also influenced by psychological and social factors. Some individuals may favour long leisure hours which they can happily fill with cheap or free activities such as reading, watching television, sleeping or walking. Other individuals may have a low boredom threshold and thus have a low marginal utility from leisure time. Equally there are cultural influences at work. There appears to be a greater work ethic in countries such as Germany and Japan than in other countries, particularly those with warmer climates.

Choice or rigidity?

The extent to which choice can actually be exercised in the work/leisure trade-off depends on flexibility in the labour market. When choosing between most goods and services, consumers can readily vary the amounts consumed in response to changing relative prices. Consumers generally have less choice in their participation in labour markets. Many jobs have standardized hours where individuals cannot choose to add or subtract hours in response to changes in wages. However workers can express their general preferences through trade unions and staff associations and these may be taken into account in determining the overall work package of pay, hours and holiday benefits.

Some jobs offer flexibility in offering overtime provision, and some individuals may have extra employment in addition to their main job. In these cases individuals will be in a position to exercise more precisely their choice between work and leisure.

Finally the unemployed are generally not acting out of choice but by lack of opportunity in their allocation of leisure time. However there has been considerable debate regarding social security benefits and incentives to work. Right-wing economists argue that benefit levels are distorting the labour market so that some unemployed maximize their total utility by remaining unemployed rather than entering the labour market.

Trends in work and leisure

There are several ways of examining these trends including analysis of:

- unemployment data
- holiday entitlement
- hours worked

Holiday entitlement

There has been a steady increase in paid holiday entitlement in the postwar period. For example, for manual workers the average holiday period has risen from 2 weeks in 1951 to 45 weeks by 1991.

Price elasticity of demand

Price elasticity of demand measures the responsiveness of demand to a change in price This relationship can be expressed as a formula, and exhibit 4.1 shows a worked example for calculating price elasticity of demand.

$$\frac{\text{Percentage change in quantity demanded}}{\text{Percentage change in price}}$$

Price elasticity of demand a worked example

When the price of Matashi 21" colour TVs rose from £160 to £180, demand fell from 3200 to 2800 sets per week. Calculate elasticity of demand:

1. To calculate percentage change in quantity demanded, divide the change in demand ($\Delta Q = 400$) by the original demand ($DO = 3200$) and multiply by 100:
2. 400 3200 x 100 = 12.5
3. To calculate percentage change in price, divide the change in price ($\Delta P = 20$) by the original price

   (PO = 160) and multiply by 100:
4. 20/160 x 100 = 12.5
5. Elasticity of demand = 12.5/12.5 = 1

Where demand is inelastic it means that demand is unresponsive to a change in price, to whereas elastic demand is more sensitive to price changes. It should be noted that, since a rise in the price of a good causes a fall in demand, the figure calculated for price elasticity of demand will always be negative. Economists generally ignore the minus sign.

Note that the demand curve, which has elasticity of demand of I throughout its length, is a rectangular hyperbola.

Factors affecting price elasticity of demand

The following are the main factors which influence price elasticity of demand:

- necessity of good or service
- number of substitutes
- addictiveness
- price and usefulness
- time period
- consumer awareness

Necessity of good or service

Goods and services which are necessities generally have a lower price elasticity of demand than goods which are luxuries.

Number of substitutes

Goods and services which are provided in conditions of near monopoly tend to have inelastic demand, since the consumer cannot shop elsewhere should prices increase. Competition in a market makes demand more elastic.

Addictiveness

Goods such as cigarettes which are addictive tend to have inelastic demand.

Price and usefulness

Cheap and very useful goods and services tend to have

inelastic demand since an increase in a low price will have little impact on consumers' purchasing power.

Time period

Demand elasticity generally increases the more time is allowed to elapse between the change in price and the measurement of the change in demand. This is because consumers may not be able to change their plans in the short run. For example, many holidaymakers book holidays 6 months in advance. Thus a fall in the value of the US dollar might have limited effect on the demand for US holidays in the short run since consumers have committed holiday plans. It may not be until the next year that the full effects of such a devaluation on demand can be measured.

Consumer awareness

Package holidays represent a bundle of complementary goods and services which are bought by consumers, and consumers may be attracted to the bottom-line price of a holiday. Consumers may be unaware of destination prices. For this reason, elasticity of demand for services such as ski passes may be inelastic for UK holidaymakers due to lack of information.

Elasticity of demand and total revenue

The concept of price elasticity of demand is useful for firms to forecast the effects of price changes on total revenue received from selling goods and services, as well as for governments wishing to maximize their tax receipts. Total revenue is defined as:

Total revenue = price x quantity sold

Consider a rise in the price of a good by 10 per cent. If demand is elastic, quantity sold will fall by more than 10 per cent and thus total revenue will fall. However, if demand is inelastic it will fall by less than 10 per cent and thus total revenue will rise. Similarly, a fall in the price of a good will lead to a rise in total revenue in the case of elastic demand and a fall in total revenue where demand is inelastic.

Income elasticity of demand

Income elasticity of demand measures the responsiveness of demand to a change in income. This relationship can be expressed as a formula:

$$\frac{\text{Percentage change in quantity demanded}}{\text{Percentage change in income}}$$

Calculation of income elasticity of demand enables an organization to determine whether its goods and services are normal or inferior. Normal or superior goods are defined as goods whose demand increases as income increases. Therefore their income elasticity of demand is positive (+/+ = +). The higher the number, the more an increase in income will stimulate demand.

Inferior goods are defined as goods whose demand falls as income rises. Therefore their income elasticity of demand is negative (- / + = -)

Knowledge of income elasticity of demand is useful in predicting future demand in the leisure and tourism sector. It also helps to explain some merger and takeover activity as organizations in industries with low or negative income elasticity of demand attempt to benefit from economic growth by expanding into industries with high positive income elasticity of demand. Such industries show market growth as the economy expands. Examples of this include Pearson plc. Pearson owns the Financial Times Group Ltd. (low income elasticity of demand), and has bought into BSkyB Ltd. (high income elasticity of demand). Similarly, First Choice has bought into the cruise market, which promises high income elasticity of demand.

Cross-price elasticity of demand

Cross-price elasticity of demand measures the responsiveness of demand for one good to a change in the price of another good. This relationship can be expressed as a formula:

$$\frac{\text{Percentage change in quantity demanded of good A}}{\text{Percentage change in price of good B}}$$

Cross-price elasticity of demand measures the relationship between different goods and services. It therefore reveals whether goods are substitutes, complements or unrelated. An increase in price of good B will lead to an increase in demand for good A if the two goods are substitutes. Thus substitute goods have a positive cross-price elasticity of demand (+ / + = +).

For goods which are complements or in joint demand, an increase in the price of good B will lead to a fall in demand for a complementary good, good A. Therefore complementary goods have negative cross-price elasticity of demand (-/+ = -).

An increase in the price of good B will have no effect on the demand for an unrelated good, good A. Unrelated goods have cross-price elasticity of demand of zero (0/+ = 0).

Demand forecasting

The supply of leisure goods and services cannot generally be changed without some planning. The supply of capital goods such as aircraft requires long planning cycles. Tour operations require considerable planning to book airport slots arid hotel accommodation. Equally, leisure and tourism services are highly perishable. It is not possible to keep stocks of unsold hotel rooms, aircraft and theatre seats, or squash courts. Whilst the supply of some leisure goods, such as golf balls and tennis rackets, can be more readily changed, and stocks of unsold goods held over, there is clearly a need for forecasting of demand for leisure and tourism goods and services.

The US-based Boeing Corporation has painted an optimistic picture for the future of the airline industry in its annual civil aviation market outlook. Vie report forecasts demand for new aircraft of $980bn (L610bn) over the next 20 years. Of this, $731bn-worth of aircraft would be needed to extend airline fleets to meet future passenger growth, whilst $249bn would be needed to replace aircraft which are wearing out.

Boeing, the largest manufacturer of commercial aircraft in the world, bases this figure on its forecast of passenger growth for air travel of around 5 per cent per year over the next 20 years.

This year's outlook represents an important turning point for the industry. Global airline losses, economic recession, the Gulf war and Chernobyl all contributed to a 4-year slump in aircraft sales. But an upbeat spokesman, Mr Richard James, Boeing's vice president of marketing, said that the second half of the 1990s looked more promising.

'The recovery is already well under way in the USA, and the widely held expectation is that Europe is on the road to recovery,' he said. In fact Boeing expects the biggest growth in passengers to take place in Asian markets. Although the Japanese economy is still suffering, the rest of Asia was witnessing a period of strong growth.

Methods for forecasting demand include:

- naive forecasting
- qualitative forecasts
- timeseries extrapolation
- surveys

- Delphi technique
- models
- Naive forecasts

Naive forecasting makes simple assumptions about the future. At its simplest, naive forecasting assumes that the future level of demand will be the same as the current level. Naive forecasting may also introduce a fixed percentage by which demand is assumed to increase, for example 3 per cent per annum.

Qualitative forecasts

Qualitative forecasts consider the range of factors which influence the demand for a good or service, as discussed. These factors are then ranked in order of importance and each of them is in turn analysed to reveal future trends. Although statistical data may be consulted at this stage, no attempt is made to construct a mathematical formula to describe precise relationships between demand and its determinants. Such forecasts rely on a large measure of common sense and are likely to be couched in general terms such as 'small increase in demand' or 'no change in demand envisaged'.

Time series analysis

A time series is a set of data collected regularly over a period of time.

Time series of sales of a product

Year	*Q1*	*Q2*	*Q3*	*Q4*	*Total*
1	112	205	319	421	1057
2	124	220	350	460	1154
3	90	245	383	503	1221
4	138	267	412	548	1365
5	160	285	450	595	1490

First this data can be seen to exhibit seasonal features. Sales of this product rise within each year to a peak in the fourth quarter and drop back sharply in the first quarter of the next year. Second there seems to be a trend. The figures for each quarter and the yearly totals nearly all display an upward movement. Third, the figure for the first quarter in year 3 does not fit in with the rest of the data and appears as an unusual figure. This may well have been caused by a random variation such as a strike or war or natural disaster.

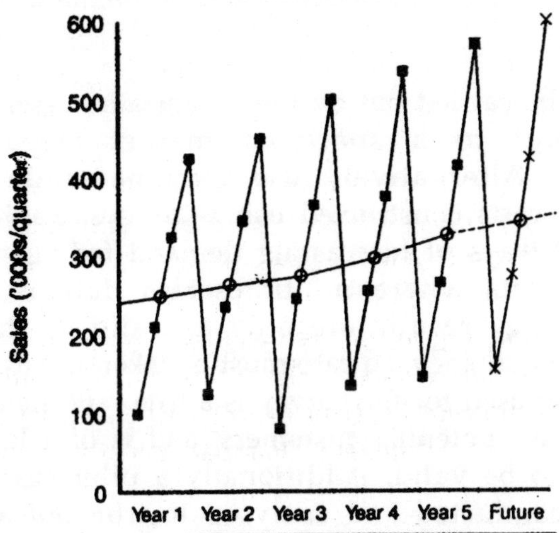

Time series data, trend and forecast

Forecasting using timeseries data first averages seasonal and random variations from the data, to reveal the underlying pattern or trend. The trend can then be used to predict future data, for general yearly totals and adjusted to indicate future seasonal totals. Timeseries forecasting is useful in predicting future seasonal demand and adjusting supply to anticipate seasonal fluctuations. This is particularly important in the leisure and tourism sector where demand tends to be very seasonal. However care must be taken in using timeseries data. Planning ski holiday capacity using timeseries data may be useful in predicting market growth, but seasonal fluctuations due to school holidays are not best predicted from past events (which would give the average date) but by looking to see when Easter falls to find the precise date. Equally it is random events that can cause significant changes in the demand for ski holidays. Clearly snowfall and exchange rates are two key factors that cannot be forecast using timeseries analysis. It is important therefore that timeseries analysis should be used as part of a package of forecasting techniques.

Surveys

Surveys may be carried out by the organization itself or contracted out to a specialist market research organization. Alternatively use may be made of published forecasts constructed using surveys. Surveys can be useful ways of forecasting demand for new or revised products where no timeseries data exist. However, survey results are only as valid as their underlying methodology, so care must be taken to ensure that the sample used for the survey is a true reflection of an organization's potential customers, and is of a large enough size to be valid. Additionally a pilot survey needs to be conducted and analysed to iron out any problems of interpretation of words or leading questions. In fact, surveys turn out to be more useful for testing ideas such as advertising campaigns or design, where respondents are asked to choose between real and concrete alternatives. Hypothetical questions are generally used in demand forecasting, and respondents' answers may not necessarily reflect what they would actually do if they had to spend money.

Delphi technique

The Delphi technique is a method of forecasting which

attempts to harness expert opinion on the subject. Questionnaires are used to discover opinions of experts in a particular field. The results of the forecasts are then fed back to the participants with the aim of reaching a consensus view of the group.

Modelling

More complex forecasting methods attempt to describe accurately the relationship between demand for a product and the factors determining that demand. They consider a number of variables, and use statistical techniques of correlation and regression analysis to test relationships and construct formulae. Some include econometric techniques which forecast key economic variables such as growth rates, interest rates and inflation rates to construct a comprehensive model which relates general economic conditions to the factors affecting demand for a particular product to the demand forecasts for that product.

Problems with forecasts

There are several problems which arise from using forecasts. First the forecasts are only as good as the assumptions of the model being used. For example the assumption that the past is a good guide to the future limits the validity of extrapolation using timeseries analysis. However, there are equally questionable assumptions included in some very complex models. It is important to know what these assumptions are so that should any of these assumptions prove to be incorrect, forecasts can be re-evaluated.

'The major problem, however, is the unpredictability of economic trends and outside events such as wars or strikes or disasters. For example, the recession of the late 1980s undermined the accuracy of many forecasts and caused severe financial problems to those who had relied on overly optimistic predictions of future levels of demand. This does not mean that forecasts are useless, but that those who use them should be constantly monitoring their operating environment to detect any factors which will upset the forecasts they are using.

11
Investment Appraisal

With hindsight it is not difficult to analyse the factors that have made some investment projects in the leisure and tourism sector such successes and others such dismal failures. The failures include the Sinclair C5 electric vehicle, the Battersea Power Station leisure project and British Satellite Broadcasting. The successes include projects as diverse as films, visitor attractions, electronic games and satellite TV (BSB). However, at the planning stage, it is much more difficult to forecast the success of investments, largely because of the uncertainty surrounding the future. This chapter seeks to define the meaning of investment, consider how potential investment projects are appraised and stress the shortcomings of quantitative techniques.

In general usage people use the term 'investment' to include bank and building society deposits and the purchase of stocks and shares. Economists are more specific in their use of the term. Investment may be defined as expenditure on capital goods and working capital. Capital goods can be contrasted with consumer goods. The latter are produced because of the direct satisfaction they yield (e.g. food, CDs, clothes), whilst the former are produced because they improve efficiency of production. Fixed capital goods therefore consist of buildings, plant and machinery, and in the leisure and tourism sector examples include hotel buildings, computer reservation and booking systems, aircraft, and golf-ball making machinery. The total expenditure on such items is recorded as 'gross domestic fixed capital formation' in government statistics.

Working capital consists of stocks of raw materials, semi-manufactured goods and manufactured goods which have not yet been sold. Manufacturers monitor stocks of unsold products closely and these tend to be the key signals in a market economy to reduce or increase production. Working capital is an essential part of production, although modern Just-in-time' production techniques have reduced the need for large stocks of raw materials and components to be held in factories. Expenditure on these items is recorded in government statistics as 'increase in stocks and work in progress'.

It can be seen that gross fixed capital formation increased in the period 1987 to 1989, fell to around its 1987 level by 1992, and recovered slightly by 1993.

Investment can also be divided into gross investment and net investment. Gross investment includes all investment, including that which is for replacement of worn-out machinery, whilst net investment only includes investment that adds to a country's capital stock.

Net investment = gross investment — depreciation

Factors affecting investment

Investment in the private sector is undertaken to increase profitability. Since we assume that the motive of private sector organizations is the maximization of profits, such organizations will seek to invest in those projects which yield the highest return. Investment projects will incur planning, construction and running costs and yield revenue when in operation. Thus the profitability of an investment project can be analysed by investigating its costs and revenue.

Holiday Inn: Europe

The UK brewery and leisure group Bass plc has announced new investment plans for extending its Holiday Inn hotels into Europe. Its chosen strategy is to expand mainly by franchising, and to extend its presence in the budget market. The vehicle for this is the Holiday Inn Express concept aimed at price-conscious travellers. By avoiding costly city-centre sites and concentrating instead on roadside locations, the investment cost to franchisees is expected to range between *£28000* and £30000 per room and rooms are likely to cost an average of E35 a night.

Cost of investment

The main costs of an investment will be:

— planning costs
— costs of capital goods
— cost of financing investment
— running costs of the investment

Planning costs

The planning costs of an investment include consultancy costs for technical feasibility, market research, competitor scanning, financial appraisal and overall project planning. For large-scale projects, planning costs can be considerable and add to the overall project timetable. For example, BAA's plan to build a new terminal, Terminal 5, at London Heathrow airport had to go before a public inquiry with all the attendant legal costs, and the planning and consultation phase has doubled the timescale for the development.

Chocks away for Concorde 2?

British Aerospace, Aerospatiale of France and Deutsche Aerospace are working on plans for Concorde 2. They

Table 1 Terminal 5 timetable

Year	Projected stage
1992	Local consultations
1992	Submission of planning application
1994	Start of public planning inquiry
1995	End of public planning inquiry
1997	Govenimment decision expected
	Subject to planning approval being granted
1997	Start of construction
2001	Completion of phase 1 construction
2002	Opening of phase 1
2016	Terminal reaches maximum capacity

have recently made a request for up to E60m from the government and the EU to finance a continuation into their feasibility studies. There is however considerable disagreement between the aircraft manufacturers, airline chiefs and industry experts as to the likely feasibility of the project.

The manufacturers would need a production run of over *500* aircraft to break even, but few commentators can foresee a market of more than 100 planes. Even then reaction is guarded. Whilst design teams dream of more seats, and increased range, Ron Muddle, director of planning at BA, has his feet firmly on the ground, noting that running costs per passenger for today's Concorde are several times those for a Boeing *747*. He says that only a radical design breakthrough would make the aircraft a commercial proposition.

Costs of capital goods

The capital costs of an investment are the costs of buildings, plant and machinery. In some cases these are known costs, since there is a market in commonly purchased capital goods such as computer systems, vehicles and standard buildings. For more complex investments capital costs can only be estimated in the planning stage and for large construction projects, estimates of costs are notoriously unreliable. The original estimate for building and equipping the Channel Tunnel was G10bn but by 1993 the figure had been revised to E10bn. Such escalations in costs are typical of large construction projects. In the case of the Channel Tunnel, factors such as price increases in materials, increased wages, unforeseen technical difficulties in boring the tunnel, specification changes to improve safety, and legal disputes over costs between Eurotunnel and the construction company Trans-Manche Link (TML) have all added to the increased costs.

Cost of financing investment

Finance for investment projects may be found internally out of a company's profits, or externally from the capital markets, for example, through banks or share issues. External funding by loans carries costs in terms of interest rates that have to paid for the duration of a loan. These interest rates may be fixed or variable. External funding by share issue incurs issue costs but the costs of funding (i.e. the dividend payments to shareholders) are then tied into future profits.

It might appear that internally generated funds do not carry any special costs, since a company does not have to pay interest on its own funds. However there is an opportunity cost of using internal funds. That is the cost in terms of other uses to which the funds could have been put. A company could put funds on deposit in the money markets and gain interest on such deposits. Thus even where internal funds are used for investment, a notional interest rate will be used to represent their opportunity cost. In general, higher interest rates will act as a disincentive to investment.

Running costs of the investment

The running costs of an investment will include all the other costs of operating the project. These include labour costs, maintenance costs and raw material costs. New technology which reduces running and production costs can be an important cause of investment.

Revenue from investment

Total revenue from sales resulting from an investment project can be calculated by multiplying the selling price by the quantity sold and thus the main factors affecting the revenue obtained from an investment are:

- price of output
- quantity of output sold
- other factors

Price of output

The price of the output of an investment project will largely depend on demand and the competition in the market under consideration. This is discussed fully in Chapter 6, and in general the less competition, the more power a supplier will have to set price. Where a monopoly or near monopoly exists, price can be producer-determined (but quantity sold will reflect demand). However, potential competitors will move quickly to produce near substitutes where possible, particularly if a premium price is being charged. Where a few producers exist in a market (oligopoly or monopolistic competition), the impact of a new entrant will change the actions of those already in the market and thus lead to unpredictability. In a perfectly competitive market prices will be driven down to reflect the lowest average costs in the industry.

Thus, although a company may have market intelligence about current prices in the market where its investment is to take place, any estimate of prices in future years is likely to be very uncertain. Channel Tunnel prices, for example, have changed considerably between the planning stage and the present. This reflects the changing marketing strategies of competing ferry and airline companies.

Quantity of output sold

Quantity sold will be closely related to price charged. However it will also be related to factors including consumers' income, competitive prices and advertising. Clearly there are a range of factors, for example environmental pressures, taxes, fuel costs, which might cause the forecasts to be wrong.

Other factors

Government policy may affect the revenue that derives from an investment project in several ways. First, government taxation policy may affect prices (VAT), or spending power (income tax) or profits (corporation tax). Second government legislation may affect the demand for goods, and finally monopolies and mergers legislation may have an impact upon prices that can be charged. Expectations play a key part in investment decisions. Expectations reflect views about how successful the economy will be in future years. Where investors have a pessimistic view about the future economy they will generally defer investment decisions.

Property development is a prominent feature of much leisure and tourism investment. Whilst rental income is a part of the anticipated revenue from such developments, capital appreciation can also be an important factor. Thus, such developments are often sensitive to expectations about future prices of property.

Above all, the factors surrounding an investment decision are subject to a great deal of uncertainty. Few of the factors have known values. Current interest rates are known, and where an investment obtains funds at fixed rates, this provides a predictable element. However, where funds are obtained at variable interest rates, considerable uncertainty will exist. Similar uncertainty surrounds the final costs of complex capital projects, price of output and demand for the final good or service. These are all subject to changes in the competitive and political, economic, sociocultural and technological (PEST) environments.

Appraisal techniques

Having identified the factors affecting the profitability of an investment, these can be used in a variety of quantitative methods to aid decision making. Investment appraisal reports may appear very authoritative, neatly summarizing projects in figures. However in view of the uncertainties discussed in the previous section, care should be taken to examine the assumption on which appraisals are made. The main appraisal techniques are:

- payback method
- average rate of return
- net present value
- internal rate of return

Payback method

This method compares investment projects by measuring the length of time it takes to repay the original investment from the revenues earned. It therefore favours projects which have the earliest payback. The key problems with this method are first that earnings that an investment may make after the payback period are not taken into account, and second revenues are not discounted so earnings within the payback period are given equal weight irrespective of the year they appear in. On the other hand, the sooner the payback, the less a project will be subject to uncertainties, and some companies may see speed of return as a priority over total return.

Average rate of return

This method calculates the total earnings from an investment and divides this by the number of years of the project's life. This figure is then expressed as a percentage of the capital costs of the project. For example, if an investment project had a total cost of £100000 and earned a total of £500000 over 5 years, the annual earnings would be £10000, which represents an annual average rate of return of £10000/£1000000 or 10 per cent on the capital employed. This method also fails to discount future earnings.

Net present value

The net present value method takes into account the fact that future earnings have a lower value than current earnings. For example, £100 today could be invested at a rate of interest of 10 per cent to give £110 in a year's time. Working this backwards, £100 in a year's time is only worth £90.91 today at a rate of interest of 10 per cent.

In other words, it has been discounted at a rate of 10 per cent to find its present discounted value. Discount tables exist to assist such calculations but there is also a formula for calculating present discounted value (PDV):

$$\text{PDV} = R_t/(1 + i)^t$$

where R = return, t = year and i = rate of interest or discount rate (expressed as decimal).

The net unadjusted revenues sum to £19rn and thus the project appears to show a net surplus of £3m. However, the net present value technique compares costs and revenues discounted to their net present values. The total net revenue falls to £14.55m when discounted to present value, and the project shows the following net present value;

Costs at present value	£16.00m
Revenue at present value	£14.55m
Net present value	£1.45m

This negative figure indicates an unprofitable investment.

Internal rate of return

The internal rate of return method also uses discounted cash flow. It calculates the discount rate that would equate the net present value of future earnings of an investment to its initial cost. This rate is called the internal rate of return. An investment will be profitable if its internal rate of return exceeds the rate of interest that has to be paid for borrowing, funds for the investment, allowing a margin for risk. A feasibility study into a fixed channel link by Coopers and Lybrand and Setec Economie in 1979 concluded that the internal rate of return on the project would be between 11 and 18 per cent.

When comparing investment projects those with the highest internal rate of return will be selected.

Changes in the level of investment

Changes in the level of investment will be caused by changes in the costs and predicted revenues of investments.

Investment activity in economies tends to be volatile, that is subject to considerable fluctuations. One of the explanations of this is the accelerator principle.

When demand for consumer goods and services is relatively stable in an economy, much of the demand for capital goods will take the form of replacing worn-out plant and machinery. However, if demand for final goods rises and there is no spare capacity in an industry, then new machinery will have to be purchased. Thus the demand for capital goods will significantly increase to include new machines as well as replacement machines. Similarly, if the demand for final goods in an economy falls, firms will find they have overcapacity and too many machines. They will reduce the stock of machines to the new lower levels needed by not replacing worn-out machines, so the demand for capital goods will fall. Thus a rise in the demand for final goods will cause an accelerated rise in the demand for capital goods, and a fall in the demand for final goods will cause an accelerated fall in the demand for capital goods. The accelerator theory helps to explain the sudden fall in investment in 1990, in response to a fall in consumer demand.

Risk and sensitivity analysis

Sensitivity analysis is a technique for incorporating risk assessment in investment appraisal. It works by highlighting the key assumptions upon which investment appraisal figures were based. For example, revenue forecasts for an investment might be based upon

- sales of 100000 units per year
- market growth of 3 per cent per year
- price of £3 per unit
- exchange rate of £l = $1.5

Sensitivity analysis would calculate the effects on an investment appraisal of changes in these assumptions. Such analysis would demonstrate the effects of, for example:

- sales of 80 000 units per year
- market growth of 1 per cent per year

- price of £2.50 per unit
- exchange rate of £l = $1.5

and thus illustrate a project's sensitivity to a variety of scenarios.

Government policy

The policy of the Conservative party is to interfere as little as possible in the free market. However it does offer financial assistance where a project provides employment in areas of high unemployment and where there are wider benefits to the community.

12

Coordination

All leisure and tourism organisations set themselves objectives or goals in order to provide a framework within which all their resources can be used to best effect and their performance measured. Objectives for individual organisations will be very diverse and will reflect the philosophy of the owners or managers, the size of the organisation, its stage of development and whether it is in the commercial or non-commercial sector. Objectives of leisure and tourism organisations will be developed and refined by all those who have an interest in the organisation, including:

— The owners.
— The managers.
— The staff.
— Visitors or users.
— Shareholders.
— Local councillors.
— Members (of a club or association).
— The local community.
— Society in general.

Owners and managers will be concerned that the objectives are realistic and achievable and provide a reward for their effort, skill and management expertise; staff will want to be sure of their conditions of employment and future prospects in terms of promotion and the growth, or otherwise, of the organisation. Visitors will be concerned with the experience they receive and whether they think the organisation gives value for money. Shareholders will be looking to the owners and/or managers to provide them with a growing return on capital invested in the organisation. Local councillors, representing the local community, will be keen to see that public facilities are being used to the maximum, objectives are being achieved and that local authority funds are being wisely deployed. The members of a club or association will be actively involved in setting objectives and helping to achieve them. Society in general has, to a greater or lesser extent, a stake in the aims and objectives of leisure and tourism organisations. The benefits of faster travel, instant entertainment and access to a wealth of activities and facilities needs to be balanced against the wider issues and concerns of social and environmental exploitation, problems of congestion and changes in the nature of work and leisure in society.

Non-commercial organisations

Non-commercial leisure and tourism organisations, falling within the public or voluntary sectors of the economy, do not have 'profit maximisation' as their primary objective. They have been developed with wider social objectives in mind; a council-run leisure centre, for example, will have as a primary aim, 'the provision of a wide range of leisure and recreational services and facilities for the benefit of local people'. There are many examples of non-commercial organisations in leisure and tourism, including:

— *Local clubs and societies set* up by local people with a specific purpose in mind, these organisations will aim to break even on their finances and may apply for some financial help from their local authority. A good example is a local photographic society.

— *Charitable trusts many* trusts are established to conserve or preserve our national and local heritage. The most well-known and respected is the National Trust which today protects more than 600,000 acres of land in England, Wales and Northern Ireland as well as over 200 houses and parks. The Civic Trust, established in 1957, is a registered charity that aims to uphold high standards of environmental quality and management throughout the United Kingdom.

— *Local authorities local* councils play a major role in the provision of leisure and tourism facilities in Britain. Without their involvement, facilities such as recreation grounds, parks, libraries, museums, leisure centres, tourist information centres and visitor attractions would not exist. The general move towards privatisation, market testing and compulsory competitive tendering, has meant that local authorities are now functioning much more like private sector operators and the distinction between commercial and non-commercial is becoming blurred.

— *Public corporations* the main public corporation linked to the leisure and tourism industry is British Rail, offering a service to both business and leisure travellers. Privatisation has meant that the former state-owned enterprises of British Airways and the British Airports Authority (BAA) are now in private hands. BR is itself scheduled for privatisaton in the not too distant future.

— *Quangos* these are quasi-autonomous non-governmental organisations which are primarily financed from the public purse but which have a high degree of autonomy. Examples in leisure and tourism are the Sports Council, Countryside Commission and the British Tourist Authority.

Although profit maximisation is not the primary objective of non-commercial organisations in leisure and tourism, those which are part of local government or are agencies of central government (e.g. the quangos), are expected to offer value for money and meet targets and agreed performance criteria. Many local authorities have recruited staff from the private sector and have implemented private sector management practices in order to help achieve their objectives.

Commercial organisations

The leisure and tourism industry in the UK is dominated by commercial or private sector organisations. Some of the best-known names in the industry are private companies, such as Nike, British Airways, Mecca, Forte, Thomson Holidays and Alton Towers, to name but a few. The private sector is made up of large and small organisations owned by individuals or groups of people whose primary aim is to make a profit. Many individuals rely on the profits generated by commercial organisations for a substantial part of their income. Profit maximisation is an important objective for a number of reasons:

— In order to provide resources for further expansion of the business.

— To reward risk taking.

— To enable the business to respond to the needs of its customers.

— To encourage efficiency and innovation.

Although profit maximisation is the primary objective of most private sector companies, it is by no means the only objective of all commercial leisure and tourism organisations. A lot of small businesses in the leisure and tourism industry are run by people who used to work for larger companies, but became frustrated with the high level of bureaucracy they encountered. Operating your own business in leisure and tourism can give a great deal of job satisfaction and the feeling that you have control over what decisions are made. However, that there are also disadvantages to being a sole trader or partner. Some owners will not seek to maximise profits to the full, but may be content with a level of profit that gives them the type of lifestyle they are happy with; after all, why work in an industry concerned with leisure, holidays and travel and have no time to enjoy yourself and have fun!

The role of mission statements

It is currently very fashionable for organisations, whether in the public, private or voluntary sector, to develop a mission statement. The mission statement is intended to convey to all those with an interest in the organisation, be they staff, shareholders or the public in general, what business it is in and where it sees itself going. Some mission statements introduce an element of the organisation's philosophy and values.

The aims of the Arts Council of Great Britain

— to open the arts to all;
— to promote excellence among artists of all kinds;
— to encourage innovation in the arts;
— to keep alive our heritage in the arts; and
— to serve as a national forum of thinking and planning in the arts by
— encouraging people to recognise the contribution made by artists and
— those who work in the arts to the quality of life;
— pressing the case for the arts and their public funding;
— encouraging and supporting all other sources of arts funding,
— using our financial resources to achieve our aims in Scotland, Wales and England;

— collaborating with individuals and organisations who share our aims; and
— making our own organisation open and accessible.

Some people are very sceptical about the value of mission statements and see, them as nothing more than a public relations exercise. What the mission statement can do is set out in very broad terms the direction in which an organisation is hoping to progress in the future and provide a framework for the development of its more specific objectives. British Airways is a very good example of this; although" its mission statement is very succinct, the Annual Report 199293 lists the seven detailed objectives (which it calls goals) that the company will hope to fulfil in order to achieve its mission. These are:

1. *Safe and secure to* be a safe and secure airline.
2. *Financially strong to* deliver a strong and consistent financial performance.
3. *Global leader to* secure a leading share of the air travel business worldwide with a significant presence in all major geographical markets.
4. *Service and value to* provide overall superior service and good value for money in every market segment in which we compete.
5. *Customer driven to* excel in anticipating and quickly responding to customer needs and competitor activity.
6. *Good employer to* sustain a working environment that attracts, retains and develops committed employees who share in the success of the company.
7. *Good neighbour to* be a good neighbour, concerned for the community and the environment.

Mission statements were first developed in private sector companies, principally in the United States, but are now to be found in public and voluntary sector leisure and tourism organisations. Some local authorities, however, have chosen not to follow the trend of developing a mission statement and prefer to continue to summarise their work in a policy statement. A policy statement for a typical, progressive borough council would be as follows:

> Blueridge Borough Council takes pride in the standards of service it delivers to the residents of the Borough. Our primary responsibilities are to promote services of the highest possible quality within the resources we have, at a cost acceptable to Council Tax payers, tenants and users of our leisure services. We, therefore, place great emphasis on caring for the needs of our customers and on being cost conscious and efficient.
>
> We aim to deliver services through an effective partnership of councillors and employees. We endeavour to ensure that our staff are well trained and are aware of the aims and objectives of the Council.
>
> The Council's belief is that the residents of the Borough expect a high level of efficiency in the services they use, and are looking for a dynamic and forward looking approach towards building on its services for a growing population, thus enhancing the quality of life for all.

Hierarchy of objectives

The examples of British Airways and the Arts Council of Great Britain show that it is often sensible to think of setting objectives within a hierarchy, with the mission statement, giving the general direction and policy of the organisation, at the top of the apex. The mission or policy will then be translated into organisational objectives, which may, depending on the size and structure of the organisation, be converted into objectives for particular departments or divisions. Targets for team or individual performance will then be developed so that measurement of success or attainment can take place.

Conflicting objectives

We have seen that leisure and tourism is a dynamic industry, constantly adapting in response to changing customer expectations, new technological developments and wider changes in the nature of society in general. Leisure and tourism organisations must reflect this dynamism by constantly reviewing their objectives and methods of operation. The setting of objectives cannot be seen as a once-and-for-all operation, but as an evolving process concerning all those who have a stake in the organisation.

The process of modifying objectives can sometimes lead to conflict within organisations. A local museum, for example, funded by the town council, which has for many years offered an excellent service to local school children may be required to adopt a more commercial approach to its activities in order to provide an income to offset against its council subsidy. This change from an educational to a financial objective may not be accepted by the staff at the museum who see their job as providing an educational resource and not running a business. At a national level, questions have been raised about institutions such as the Victoria and Albert Museum and the National History Museum charging for admission. Both museums used to admit visitors for free, but decided to introduce an admission charge to offset rising operating costs. Some people fear that commercial activities at the museums will detract from the educational and conservation objectives for which they were established.

Some tourist companies are criticised for taking little heed of the negative environmental and social effects their activities can have on destinations, particularly those fragile areas new to tourism. All too often, there is a conflict between the purely commercial objective of maximising profits by selling as many holidays as possible, and the wider social and environmental objectives of disturbing places and people as little as possible.

There may be conflict when a leisure organisation says it has one objective that states it will endeavour to provide a range of facilities and services for all sectors of the community and a second that says it will be 'a good neighbour, respectful of community feelings and concerns'. If it happens to organise events that cause disturbance late into the night, there may be bad feeling in the local community which may lead to the organisation reviewing its operation and objectives.

From time to time, all managers in leisure and tourism organisations set themselves and their staff objectives in order to get results. Some organisations have gone one step further by implementing the formal technique known as MBO (Management by Objectives), which is widespread in many sectors of the UK economy. To call MBO a technique undervalues its true purpose; it is better thought of as a total management approach or management style which encourages participation by all employees and rewards openness. The basis of MBO is the involvement of managers and employees in a setting of a mutually-acceptable set of objectives. It examines the current status of an organisation, highlights areas that need improvement or amendment, specifies means of achieving the changes, and gives time limits within which they will be made. When the time limit is reached, the results are reviewed, new objectives may be set and the process is repeated.

At *stage one,* a manager meets with an employee to discuss how that employee can best contribute to the overall effectiveness of the organisation by jointly agreeing objectives for the individual. The sort of objectives that may be agreed by an employee and manager working in leisure and tourism could include:

— Improving the level of customer service in a restaurant or fast-food outlet.
— Increase in occupancy, attendance or usage rates for a facility such as a hotel, tourist attraction or sports centre.
— Reduction in staff turnover in the reservations department of a tour operator or airline.
— Control of stock levels and wastage in the catering function of a major visitor attraction.
— Increased sales in a high street travel agency.
— Increased levels of guest spending on ancillary services in a self-catering villa complex.
— Increased turnover in the shop at a golf course or fitness suite.
— Improved security in a major out-of-town entertainment venue.

Stage two is concerned with the manager and employee agreeing targets against which to measure whether or not the objectives have been met. These targets, sometimes known as performance indicators, should be:

— Easily measurable for example, reduce the number of customer complaints by 20 per cent or increase turnover by 10 per cent.
— Realistic a target is only an incentive to the employee if he or she considers that it is realistic and achievable. A target of reducing customer complaints to zero, for example, is totally unrealistic and therefore not appropriate.

— Specific targets must be specific and unambiguous; general statements are unlikely to be measurable.
— Set within a time frame for example, increase the use of a local authority leisure centre by disabled people from I per cent to 4 per cent within 12 months.

A central feature of MBO is that objectives and targets should not be imposed by management but rather agreed between management and employees. Staff feel more comfortable with the process if they are asked to accept responsibility for achieving targets rather than being told exactly what to do without consultation.

Stage three of the MBO process involves the periodic monitoring of the performance of the individual member of staff against the agreed targets. This is likely to be an informal process and will take the form of a manager overseeing the work of a particular employee or group of employees and giving support and advice on work methods and systems, highlighting any areas that may need adjustment or further action. At stage four, manager and employee will hold a more formal review and appraisal meeting at which the performance of the member of staff will be judged against the original targets, which may have been modified as part of the monitoring process. The outcome of the appraisal may be linked to the employee's pay via a performance related pay scheme or other incentives. Stage four of the MBO process should end with a statement of objectives and targets for the next period of time, in order to continue the cycle.

Benefits and drawbacks of MBO

The Management by Objectives system has many potential benefits to the leisure and tourism industry If it is part of a wider participative style of management which encourages openness, it can:

— Let staff know exactly what is expected of them.
— Allow management to accurately measure the efficiency and effectiveness of their organisation.
— Help management to plan for the future.
— Encourage motivation on the part of employees.
— Identify staff and management training needs.
— Highlight areas of the organisation that need further development.
— Encourage the review of the organisation's structure.
— Encourage innovation from employees and managers.
— Allow management to deploy resources profitably.

Although MBO, if properly installed, has a number of potential advantages to a leisure and tourism organisation, the system does have its critics. They point to the rigidity and inflexibility of MBO, which doesn't fit well into an industry that is by its very nature very dynamic and having to respond quickly to the changing habits, fashions and tastes of its consumers. Those who favour the MBO approach would argue that all organisations must set themselves objectives and targets, since, without them, success or failure cannot be accurately measured. A well-developed MBO system should be able to take into account the dynamic nature of the leisure and tourism industry by, for example, shortening the length of time between monitoring and appraisal meetings.

Relating objectives to performance

We have seen that the MBO system offers one way for the management of a leisure and tourism organisation to set objectives and targets and review its performance. Whichever management philosophy or system is followed, one thing is quite clear; the setting of objectives is only the first part of evaluating performance of individual members of staff and the efficiency and effectiveness of the leisure and tourism organisation generally. In order that the objectives can be realised, die organisation must translate them into workable practices and achievable targets.

The personal function

Leisure and tourism is very much a 'people business'. Like all organisations in the service sector, it relies to a very great extent on the performance of its staff and management to achieve overall success. Quite simply, the staff are the most important resource in any leisure and tourism organisation. The quality of the customers' experience is dependent not only on the skills of the employees but also on their attitude and personality. What sets leisure and tourism apart from most other service sector industries is the fact that the staff are an integral and essential part of the 'product' the customer is buying. This holds true whether we are talking about an overseas holiday, when the client will deal with a range of staff from a travel agency clerk, airport check-in assistant to an overseas representative, or a 40-minute game of squash in the local leisure centre, when the attitude and efficiency of the staff will again influence the overall quality of the experience the customer receives. As Butlin's Holiday Worlds state in their handbook for all members of staff:

> We are a holiday home to many thousands of families each week. Families like your own who have been saving and looking forward all year to their visit to us. They rely on you and fellow members of your team to make their visit enjoyable. We need to ensure that they will receive five-star care.

Leisure and tourism is a very labour-intensive industry, characterised by a number of distinct features:

— A high proportion of unskilled staff.

— A large proportion of seasonal workers.

— Many part-time staff.
— High staff turnover in many sectors.
— Low rates of pay in some sectors.
— Employees who need to be mobile.

These characteristics of leisure and tourism employment place particular pressures and challenges on the personnel departments of many organisations.

Is HRM the same as personnel management?

It is difficult to argue that there is a clear distinction between human resource management and personnel management. There are many examples of leisure and tourism organisations that have simply changed the name of their personnel department to include the fashionable phrase, HRM, with little or no change to the internal operations of the department. Others have adopted the title of HRM department at the same time as they have carried out a major reappraisal and restructuring of the way in which they manage their human resources. Whereas the function of a personnel department could be viewed as rather mechanistic, bureaucratic and administration led, a unit that calls itself a human resource management department is signalling to those inside and outside the organisation that it is adopting a more long-term view of all aspects of employing, empowering, supporting, developing and rewarding their employees. At the end of the day, HRM is concerned with achieving a balance between the ambitions of the individual and the returns to the organisation. It is crucial that time and money is invested in getting the right balance, particularly in view of the fact that staff costs typically make up more than three-quarters of all costs for many leisure and tourism organisations.

What is the personnel function?

The personnel function in any organisation has traditionally been concerned with the 'hiring and firing' of staff. The personnel department of the 1990s, however, has to take a much more sophisticated approach to the management of its people, and is likely to become involved in a wide range of issues including:

— Recruitment and selection.
— Training and personal development.
— Staff retention and turnover.
— Staff appraisal and review.
— Employment legislation.
— Redundancy, retirement and pension advice.
— Skills training, e.g. customer care.

These issues, when combined with the more established personnel tasks, such as grievance and disciplinary procedures, negotiations with trade unions and staff associations on such matters as pay and conditions, and the general welfare of staff, demand an enormous amount of expertise, understanding and commitment from those working in personnel today. The tasks of those given the responsibility for managing staff, which in leisure and tourism will occur across all sectors of the industry, are, therefore, far more wide-ranging than they have ever been before, and the role of the human resource manager is rightly being acknowledged as a key function in the management of any organisation striving for excellence and long-term success.

Manpower planning

In a volatile industry such as leisure and tourism, which is constantly developing and innovating in response to changing customer requirements, the task of planning likely future staff needs is no easy matter. In such a competitive environment, however, the need to have just the right number of employees, in order to keep staff costs to the minimum, becomes even more important. Manpower planning gives an organisation the opportunity to look at its existing staffing levels and to forecast the mix of human resources it will need to meet its future objectives. Although leisure and tourism organisations vary greatly in their size and in terms of the sector in which they are operating, it is possible to identify a number of stages that any organisation will have to go through in order to draw up its manpower plan. These are:

1. An examination of the organisation's strategic plan.
2. Consideration of existing staff resources in the context of the strategic plan.
3. An estimate of any likely future changes in the supply of staff.
4. The likely demand for staff in the future.
5. Development of the future human resource 'mix'.

The organisation's strategic plan will identify where the organisation sees itself at the moment, where it wants to be in the future and what it has to do in order to get there. Obviously, a key element of this strategy will be how many staff will be needed and what type of people will need to be trained. In estimating the likely supply and demand situation in relation to staffing in the future, the organisation will need to look at both its internal strengths and weaknesses, and the many external influences that affect the situation. These external influences are likely to include:

— *Demography this* is concerned with population characteristics, e.g. the decline in the birth rate in the UK since the 1960s has led to a decline in the number of young people available for work in the 1990s (the so-called 'demographic timebomb'). This has major repercussions for an industry such as leisure and tourism which employs a large number of people under the age of 30. Although most leisure and tourism organisations appear not to have addressed the issue to any great extent, with the exception of Eurocamp and one or two other operators which now actively seek out older staff, the supply of younger staff is likely to get worse as we lead up to the year 2000. With an ageing population generally, it makes sense from an operational point of view to consider employing more mature staff who may be able to relate more easily to an older clientele.

— *The strength of the economy spending* on leisure and tourism is directly linked to the economic health of the country. A period of prolonged recession will suppress the demand for leisure and tourism facilities and so reduce the need for extra staff.

— *Technology we* have seen that leisure and tourism is an industry that makes extensive use of new technology, for example a computerised reservation system in a local travel agency or a global communications network used by an international airline. Although there are many scare stories about new technology replacing people in jobs, leisure and tourism is in the fortunate position of being reliant on so much face-to-face contact, which a machine simply could not reproduce. It is considered that leisure and tourism will be one of the fastest-growing industries because it has harnessed new technology equipment and systems.

Once the staff demand and supply has been predicted, the organisation will be in a position to implement the final stage of its manpower plan, namely the development of its future human resource 'mix'. It will use all the information made available in the first four stages to estimate the numbers of full and part-time staff, any temporary or contract appointments, training requirements and an overall manpower strategy for the future.

Personnel records

All leisure and tourism organisations will need to keep information on their current employees and people who have worked for them in the past. Some may hold on file, for future use, speculative applications from individuals seeking employment. These personnel records on individual members of staff may be supplemented by data on, for example, staff turnover on an annual basis, an analysis of staff illness patterns or details of why employees have left the organisation.

The personnel records of most leisure and tourism organisations are likely to include details of the following:

- *Personal details address,* telephone number, date of birth, bank account number (if payment is by direct transfer), details of dependents, etc.
- *Job title and grade with* details of annual holiday entitlement.
- *Accident and sickness record details* of accidents at work and reasons for sickness are kept.
- *Absenteeism details* of authorised and unauthorised absences will be held on file and, in cases where the situation is either particularly bad or good, the details may be referred to in an appraisal interview.
- *Payroll information current* remuneration with details of any annual increments or bonus payments made or planned for the future.
- *References the* names and addresses of people willing to give a reference or copies of actual references will be held.

— *Staff appraisals and reviews if* the organisation has a formal appraisal or review system in place, details of any interviews or action plans arising will be held in the personnel department.

In smaller organisations, the personnel information may be stored and updated manually. If only a small number of staff are employed, this system will prove to be quite adequate. Larger organisations, however, are likely to use a computerised personnel records system, with the benefits of greater storage capacity, speed of use and accessibility to many staff at the same time. Information on employees which is held on computer, however, does fall within the scope of the Data Protection Act 1984, which provides new rights for individuals and demands good practice from those who hold personal data on individuals. Whether a manual or automated system is used for storing data on employees, the security of the personnel records is very important. Handling such sensitive, personal information calls for a system that allows access only to authorised staff and is housed in a safe and secure environment.

Recruitment of staff

Good staff are the backbone of any organisation in the service sector, and particularly in leisure and tourism where they are an integral part of the 'experience' the customers are buying. But how can you be sure of getting the best people for the job? A thorough approach to recruitment and selection, paying attention to detail and allowing enough time to see the process through to its completion, will pay dividends to the organisation, and in particular will go a long way towards reducing the high levels of staff turnover that are found in some sectors of leisure and tourism. Management time spent on recruitment should be regarded as a wise investment for the future; all too often, more time and attention is given to choosing a new computer system than to selecting the most important resource the organisation has, its staff.

The recruitment process

Factors such as the fall in the number of young people available for work, the number of employees who no longer see a post as 'a job for life' and the general 'skill shortages' within the UK workforce mean that the task of selecting staff can no longer be left to chance. While there will always be mistakes made when it comes to employing people, a systematic and objective approach to the process of recruitment is likely to achieve the objective of getting the best person for the job.

Job analysis

Whenever a vacancy arises, whether it is to replace an employee who is leaving or if it is a new post, there needs to be a thorough analysis of what the job entails. If it is an existing post to be filled, simply finding a set of old job details and reproducing them without considering if they are still relevant is not good enough. The dynamic nature of the leisure and tourism industry is such that an approach of this sort will not achieve the desired objective of filling the post with the best candidate. Information to be included in the job analysis can be obtained from the existing postholder, previous records, other members of staff and by direct observation. A job description can then be compiled, detailing the content of the job and areas of responsibility. A typical job description is likely to include:

— *Basic details title* of post, grade, post number, department/section, location, etc.
— *Summary of the job outlining* the key objectives of the post.
— *Responsibilities clarifying* the position in the

organisational structure, detailing to whom responsible and for whom responsible.

— *Detailed duties a* list of all the relevant duties attached to the post.

— *Conditions of employment general* information on salary/wage, holiday entitlement, hours of work, pension arrangements, welfare and social facilities, trade union membership arrangements, training, etc.

The job description will be sent out to potential candidates together with an application form and further details as appropriate. Some organisations prefer to ask for a CV rather than a completed application form, while others make it very clear that CVs are not acceptable in place of an application form.

At the same time as they are compiling a job description, many organisations will also draw up a job specification, often referred to as a person specification, which provides a blueprint of the 'ideal' person for the job in terms of skills, character, previous experience and qualifications. A person specification for an Assistant Events Officer post with a voluntary sector organisation.

As well as indicating the type of experience and skills that the successful candidate will need to demonstrate, the example of the person specification shows how the extent to which the candidate meets the criteria will be assessed. In this case, the criteria will be assessed from the application form, at interview, by role play and by means of a writing exercise. Some person specifications divide the qualities, experience and skills sought into those that are essential' and those that are 'desirable'. When drawing up a person specification, organisations must be careful not to introduce bias either in favour of, or against, one particular section of society, for example disabled people. Discrimination on the grounds of sex or race are covered by legislation under the Sex Discrimination Act and the Race Relations Act respectively.

Seeking suitable applicants

Once the job specification and person specification have been finalised, the task of finding potentially suitable applicants can begin in earnest. The task may focus solely on internal candidates or may be opened up to outside applicants. The process can be carried out entirely in-house or may be partly or wholly delegated to an outside recruitment agency. In leisure and tourism, agencies tend to be used either for very senior appointments, e.g. Director of Marketing or Head of Leisure Services, or in situations where jobs are becoming hard to fill, notably some posts in the hotel and accommodation sector. Recruitment agencies specialising in leisure and tourism advertise their services in the relevant trade newspapers and journals. There are many different methods that leisure and tourism organisations use to look for suitable applicants, including:

- Advertisements in local, regional and national newspapers, e.g. the Guardian has appointments covering the arts, marketing, tourism, environment a countryside.
- Advertisements in trade journals and magazines, e.g. Leisure Management' Leisure Opportunities, Travel Trade Gazette, Caterer and Hotelkeeper, to name but a few.
- Employment agencies.
- Job centres.
- Links with universities, colleges and schools.
- A 'trawl' through any speculative applications held on file.
- Advertisements in internal staff newsletters or equivalent

— Vacancies circulated by Professional Bodies.

The selection process

If the job description and person description have been carefully prepared, and any advertisements, if used, are written in a clear and precise manner, the organisation is likely to keep the number of unsuitable applications to a minimum. The initial sift of application forms, letters or CVs will concentrate on matching the candidates' qualifications, experience and skills to the previously prepared person specification. This process will end with the drawing up of a short list of suitable candidates who will be invited to take part in the next stage of the recruitment process. This will usually take the form of an interview, either one to one or by a panel, at which the candidate will be given the opportunity of expanding on his or her written application and will be able to learn a little more about the people and the organisation he or she is hoping to work for. The candidate will also be asked questions during the interview and may be asked to carry out tasks, such as operating a computer or piece of machinery. Some organisations use other selection methods, including written tests and personality questionnaires.

Although often criticised for being too subjective, the interview is usually the central component of the selection process for any job in leisure and tourism. It has two basic aims:

— To give the organisation the opportunity to meet candidates face to face and find out more details about the applicants and their achievements to date.

— To give the candidates the chance to formulate their assessment of what the job entails and the people they will be working for and with.

Much of the criticism levelled at interviewing as a way of selecting staff is that it is by its very nature personal and, therefore, open to bias on the part of those carrying it out. In order to make the interview as objective as possible, it needs to be carefully planned in advance, with each candidate being asked exactly the same set of questions. In this way, candidates' responses can be more accurately compared and evaluated. There are a number of 'golden rules' in interviewing, including:

— Draw up a list of questions in advance of the interview.

— Take brief notes during the interview, as it is very easy to mistake one candidate for another, particularly if several are being interviewed on the same day.

— Invite the interviewees to take notes if they wish.

— Get the interviewee to expand on the information contained in the application form or on the CV.

— Be alert to the interviewees' strengths and weaknesses.

— Ask open questions that invite an answer other than 'yes' or 'no'.

— Ask for information on future career plans. A question often used at interview is 'where do you see yourself in x years' time.

— Give applicants plenty of opportunity to reveal all relevant information and ask any questions.

— Avoid asking personal questions.

There are occasions when, after having carried out the painstaking task of interviewing several candidates, the interview panel does not consider any of the applicants suitable for the job. This should not necessarily be seen as a failure of the selection process, but rather the fact that the process has worked well even though no suitable candidate has been found. On these occasions, the organisation may decide to re-interview a selection of candidates or start the whole process again by seeking new applications.

Appointment

If the interviewer or interview panel are sure that a suitable person has been found, a formal written offer of appointment can be made, subject to satisfactory references and possibly a medical examination. The successful candidate will be invited to reply in writing that he or she accepts the offer of the job. Once this letter of acceptance is received, those candidates who were unsuccessful should be informed of the decision as a matter of courtesy and to maintain the organisation's professional image.

Induction

It is vital to maintain the momentum of the recruitment process by providing *the* successful candidate with a structured induction to the organisation.

An induction programme should be designed to help new members of staff familiarise themselves with their new environment, to settle easily into their new jobs and to establish good working relationships with other members of staff. Induction is, particularly important in those sectors of the leisure and tourism industry which have a higher then average staff turnover, since it can help to build relationships over the crucial first few months of a new appointment. A comprehensive induction programme should include the following details

— Brief information on the scope and importance of the leisure and tourism industry.
— The structure, aims and philosophy of the organisation.
— The main features of the job with an indication of lines of responsibility

— The principal conditions of employment.
— An introduction to work colleagues.
— A tour of the facilities.
— Rules on dress, personal appearance, eating, drinking, smoking, etc.
— Health, safety and security procedures.
— Staff representation, including trade union membership and trade associations.
— Social and welfare facilities.
— Training and personal development opportunities.

Some organisations identify an existing member of staff to help the new settle in to their new surroundings, a process known as mentoring. The plays an important role in the induction process, which, if planned well carried out with enthusiasm, will give the new employee an early opportunity becoming an effective and valued member of the team.

Staff training and development

There can be little doubt that a well-trained workforce is any leisure and tourism organisation's best asset. Offering opportunities for training and development increases staff morale and motivation, which in turn feed through into in efficiency, productivity and output.

In short, training can:

— Increase profitability and efficiency.
— Improve customer service.
— Reduce staff turnover.
— Increase flexibility.
— Trigger innovation and new ideas.
— Reduce costs.

Training needs analysis

A logical starting point for any leisure and tourism organisation wanting to introduce, or improve, training for staff, is to implement a training needs analysis (TNA). A TNA is an auditing process that aims to identify:

1. The current level of technical and management skills within the organisation.
2. The required level of technical and management skills needed to be an effective organisation.
3. Any shortfall or surplus in the level of technical and management skills.

If a shortfall is identified, which is often the case in the leisure and tourism industry, which has generally under invested in training for its staff, the TNA should make recommendations on the action necessary to bridge the training gap. TNAs can be carried out by staff within the organisation or by employing outside consultants who specialise in the field. Either way, the senior management must give full commitment to the initiative, since it wili require additional resources over a long period of time. A fully planned and costed staff training plan is not a 'quick fix' solution, but one that will take time to achieve its aims. The TNA may well identify the need for increasing the level of technical and management skills through a mixture of on-the-job and off-the-job training.

On-the-job training

As its name implies, on-the-job training is when employees gain and develop their skills and knowledge while carrying out their normal everyday duties. Many jobs in leisure and tourism are ideally suited to this type of 'hands-on' training, for example operating a VDU in a travel agency, working in the plant room of a leisure centre, training to be a chef in a restaurant or hotel, working behind the counter in a tourist information centre, to name but a few. On-the-job training often leads to qualifications such as National Vocational Qualifications (NVQs), SVQs in Scotland and General National Vocational Qualifications (GNVQs), all of which give employees credit for training related to the world of work.

Off-the-job training

Training that takes place away from the normal place of work is sometimes preferred by staff and employers as a way of achieving a specific training objective. Some leisure and tourism organisations make extensive use of 'day release' courses offered by local colleges and private training providers, often leading to industry-related vocational qualifications. Evening classes are also popular in sectors such as travel and leisure centre management. Some organisations encourage their senior staff to work towards management and supervisory qualifications, either by the traditional route of going on a course, or perhaps by following a distance-learning programme based around home study and a small amount of tutorial support. Many organisations have found that the areas of customer care and foreign language training are particularly beneficial for staff working in leisure and tourism.

Staff appraisal

The main function of staff appraisal, sometimes referred to as staff development review, is to give an employee and his or her immediate superior the opportunity to discuss current performance and to agree a working plan for the future, in relation to specific targets and objectives. The appraisal, usually taking the form of an interview between the two parties, is also likely to highlight training needs for the individual which will have time and cost implications for management. Some leisure and tourism organisations, particularly in the commercial sector of the industry, use the staff appraisal process to determine what level of bonus or performance-related pay the employee should receive. Others prefer to keep the two issues quite separate. Staff appraisal has been widely used in private sector leisure and tourism companies for many years. More recently, in response to the 'privatising' of many local authority leisure and tourism services through such measures as CCT and market testing, the public sector has begun to introduce the concept of appraisal of staff performance as part of a wider process of increasing efficiency and becoming more competitive.

In order to be of maximum benefit to any leisure and tourism organisation, whether it is in the private or public sector, an effective system of staff appraisal needs:

— Careful preparation by both the supervisor/ manager and the employee. 0 A procedure that is clearly understood by both parties.

— A well-designed appraisal form with space for comments by both parties.

— An appraisal interview that is structured, but flexible enough to incorporate new ideas and developments.

— An objective, written summary of the key points of the interview and agreed future targets and plans.

— Feedback from employee and supervisor /manager on the effectiveness of the process.

— An informal yet 'business like' atmosphere.

Most organisations recognise the benefits of introducing a staff appraisal system, although it can have one or two drawbacks if not carefully planned. The benefits include:

— Assisting in meeting organisational objectives. 9 Helping managers improve the effectiveness of their staff.

— Assisting the employee to identify his or her role in the organisation.
— Improving communication between staff and management.
— Building commitment and loyalty.
— Helping managers understand better the jobs that their staff carry out.
— Identifying training and personal development needs.

Because staff appraisal is understandably a very sensitive issue, introducing such a scheme without a supportive and positive approach on the part of management and employees can sometimes lead to problems. There is often a great deal of uncertainty and suspicion surrounding the process when appraisal is linked to pay and bonuses, which is why many organisations, choose to treat the two issues separately. Managers and supervisors must be aware of the importance of confidentiality in the whole process in order to gain the confidence of the staff. Management must also be careful not to raise expectations in their staff which cannot be met; for example, promising staff training opportunities that fail to materialise. If staff appraisal is well planned and has the commitment of management and employees, it can be a very useful tool for improving performance and helping meet overall objectives.

Staff motivation

We have seen in earlier units that leisure and tourism employs a large number of unskilled, lowpaid workers who are often called upon to work unsocial hours; it is a fact of life that those employed in leisure and tourism are asked to work at the very time that most people are 'at leisure'. Add to these factors the high level of direct contact that leisure and tourism employees have with their customers and we can begin to see the challenges that face managers when it comes to motivating their staff. The motivation to work well is usually related to job satisfaction, a complex issue that depends on many inter-linking factors, such as the working environment, attitude of senior management, cooperation with colleagues, pay and reward systems, terms of employment, recognition of achievements, personal circumstances, status, etc.

Leisure and tourism organisations that put people first and treat staff requirements as a high priority are likely to be rewarded with employees who:

— Attend work regularly.

— Display high morale.

— Project a good company image.

— Are happy at their work.

— Give a high level of customer service.

— Achieve greater productivity.

— Are motivated to achieve.

— Work well as members of teams.

Above all, an employee needs to feel a valued part of the organisation, recognised for his or her achievements and managed by senior staff who provide a supportive and effective environment. With all of these points in place, staff motivation will be high and the organisation will be in excellent shape to achieve its aims.

Tourism organisations

In order to analyse and understand the behaviour of organizations in the leisure and tourism sector, we need to be able to clarify their aims and objectives. The National Trust for example will follow different policies to English Heritage which itself will have different policies to Alton Towers. The similarity between these three is that they all have historic houses open to the public. The key difference is in their forms of ownership the first being a voluntary organization, the second a government-funded organization and the third a private sector organization.

Public sector organizations are those owned by the government. This can be national government or local government.

Local government organizations

Leisure and tourism provision in the local government sector includes:

— leisure centres and swimming pools
— libraries
— arts centres
— parks and recreation facilities
— tourism support

It should be noted that some provision occurs in the commercial marketplace. For example, customers of arts centres and leisure centres have to pay for the services provided. On the other hand facilities such as parks and children's playgrounds are generally provided without charge.

Sources of finance

The finance of these organizations comes from:

— charges for services where applicable central government grants
— grants from other sources
— local government taxation
— local government borrowing

The ability of local government to provide the level of services it wishes has been severely curbed by government legislation in recent years. Local government no longer has the power to set its own level of spending but is regulated through a system of central government-determined expenditure targets, council tax capping and financial penalties for exceeding central government spending targets.

Ownership and control

In essence local government organizations art, owned by the local population. Policy decisions or decisions of strategic management are taken on their behalf by the local council. Each local government area elects councillors or members to represent them, The political party which holds the majority of seats on the council will generally be able to dictate policy and such policy will be determined through a series of committees such as:

— libraries and arts
— recreation and leisure
— planning and resources

The planning and resources committee is a particularly powerful one as it determines the medium to long-term strategy of the council and thus provides the financial framework within which the other committees must operate. The day-to-day or operational management of local government-run services depends on the nature of the service being provided. The council officers are responsible for overall management and services which are spread out across a local government area, such as parks, will be run from the council offices. Larger services such as leisure centres will have their own management which in turn will be responsible to a service director at the council offices.

Aims and missions

The aims of local government and its organizations are largely determined by the political party or coalition of parties who hold the majority. This often means that leisure provision for example will vary between neighbouring local authorities which have different political parties in power. Administrations to the right of the political spectrum favour lower local taxes and market-driven provision, Those to the left favour public provision and subsidized prices.

To determine the differing aims of political parties we need to consult their manifestos as well as review their actual provision. However political parties do not operate in a vacuum. They

— pressure groups
— a trade unions
— local press
— national government

National government organizations

National government-owned organizations can be further subdivided into public corporations, other quangos and government departments.

Public corporations

There are few public corporations left after the privatization programme post 1979. Those privatized in the leisure and tourism sector included BA and BAA. The BBC remains in the public sector but it is increasingly being subjected to private sector objectives and management techniques.

Other quangos

There are a whole range of leisure and tourism organizations which are known as quangos quasi autonomous non-governmental organizations. Their autonomy stems from the fact that they are not directly answerable to ministers or parliament. The 'non-governmental' description of them is only partially true as they are funded by government.

Government departments

There are a number of government departments which impinge on the leisure and tourism sector of the economy, including:

— the Department of National Heritage (DNH)

— the Department of Transport

— the Department of the Environment

Of these, the DNH is the most significant, having responsibility for:

— the British Tourist Authority

— the English, Welsh and Scottish Tourist Boards

— royal parks and palaces arts and libraries

— sport

— broadcasting and the press

— heritage sites

Preserving the past, shaping the future

The Department of National Heritage (DNH) has spent a small part of its Elbn-a-year budget on setting out its stall in its new publication *Preserving the Past, Shaping the Future.* In it, the DNH reveals its aims:

— to preserve the heritage of the past

— to help create the culture of today and add to the heritage for future generations

— to broaden opportunities for people to enjoy the benefits of their heritage and culture

The DNH, significantly, is headed by a minister of cabinet rank. It brings together government responsibility for heritage, museums and galleries, libraries, arts, film, broadcasting, the press, sport, tourism and the national lottery. Thus its responsibilities include ensuring safety at sports grounds, broadcasting and press standards, subsidizing arts, and allocating national lottery proceeds. It performs these tasks by direct spending, legislation, through intermediaries such as regional arts boards and in conjunction with private sector providers.

But whilst the *Sun* was exercising its leader-writing skills on the sexual antics of the DNH minister, *The Times* was conducting a more reflective debate. It cautioned against the recent obsession of value for money which has permeated almost every aspect of public spending. Instead it suggested that the priority ought to be money for values. In this it highlighted the danger of allocating DNH expenditure only where measurable economic effects such as urban regeneration or tourism revenue could be proven. It argued that arts expenditure needs to be informed by wider values.

Aims and missions

Before the 'Thatcher revolution' of the 1980s there was a much clearer difference between public corporations such as the BBC and private sector organizations. Public corporations tended to aim for public service and without the discipline of the profit motive were able to provide services that were loss-making. The rigours of efficiency and private sector management styles were rarely apparent. The old stereotypes are less true today. Public corporations have been subjected to efficiency targets, performance indicators, target rates of return on investment and citizen's charters, all of which have made them more closely mimic private sector organizations. The aims of public corporations are contained within their charters or constitutions. The BBC charter is due for renewal in 1996.

The aims of other quangos are specific to each organization. For example, the aim of the Countryside

Commission is to promote the conservation and enhancement of landscape beauty and to encourage the provision and improvement in facilities in the countryside. The aim of the Sports Council is to promote the development of sport, In doing so it has developed a strategy which emphasizes participation and access. By its distribution of grants the Sports Council is able to encourage organizations which support its strategy. Both of these organizations support smaller, often voluntary organizations, and there is some tension between their government funding and their ability to support particular lobbies. The aim of government departments is to carry out the policy of the government of the day and includes the planning, monitoring and reviewing of provision and legislation.

Sources of finance

National organizations in the public sector are financed in the main from:

— taxes

— trading income

There has been continuing pressure from the government for more contribution from sponsorship and trading activities. The dependence on tax funding makes public sector organizations subject not only to the whims of the government of the day but also to the state of the economy as a whole.

Staff fear more cuts as ETB funds diminish

Staff at the English Tourist Board (ETB) are awaiting the next round of job cuts. The ETB has seen staff levels severed since the government announced drastic cuts in funding in 1992. Funding of C15.4m in 1992/93 is down to E13.9m in 1993/94 and will drop to El 1.3m in 1994/95. In 1995/96 funding will be down to E10m representing an investment of about 12p per domestic visitor.

Ownership and control

National government organizations are owned by the government on behalf of the population at large. However, each type of organization is controlled in a different way. Public corporations are given some autonomy and have a legal identity separate from the government. An act of parliament outlines aims, organization and control for each industry. The basic structure is one where a board is established responsible for day-to-day running of the industry. The chair of the board and its other members are appointed by an appropriate government minister. Strategic decisions will be taken by the minister in consultation with the government.

Despite their non-governmental status, the government exerts considerable control over other quangos by its power of appointment. The Sports Council, for example, which meets four times a year has its chair, vice chair and members appointed by Under Secretary of State for National Heritage.

Arts boss bound by bureaucracy

The Secretary General of the Arts Council has criticized the growing managerialist culture which the government is importing from industry as counterproductive. He complained that a succession of ministers had insisted on structural changes, internal reviews and performance monitoring, so that he and other senior staff spent more time in meetings than in attending the arts events. Government departments are headed by a minister and staffed by civil servants. The degree of political control is thus more direct than for public corporations and other quangos.

Private sector organizations

Private sector organizations are those which are non-government-owned. They can be further subdivided into profit-making organizations and non-profit-making organizations.

Profit-making organizations

Profit-making private sector organizations consist of sole proprietors, partnerships, private limited companies and public limited companies. There is an important distinction between these types of company in terms of the liability of investors.

Limited and unlimited liability

Sole proprietors and unlimited liability partners both operate under conditions of unlimited liability. Unlimited liability means that the owners of such companies face no limit to their contribution should the organization become indebted. Most of their personal assets can be used to settle debts should the business cease trading. This includes not only the value of anything saleable from the business, but also housing, cars, furniture, stereos the only exceptions being a person's 'tools of the trade' and a small amount of bedding and clothes. In contrast to this, limited liability places a limit to the contribution by an investor in an organization to the amount of capital that has been contributed. This applies to private and public limited companies as well as some partners who enjoy limited liability. Should one of these organizations cease trading with debts, an investor may well lose the original investment, but liability would cease there and personal assets would not be at risk.

Sole proprietors

Because of the discipline that unlimited liability brings, there are very few formalities required to start trading as a sole proprietor. The main requirement dictated by the Business Names Act 1985 is that the name and address of the owner must be displayed at the business premises and on business stationery.

The advantages of the sole proprietor include:

— independence
— motivation
— personal supervision
— flexibility

The problems of the sole proprietor include:

— unlimited liability
— long hours of work
— lack of capital for expansion
— difficulties in case of illness

Partnerships

The usual maximum number of partners is 20. A Deed of Partnership is generally drawn up to determine contribution of capital and sharing of profits. The Limited Partnership Act 1907 permits the admission of partners with limited liability as long as they do not take part in the management of the firm and as long as at least one partner retains unlimited liability.

The advantages of partnerships include:

— more capital available
— more expertise available
— flexibility
— motivation

The problems of partnerships include:

— unlimited liability
— disagreements

Private and public limited companies

The main difference between these is that public limited companies must have a minimum share capital and that shares in the private limited companies can only be transferred with the consent of other shareholders. Shares in public limited companies can be freely traded on the stock market. The similarities between the company forms are that they are bound by closer rules and regulations than are unlimited liability organizations. Recent examples of leisure and tourism sector organizations that have been floated on the stock market (i.e. changed from private to public limited companies) include:

— Eurodollar (car hire) 1994
— Servisair (aircraft handling) 1994
— BSkyB (satellite TV) 1994
— Telewest (cable TV) 1994
— Sunset Holidays (tour operator) 1994

Trade weighs taking the plunge

Airtours profits have rocketed from Urn in 1987 to E45m in 1993—that could never have happened without Airtours floating on the stock market. Perhaps that explains why travel companies continue to make cash calls on the City either by going public or seek venture capital investment. One person who believes more holiday companies should float has just done it himself Inspirations managing director Vic Fatah. 'If you float on the stock exchange you give up less than if venture capitalists come in', said Mr Fatah. Companies could also consider raising private funds. 'The advantage of venture capitalists is that you can get people in at an earlier stage of your development.' Another advantage in taking the private route is that a company does not have to pay fees to advisors such as merchant bankers, brokers, lawyers and public relations firms.

Expense is one reason why former Eurocamp group sales and marketing director Julian Rawel advises caution before opting to float. Mr Rawel helped steer Eurocamp through its flotation in 1991. The demands on a quoted company are always great, says Chris Parker, who has taken Unijet to the brink of floatation on two separate occasions: 'A quoted company always has to perform in the short term, which can be very difficult in a volatile industry'.

Some of the debate in the travel sector over moving from a private limited company to a public limited company. Airtours sees access to capital as being a key advantage of becoming a public limited company.

On the other hand Eurocamp stresses the costs of flotation and Unijet voices concerns about the constant need to perform as a public limited company, and the possible loss of control. The extent of share ownership and lack of control on transfer of shares mean that it is more difficult to retain control of public than private limited companies.

To commence business, limited liability, companies must obtain a Certificate of Incorporation and a Certificate of Trading from the Registrar of Companies.

The following must be provided:

— Memorandum of Association. The key points included in this are the name and address of the company, the objectives of the company, and details of share capital issued.
— Articles of Association. This details the internal affairs of the company including procedures for annual general meetings, and auditing of accounts.

Incorporation confers separate legal identity on the company. This may be contrasted with the position of unlimited liability organizations where the owners and the organization are legally the same.

Sources of finance

Sources of finance available to and partnerships are limited to:

— capital contributed by the owners

— ploughed-back profits

— bank loans

This is a key reason why small firms remain small.

Companies are able to raise capital through the additional routes of:

— shares (equity)

— debentures

Shares can be seen from the shareholder and company perspective. From the company point of view, share capital is generally low-risk since if the company doesn't make any profits then no dividends are issued. Shareholders seek dividend payments as well as growth in the value of shares. Debentures can be seen as a form of loan as they carry a fixed rate of interest. Thus to the company they pose a problem when profits are low, but their fixed interest rate is attractive when profits are high. Debenture holders get a guaranteed rate of return. First, Eurotunnel's capital represents a mixture of loans from banks which carry interest payments until they are repaid, and share issues which will not pay dividends until profits are earned. If profits from the tunnel are insufficient to repay loans and interest, the company may be forced into liquidation by the banks. The assets of the company would then be sold to repay the banks. Under this scenario, shareholders would get nothing. However because their liability is limited, neither would they stand to lose any personal assets. Under a more optimistic, high-profit scenario, payments to the banks are limited to previously negotiated rates, leaving substantial profits to be distributed in the form of high dividends to shareholders.

Second, three different forms of share issue are illustrated:

— A placing in 1986. This is where Eurotunnel's shares were placed directly with institutions such as pension funds and insurance companies.

— An offer for sale in 1987. This is where shares are advertised and offered to the public.

— A rights issue in 1990 and 1994. This is where existing shareholders are able to buy new shares at a discount.

Finally, the underwriting of share issues means that insurance has been taken out against the eventuality of shares remaining unsold.

Share prices and the stock market

Shares which are sold on the stock market are second-hand shares and thus their purchase doesn't provide new capital to companies. Prices of shares are determined by supply and demand. The stock market approximates to a perfect market and thus prices are constantly changing to bring supply and demand into equilibrium. The demand for and the supply of shares depend upon the following:

— price of shares
— expectations of future price changes
— profitability of firm
— price of other assets
— interest rates
— government policy
— tax considerations

Aims and missions

Objectives in the private sector are generally to maximize profitability. Many organizations have elaborated their aims into mission statements.

BAA's mission statement

'Our mission is to make BAA the most successful airport company in the world.'

This means:

— always focusing on our customers' needs and safety
— seeking continuous improvements in the costs and quality of our services
— enabling our employees to give of their best

Ownership and control

Understanding small business organization is straightforward. The owner is the manager. This may mean that profit maximization is subject to personal considerations such as environmental concerns or hours worked.

For companies, size of operations and number of shareholders make the picture more complex. Companies are run along standard lines: the managing director is responsible for directing managers in the day-to-day running of the organization. The board of directors is responsible for determining company policy and for reporting annually to the shareholders. This can lead to a division between ownership and control and a potential conflict of interests. Shareholders generally wish to see their dividends and capital gains, and thus company profits, maximized. Managers will generally have this as an important objective since they are ultimately answerable to shareholders. However, they may seek other objectives in particular, maximizing personal benefit which may include kudos from concluding deals, good pension prospects and a variety of perks such as foreign travel, well-appointed offices and high-specification company cars.

Non-profit-making organizations

Non-profit organizations in the private sector vary considerably in size and in purpose. They span national organizations with large turnovers, smaller special interest groups, professional associations and local clubs and societies, and include:

- the National Trust
- the Council for the Protection of Rural England
- the Ramblers Association
- the Tourism Society
- the Institute of Leisure and Amenity Management
- the British Amateur Gymnastics Association

The National Trust

The National Trust is a charity and independent from the government. It derives its funds from membership subscriptions, legacies and gifts, and trading income from entrance fees, shops and restaurants. It is governed by an act of parliament the National Trust Act 1907. Its main aim is to safeguard places of historic interest and natural beauty.

Aims and missions

Aims and missions of voluntary groups include protection of special interests, promotion of ideas and ideals, regulation of sports and provision of goods and services which are not catered for by the free market.

Index